MAPPING FATE

Also by Alice Wexler

EMMA GOLDMAN IN AMERICA
EMMA GOLDMAN IN EXILE

MAPPING FATE

A Memoir of Family, Risk,
and Genetic Research

ALICE WEXLER

TIMES BOOKS

RANDOM HOUSE

Library of Congress Cataloging-in-Publication Data

Wexler, Alice
Mapping fate: a memoir of family, risk, and genetic research/Alice Wexler.
p. cm.
Includes bibliographical references and index.
ISBN 0-8129-1710-3 (acid-free paper)
1. Wexler, Alice. 2. Huntington's chorea—Patients—United States—
Family relationships. 3. Huntington's chorea—Research—United
States—History. I. Title.
RC394.H85W49 1995
362.1'96851'0092—dc20 94-25295
[B]

Book design by Susan Hood

Manufactured in the United States of America on acid-free paper

4   6   8   9   7   5   3

To the memory of my mother,
Leonore Sabin Wexler

. . . for he knew then that his fate was written in Melquiades' parchments. He found them intact among the prehistoric plants and steaming puddles and luminous insects that had removed all trace of man's passage on earth from the room, and he did not have the calmness to bring them out into the light, but right there, standing, without the slightest difficulty, as if they had been written in Spanish and were being read under the dazzling splendor of high noon, he began to decipher them aloud. It was the history of the family, written by Melquiades, down to the most trivial details, one hundred years ahead of time.

—GABRIEL GARCÍA MARQUEZ,
One Hundred Years of Solitude

Everyone, real or imagined, deserves the open destiny of life.

—GRACE PALEY,
"A Conversation with My Father"

CONTENTS

Contents

"THAT DISORDER":
AN INTRODUCTION

For I the Lord your God am an impassioned God, visiting
the guilt of the fathers upon the children, upon the third and
upon the fourth generations.

—EXODUS 20:5

First there is the grandfather who has died of "nervous trouble"
on the back ward of a state hospital, the uncle who attracts
whispers and stares from the neighbors as he staggers down the
street, the doctor who says, "Women do not get it." Rumors of
hereditary insanity linger about the family in question, along
with a certain atmosphere of secrecy and suspicion. Divorce, ar-
rests, abandonment, suicide punctuate the action. There is always a moment of discovery, when the protagonists finally learn
the truth, usually after having had several children. In the end,
the characters all come to resemble one another, and the action
winds down to a predictably gruesome close, with no resolution or release and always the promise of more performances to
come. This is the drama of families with Huntington's disease
(formerly called Huntington's chorea), played out with minor
variations on stages around the world.

In the summer of 1968, my sister and I discovered that this
drama was also our own, when our fifty-three-year-old mother
was diagnosed with Huntington's disease. In our mid-twenties,

we learned for the first time the hidden history of our family, summed up in the awful word "chorea." We learned that our maternal grandfather and all our uncles had died of this disease and that our mother would repeat their fate. Nancy and I each faced a fifty-fifty chance of inheriting her disease ourselves.

Back in 1872, the physician George Huntington wrote the classic account of the disease that would become associated with his name. He had learned about it from his father and grandfather, both physicians, who had seen it among their patients on Long Island, New York. It was "confined to certain and fortunately a *few* families, and has been transmitted to them, an heirloom from generations away back in the dim past." It was spoken of by those "in whose veins the seeds of the disease are known to exist, with a kind of horror, and not at all alluded to except through dire necessity, when it is mentioned as *'that disorder.'* "

The symptoms began extremely gradually, "by the irregular and spasmodic action of certain muscles, as of the face, arms, etc." The movements grew progressively worse over a period of years "until the hapless sufferer is but a quivering wreck of his former self." In the end, every muscle in the body was affected "(excepting the involuntary ones), and the poor patient presents a spectacle which is anything but pleasing to witness." Nor could the patient hope for remission. "I have never known a recovery or even an amelioration of symptoms in this form of chorea; when once it begins it clings to the bitter end."

Huntington described three notable peculiarities of the disease. One was a marked tendency to insanity and sometimes to suicide. "As the disease progresses the mind becomes more or less impaired, in many amounting to insanity, while in others mind and body both gradually fail until death relieves them of their sufferings." Another was that of late onset: rarely before the age of thirty or forty, "while those who pass the fortieth year *without* symptoms of the disease, are seldom attacked." (In fact, onset may occur both earlier and later.)

The pattern of hereditary transmission was perhaps the most striking aspect of the disorder. If a parent was afflicted, "one or more of the offspring almost invariably suffer from the disease, if they live to adult age. But if by any chance these children go through life *without* it, the thread is broken and the grandchildren and great-grandchildren of the original shakers may rest assured that they are free from the disease." This illness never skipped a generation to reappear in another. For those who were stricken, however, no treatment helped, "and indeed nowadays its end is so well known to the sufferer and his friends, that medical advice is seldom sought. It seems at least to be one of the incurables."[1]

Our mother's diagnosis in 1968 prompted my father to organize the Hereditary Disease Foundation to support research, and my sister to become a researcher herself. The research in which she participated led to a breakthrough in 1983. That summer, scientists localized the Huntington's gene on the short arm of chromosome 4 by identifying a genetic marker for the disease—a neighboring stretch of DNA indicating the proximity of the Huntington's gene. This event marked the first significant advance in Huntington's research, since the marker would make possible the identification of the gene and, it was hoped, lead to an understanding of how that gene caused brain cells to die. The marker also enabled researchers to identify who would develop the illness years, even decades, in advance of any symptoms. The dream of prediction long cherished by geneticists and counselors and even by affected families became a reality.

The marker discovery reverberated throughout the biomedical community. It demonstrated for the first time the power of a controversial new technology for mapping genes and opened the way to accelerated advances in many areas of human genetics. Never before had this technique been used to locate a disease gene that could have been anywhere on any one of the twenty-three pairs of human chromosomes. Moreover, the localization of the Huntington's gene marked a significant step in the union of human genetics, which had been largely clinical and descriptive, and molecular biology, which had been highly reductionist and focused on mechanics. The coming together of these two worlds fundamentally transformed each of them.[2]

Second, the extensive dialogue that developed around presymptomatic testing for Huntington's has served as a model for thinking about all kinds of genetic testing. The cautions that scientists, doctors, health professionals, and HD activists have built into the procedures for testing have served as examples for those developing ways of testing for other illnesses as well. In a world in which growing numbers of disorders may be diagnosed before symptoms appear, even though there may be no effective therapy for them, the response of the Huntington's disease community has been carefully watched throughout the biomedical world.

Third, the way in which the research on Huntington's has unfolded—through interdisciplinary workshops, collaborative efforts, and a high degree of cooperation between families and investigators—has also served as a model for other research ventures. Although scientists collaborate on all sorts of projects, molecular biology and biomedical research have been arenas of especially fierce competition. The Huntington's Disease Collaborative Research Group, organized under the auspices of the Hereditary Disease Foundation, has been considered by many to be a model of a successful, large-scale collaborative effort in biomedical science.

Fourth, many have seen the status of being at risk for Huntington's as an extreme example of what it means to be at risk for a wide range of other conditions, including AIDS.

Huntington's poses stark questions about the meanings of certainty and uncertainty and what it means to occupy a "third space" outside the categories of either-or that we conventionally use to organize experience.[3]

Finally, Huntington's is also about nonscientists playing an active role in science, not only through fund-raising and lobbying but by participating in decision making about which research to support and working with scientists to organize research efforts. By intervening directly in the scientific world, these Huntington's activists have significantly influenced the priorities and practices of biomedical research.

My family's involvement began at a moment when biomedical interest in this disease had already started to revive, on the eve of the recombinant DNA revolution and the blossoming of neurobiology in the late 1960s. The scientific milieu was highly favorable to the intensification of interest in a disease like Huntington's, with its combined neurological and genetic dimensions. At the same time, its late onset made it peculiarly difficult to study, since it was hard to distinguish those who were unaffected from those who might develop the disease later on.

The decade of the 1960s, with its blossoming of social activism, also helped foster a political atmosphere favorable to mobililizing families directly affected by the illness. Civil rights activism, the feminist health movement, and patients' rights movements of the sixties and seventies all created an environment that encouraged families with Huntington's to act on their own behalf. Moreover, Woody Guthrie, the great poet and songwriter of the Dust Bowl, had died of Huntington's in 1967, the year before our mother was diagnosed. His long illness had inspired Marjorie Guthrie, his ex-wife, to start an organization of people with Huntington's in their families. Founded in 1967, the Committee to Combat Huntington's Disease, or CCHD, grew into a national, grassroots organization—later called the

Huntington's Disease Society of America, or HDSA—which lobbied Congress, developed services for families, and organized educational campaigns for the public and for health professionals.

Although inspired at the beginning by Marjorie Guthrie and CCHD, my father's deepest commitment was basic research. Imbued with a profound faith in science, he wanted to find a cure. At a time when the disease was of interest primarily to a few neurologists and geneticists, my father and sister helped create a support system—seed money, tissue banks, pedigrees, and workshops—that enticed many basic scientists to study Huntington's. In doing so, they pioneered imaginative ways of working with scientists, and of fostering dialogue among scientists, which would have implications far beyond the Huntington's research community, a community they helped to create.

This book began as a project of documentation in that heady summer of 1983, when we thought Huntington's might soon come to an end, like polio after the invention of the Salk and Sabin vaccines. As a historian, I wanted to record this first major turning point in the history of an obscure, seemingly hopeless illness and in the development of human neurogenetics. That summer, I began to interview the scientists who had been involved in the marker discovery, as well as others who had been associated with the Hereditary Disease Foundation. I hoped to collect memories before they became too encumbered by myth and before all the publicity in the press began to feed back into the scientists' recollections.

I soon realized that, as a member of a family that had been deeply involved with this effort and had helped to fund it, I could not write as an outsider. Although my own role has been primarily that of an observer, I was too close to the participants to write about their efforts with much critical distance. And, as a person at risk for Huntington's, I was too emotionally involved in the outcome of this research to regard it with much detachment.

I realized further that I did not want to write as an outsider, nor did I wish simply to document an exciting moment in the history of biomedical science. In my early forties and approaching the age at which my mother had begun showing symptoms, I wanted to explore the emotional meanings of being at risk, for my mother as well as for myself. Although my sister and others had studied the psychology of being at risk for Huntington's, few people actually in that position had written personal accounts of their experience outside the context of psychiatric testing, genetic counseling, the neurological exam, or the journalistic interview. As a feminist I particularly wanted to examine the relations between genetics and gender in our family, since I knew it somehow mattered to my own experience of growing up female that my mother—my same-sexed parent—was the parent at risk and that she was the one who had developed the disease. I wanted to see how our lives intersected, the rhythms of her hopes and anxieties informing those of my sister and me. Huntington's, I thought, could even be seen as a metaphor for the fear of many daughters of my 1950s generation—that we would somehow turn into our mothers, that our mothers were mirrors of our future selves—and for that common guilt of our mothers, that they had inflicted suffering on their children. What was the mother-daughter relationship, when viewed through the lens of Huntington's disease? *If the mirror, whose precursor is the mother's face, offers an illusion of wholeness to the child's body of bits and pieces, what then of the daughter who sees the mother imagining herself and imagining her daughter as the fragmented body she fears to become? What psychic map of the body is projected by a mother who recalls her own parent's choreic body? What map of the body is taken in by the daughter who sees chorea memories written on her mother's face?* [4]

Finally, I wanted to explore the meanings of secrecy and silence within our family, the ways in which what could not be said reverberated as loudly as the words that were spoken. Feelings cannot be buried as easily as facts. Denial creates its own emotional force fields, even if the relevant information remains hidden. Secrets, moreover, especially so dramatic a secret as Huntington's, may form part of a family's emotional inheritance, a psychological legacy handed down along with the family Bible, affecting every aspect of family life for generations. Since Huntington's had been a secret in our family, long hidden from my sister and me, our mother's diagnosis had implications far beyond the medical. Learning of our mother's failure for many years to tell our father about Huntington's disease in her family, and discovering our parents' decision not to tell my sister and me of our mother's risk, and therefore our own, meant recasting my entire understanding of our family history.

Our situation, then, had much in common with that of other families whose secrets differed in their content. Certainly any stigmatized condition may be surrounded by webs of secrecy, whose maintenance requires hard work and active effort. As the historian Michel Foucault argued, "Silence itself—the things one declines to say, or is forbidden to name, the discretion that is required between different speakers—is . . . an element that functions alongside the things said, with them and in relation to them . . . we must try to determine the different ways of not saying such things, how those who can and those who cannot speak of them are distributed, which type of discourse is authorized, or which form of discretion is required in either case. There is not one but many silences."[5]

In exploring the impact of secrecy in our family, I also wanted to consider the ways in which our silences were gendered. In recent decades, much feminist writing has addressed the costs for women of socially imposed silence, especially the silencing of our own deepest thoughts and emotions. Feminist historians in particular have described how the female body became the arena in which forbidden speech was acted out through physical symptoms. In our family, much remained unspoken and unspeakable until that day in 1968 when our mother's body spoke that (death) sentence. This book, in part, is my translation.

My decision to write about HD in our family raised many questions for all of us as to what kind of book this would be, particularly because there is still no effective treatment for Huntington's and the research and fund-raising efforts continue. Would this book affect those efforts? Would I write an "official story," celebrating the successes of the Hereditary Disease Foundation? a family romance to inspire others? a publicity piece for fund-raising purposes? What about those family members who did not want their personal lives publicly disclosed, particularly by someone who might not represent them as they wished to be shown? The fact that my father is a psychoanalyst, and a most unorthodox one at that, further complicated the project because of the involvement of some patients and former patients with the Hereditary Disease Foundation. There was also the fact that I was challenging Dad on his turf by interpreting our family, often differently than he did. As the book grew more autobiographical, my anxiety deepened. I realized I was no longer writing a "family story" but rather a memoir of my own.

The book I have written is far more personal than the one I intended when I started, partly because I began to see just how profoundly Huntington's had colored our family's history and, conversely, how our family history, in all its particularity, has shaped the ways in which we have responded to the illness. Unresolved angers and resentments from the past often got displaced onto arguments about the disease, while the disease, in shadow on multiple aspects of the family history, even before we knew of its existence. In short, we made emotional and metaphorical meanings out of the disease that were not determined solely by its biomedical character. The disease was often the vehicle for expressing feelings only tangentially related to it. As the medical writer Arthur Kleinman put it, "Acting like a sponge, illness soaks up personal and social significance from the world of the sick person."[6] To tell the story of the disease, then, I would have to address these other dimensions.

This wider aspect of the story has proven to be the most difficult to write, since each of us brought a different set of associations to bear on the problem of Huntington's and distinct conceptions of what counted as important in telling the story; indeed, different constructions of "the story." Certainly, in any family history, questions of privacy and confidentiality emerge in relation not only to the past but also to the present; what one person considers as central to his or her narrative of identity may involve information that others in the family consider private and "no one else's business." All members of a family, in some sense, compete for control over the family narrative, at least when it comes to public speech, and perhaps even in private as well. Whose voice may be heard, whose speech is legitimate, who can tell their own story when it also involves the stories of others—these are questions every writer who ventures out onto the thin ice of autobiography must face. When inherited illness confronts a family, such questions become especially charged, as feelings of anger, guilt, blame, and loss inevitably come into play. To erase those parts of our history that were traumatic or embarrassing, to others as well as to myself, in the hope of presenting a more heroic image, seemed to me not only false but unfair to those who are currently struggling with similar dilemmas. I wanted to show how even a family with all kinds of advantages, like ours, can still struggle mightily with such a disease. Yet I have continually wrestled with the knowledge that my speech was capable of causing others considerable pain.

Another set of questions concerned the audience to whom this book was addressed. For whom was I writing this book? For the "general public" interested in medicine and science? For medical students or genetic counselors? For scientists who wanted to learn about the emotional aspects of a disease they know only in the lab? For other people with Huntington's in their families? Was it possible to draw on some of the recent feminist critiques and cultural studies of science while still writing in a way accessible to these groups?

In the course of writing this book I have grappled continuously with these questions. At the very least, I have tried to be aware of my position as a white, Jewish, upper-middle-class woman who writes from within an academic community but outside the structure of an academic institution. Even while maintaining a critical perspective, I have tried above all to speak in ways accessible to those most affected by this story— people in the Huntington's community—in the hope that this story may encourage others to tell their stories as well.

In weaving together a personal narrative of a family confronting Huntington's disease with a more detached account of biomedical research, I have utilized several approaches. On the one hand, I have drawn on the traditional resources of the historian and journalist in investigating the past—interviews with many scientists, archival materials, and reports in the scientific, medical, and popular press, as well as personal observation at meetings and workshops. At the same time, I have pored over family papers and photographs, old letters, newspaper clippings, scrapbooks, transcripts, conversations over many years, even dreams and memories, diaries and journals. I hoped my doubled perspective as insider and outsider, as participant and observer, might be a useful position for approaching a topic that is both scientifically significant and emotionally volatile.

While my story shares some of the elements of the illness narratives written about cancer and AIDS, it is really less about an illness than about the possiblity of an illness, less about the medical dilemma of living with disease than about the existential dilemma of living at risk.

In writing this book, however, I have come to realize how privileged my sister and I have been in relation to other families with Huntington's. We have had more resources, financial and professional, than most other families with the disease. Moreover, our family is small, so that the illness has not multiplied through the generations—of my mother's family, only she had children, while her three brothers who had the illness had none. Besides my sister and me, there are no other direct descendents of our grandfather, Abraham Sabin. Most of all, our mother developed symptoms late, after my sister and I had left home, so we did not grow up under the frightening shadow of this disease that haunted so many other young people, watching their parents and grandparents, uncles and aunts, siblings and cousins growing ill and dying. A more typical experience is that narrated by a woman who testified before the Congressional Commission for the Control of Huntington's Disease and Its Consequences in 1977: "As we were growing up, all of us felt that our family suffered from hereditary insanity and that we were singled out as a family with this 'crazy streak.' We were taunted with 'Your mother is in the crazy house!' I did not then even know that my mother was alive, and if she was alive and in the crazy house, I did not know why. My mother, two uncles, two brothers and one sister have been diagnosed with HD. My brothers' and sister's spouses all divorced them immediately after committing them to the state mental hospital." Or, as another woman testified, "Now this insidious killer has a possibility of forty-five victims in our family alone."[7]

Huntington's is a devastating disease. Yet not all of its misery comes from the illness. People with Huntington's can and sometimes do live active lives for a number of years after the diagnosis, if they have the necessary supports and services. The suffering associated with the disease and with living at risk is intensified by the lack of resources available in our privatized, for-profit medical system. Nearly all of the people from families with HD who testified before the 1977 Congressional Commission spoke of the limitations of health insurance and lack of access to services. That people with Huntington's who are still relatively intact intellectually and emotionally often end up in state mental hospitals merely underlines the failures of our current health care system and the need for a national program that addresses the needs of chronic, long-term illness.

Human genetics in the 1990s inhabits a volatile space at the intersection of medicine, biology, corporate profits, law, government funding of science, state health programs, private insurance companies, genetic counseling services, schools, courts, and popular culture. Issues of race, gender, and class figure in the discourse of the new genetics, reviving old debates about the distribution of traits such as intelligence and aggression, dominance and disease, within different groups of the population. Genetic engineering is a multibillion-dollar industry, with companies competing for control over diagnostic tests for newly discovered genes or markers of lethal illnesses, whose discoverers are often shareholders and members of the board of directors of the companies that will market the tests. Clearly many groups of people have strong stakes in the technologies that are revolutionizing all of biology.

The new genetics has already opened a vast arena for contests of power over what it means to be human, who has the power to define what is normal, who has access to what resources and when. Who will control the knowledge of our bodies after the Human Genome Project has mapped and sequenced all human genes? How can we ensure that this will not be another project for enforcing narrow norms of "human nature," as the historian of science Donna Haraway has put it, for legislating "genetic destiny"? How can we respect the diversity and difference that the Human Genome Project also establishes as "normal"?

Although Huntington's affects a limited population—some seven to ten people per 100,000, or about 30,000 in the United States, with another 150,000 at risk—it has usefully been considered a prototype for biomedical research since it destroys such a wide range of functions. Understanding Huntington's may shed light on more common inherited, neurological and psychiatric disorders, such as Parkinson's, schizophrenia, and sickle-cell disease.[8] Because it is caused by one gene, however, some have argued that Huntington's may be an inappropriate model for thinking about disease, since most diseases are caused by complex interactions of genes and environment, or by a combination of genes. As the historian of science Evelyn Fox Keller has written, only for very exceptional diseases can "genetic components be considered apart from the environment. For such cases—e.g., cystic fibrosis and Huntington's disease—there is no question that molecular genetics is providing powerful and unambivalently welcome tools. But most diseases are not so simple." Indeed, the ever-expanding category of genetic disease has recently threatened to claim such social conditions as homelessness, while what Keller calls "the geneticization of health and disease" threatens to move discussions of disease from individuals to their DNA.[9]

But even Huntington's, with its straightforward genetics, may not be entirely reducible to DNA, since the cellular environment and even social milieu may also influence its expression. My hope is that the Huntington's story may suggest the ways in which even this obviously pathological, genetically determined killer may acquire distinct meanings for different individuals, families, and cultures. Biology itself, in this view, is are partially shaped by its social, political, and cultural contexts. Moreover, as recent social studies of science have argued, what counts as biological "fact" may be partly a product of cultural struggles over power.[10] Part of the fascination of the new genetics concerns the questions it raises about the construction of knowledge—how, for whom, and for what is this knowledge being constructed? In this context, then, Huntington's disease may serve as a space where many discourses collide and therefore help make visible the hidden stakes in this contest for human survival and identity in which all of us are at risk.

Huntington's is, above all, a disease of endless replication, reducing the wonderful multiplicity of human lives to a dreary, deadening sameness, repeating over and over again the same awful saga. In this connection, I have often thought of a story by Jorge Luis Borges, in which a modern-day gaucho dies in Buenos Aires in order that a scene from the life of Caesar may be reenacted. In the story I have written, the gaucho lives to tell her own tale.

—*Santa Monica, California*
January 1995

THE BODY IN QUESTION

In the summer of 1940, Mom and Dad spent a month in New Hampshire, where Dad was helping his former analyst, Theodor Reik, revise an English translation of *Masochism in Modern Man*. Mom was teaching biology at a junior high school in Harlem.

Nancy and I at Nancy's high school graduation in 1963. When the second of Mom's three brothers died that year of Huntington's (with a third terminally ill), Dad told Nancy the name of the disease. Mom, however, never mentioned it. Five years later, she too was diagnosed.

fish dreams

When I was a child in Topeka, Kansas, my father had a friend, a fellow psychoanalyst at the Menninger Clinic, who came to our house every Saturday night to discuss schizophrenia and "mortido"—Freud's death instinct—over lox and bagels. Bill was a quiet, scholarly man, serious and rather shy, a collector of rocks—"He had hobbies instead of friends," said my father. He was also a great fisherman. One day Bill's car pulled up to our house and he jumped out beaming. Gasping on the rear floor lay a tremendous carp, ancient and ravaged. This carp had apparently survived many years hidden in the murky shallows of a pond in Topeka. No one had imagined the presence there of anything more substantial than small goldfish until Bill, practicing his casting, hauled up this monster.

I forgot about that fish as I grew older, despite my fear of touching live fish and a morbid fascination with dead ones. After Dad told us the facts of our family history, this carp swam back into my dreams. In my mind's eye I saw it sliding through

3

the shadows of that Topeka pond, silent and unsuspected until the day of its discovery, and I wondered whether it had spawned other monsters who would someday also come to light.

One

AFTER WOODS HOLE

We think back through our mothers if we are women.

—VIRGINIA WOOLF
A Room of One's Own

All that remains today of my mother's love of nature is her large yellow volume of Homer D. House's *Wild Flowers* and a Peterson's *Field Guide to Western Birds,* carted through each of the family moves. By the time I cared enough to listen, she had forgotten the beautiful names. She had already begun the slow decline that would end many years later in a Santa Monica convalescent hospital. Her traces, faint in life, have now almost vanished. That is why I am greedy for old memories, hijacking my family for the ransom of stories about my mother before the illness began. If I could catch a glimpse of her whole, perhaps I could look into the mirror each day without the everlasting search for symptoms. Maybe if I could write her story, she would no longer push herself into my dreams, scratching my arms to drag me down with her.

Maryline, our family friend, calls me a Sherlock Holmes because of all the questions I ask. "When did you first know?" I badger my father. "How did you find out? Did Mother know she was at risk? When did she first begin to change? Would you have had children if you had known?" Maryline thinks it is better to forget the past and think of the future. Still I hunt my mother's tracks, hoarding transcripts, diplomas, yearbooks, diaries, clippings, old letters, and family photographs so that one day I can reassemble her from the scraps. I do this not for her sake but for my own.

When I was six I discovered my fat thumb. It was short and broad, with a nail that was wider than it was long. I remember running to my mother, sticking my fat thumb into her face and shouting "What's this?" as I burst into tears. She sat me down and explained calmly that it was a mutation, a slight difference that could be inherited within the family. Her father, my grandfather Abraham, had had a fat thumb, and two of Mom's brothers had it as well. It was neither good nor bad, just different. Something in the way she gave this explanation made me feel proud to possess a mutation. After that I was pleased with my thumb and showed it off to all my friends.

That was my first lesson in genetics, given to me by my mother, who had studied *Drosophila* in the famous "fly room" set up by Thomas Hunt Morgan at Columbia University, where she had earned a master's degree in zoology back in the 1930s. I never thought of my mother as a scientist. To me, at that time, she was just a mommy. Not an entirely reliable one at that, especially since the day, when I was three, that she had arrived home carrying a tiny bald bundle. In protest, I had hurled myself down a flight of stairs and after that had devoted myself to the task of trying to poison my blond baby sister by stuffing grass through the bars of her playpen. Mom took all my efforts in stride and made up for her betrayal by reading my favorite Uncle Wiggly stories every night and reciting poems, over and over, from *Now We Are Six,* especially the ones about Christopher Robin and Alice. Later, when we lived in Topeka, she introduced us to Fanny Brice in *Baby Snooks,* organized

birthday hayrides and picnics, tried without success to teach us
the names of the trees and birds she knew so well. She bought
us parakeets, fish, turtles, hamsters, ducks, rabbits, guinea
pigs, and in Topeka a wonderful white collie named Lucky
who barked at strangers and bit the postman but merely nuz-
zled my sister and me. She tried hard to train our dogs—we
had several over the years—but she never had much luck with
any of them. They were all headstrong and willful, terrible
watchdogs, given to chasing cars and stealing food off the dining room table when they thought no one was looking. Mom
laughed at their misdeeds and loved them all, especially Sheba,
a beautiful silver weimaraner who lived with us later in Los
Angeles and kept my mother company through long, lonely afternoons when there was no one else to share her sorrow.

In the stories Mom told about her life, Woods Hole stood out
as a kind of touchstone. She was nineteen that summer of
1934, just graduated *cum laude* from Hunter College in zoology
and botany at the top of her class of six hundred women. She
presided over the Biology Club and, for outstanding scholar-
ship and activity in the department, she won the prestigious
Elsie Seringhaus Prize that sent her up to Woods Hole,
Massachusetts, to study embryology at the Marine Biological
Laboratory. In the snapshots she mounted on the heavy black
pages of a photo album, the only one she ever filled, our petite
mother picnics on Nobska Beach and smiles from the deck of a
boat docked in front of the MBL. She collects bugs at Bessie
Creek, up at the University of Michigan Biological Station at
Cheboygan, where she spent the summer before she graduated, and eats sandwiches in the field with her systematic
botany class. She was slender and shapely, almost pretty, with
her dark Sabin brows and quick full smile, clowning a little
self-consciously at the shore with her girlfriends, and sometimes, when the camera caught her off guard, full of intelligent

concentration and often a wry, quizzical thoughtfulness. She had changed from the sad-eyed child swaddled in coats and fur-lined caps who gazed forlornly out of old sepia photographs. By the time she entered college at the age of fifteen, she had grown lively, playful, even adventurous, for who in her family had ever dreamed of becoming a scientist? "Leonore was exceptionally bright and quick," said her friend Rose, "high-spirited," and "wonderfully exuberant," with a fine sense of humor. An admiring classmate, a "fellow politician," hoped she would run her life as well as she had run the Biology Club. She was the first in her family to finish college, the first to go to graduate school. In the fall of 1934, still working Saturdays downtown at Macy's, she entered Columbia University, where Thomas Hunt Morgan, in the early 1900s, had created the most important genetics laboratory in the country. Here she studied cytology, organic chemistry, plant morphology, the comparative embryology of vertebrates, and especially genetics. Mom earned her M.A. in the winter of 1936, writing her thesis on "Egg Counts from Females Heterozygous for Early Emergence in *Drosophila melanogaster*." She also managed to serve as vice president of Phi Sigma, the graduate honorary biological fraternity. She was proud of her Columbia degree but prouder, I think, of her summer at the MBL at Woods Hole, that finest of moments salvaged from all the sorrows of her life.

A certain mystery surrounded her family, whose history did not go back very far. Mom's father, Abraham R. Sabin, had grown up in the city of Baranovici, in Byelorussia, not far from Minsk to the east and Białystok to the west, across the border in Poland. At the age of nineteen, in 1891, when millions of East European Jews were fleeing Czarist anti-Semitism and army conscription, Abraham traveled alone to America. According to family lore, he changed his name from Zaichick to Sabin when he landed in New York, taking the name of the man ahead of him in the immigration line. Mom told us he had come from a professional family of doctors, lawyers, and dentists, though she never said much about them. I somehow imagined my grandfather springing to life at the moment he stepped off the ship into Castle Garden, as if Russia were some mysterious place whose inhabitants had no real material existence. Like many Jewish immigrants, Abraham set himself up in the garment district on the Lower East Side of Manhattan, where he made a modest living in cloaks and suits. He was a quiet, melancholy man, rather intellectual, with distinctly European manners, said a cousin. Mom, who was shy as a child and loved to read, always felt she resembled her father.

Abraham married Sabina Feigenbaum, who had come to New York as a child from Iasi, in Romania, growing into a handsome, rather formidable woman in a large apartment on East Broadway with her eight brothers and sisters, near the dry-goods shop of her parents, Bessie and Philip Feigenbaum. Sabina loved to have herself photographed. A large, fashionable woman in her sixties, she poses in her bathing suit at Miami Beach, turbanned in front of the Habana Hotel, and sits astride a fake alligator on the lawn with her hands in its jaws. In my favorite picture—one of those trick photographs that I loved as a child—she sits serenely in her polka-dot silk dress at all five places around a dining room table. Our grandmother was a proud, irrepressible Jewish matriarch, jovial and outgoing, and according to Mom, a great cook. She loved playing cards with her friends every night and much preferred parties to reading books.

Sabina took over as head of the family when Abraham developed a mysterious illness and died at the age of fifty-two. Mom told us different stories about his death. An infected boil under the arm had killed him, she said. Or he had died of a terrible flu that had carried him off almost overnight. She did not tell us until many years later of her mother's words overheard at the mortuary the night her father died, words that had sent her off to the library to discover that Abraham's sickness, Huntington's chorea, was inherited, but that only men could get it. At least that was what she told us later, after she herself fell ill. She said that Abraham had been hospitalized on Long Island when she was six. He had died a few years later, around 1929.

Mom said little about her father. She never told us of her grandfather Jacob L. Zaichick, who also had Huntington's, nor of her aunt Dinka, who died of the disease in Baranovici, nor of Abraham's other sisters, Leah and Ida, who came to New York and lived long healthy lives. The family considered Huntington's a shameful secret and did not discuss it except with close relatives, and even then only rarely. After Abraham died, Sabina moved the family from the Bronx to Manhattan, where they lived in an apartment on West Seventy-eighth Street, and Sabina sold lingerie to private customers. One or another of Mom's three older brothers would move back home from time to time, and she, the only daughter, was expected to clean up after them. Later, though, her brothers helped pay for her college education and were proud of their smart, serious sister. The eldest, Jesse, ten years older than Mom, was in the clothing business like their father. The youngest, Seymour, my mother's favorite, played saxophone in the band of the handsome middle brother, Paul, who played the banjo and had his own fourteen-piece orchestra known for "the soft romantic style of music." Mom went to hear them at the Tavern on the Green in Central Park, and the Hotel Delmonico, and sometimes she and Sabina took the train down to Miami Beach to hear the Paul Sabin Orchestra and parade on the boardwalk.

By the time I met Seymour (whom everyone called "Hap" on account of his amiable disposition), he no longer played sax, except in old family photos. But Nancy and I howled with delight as we watched him make nickels stick to his forehead, dimes ooze from his palms, and quarters spring suddenly out of his ears. He was a friendly, fidgety, graying bachelor in his early forties who ran a small bar and grill with Paul on upper Broadway. Even then, when we visited from Topeka, I could not help noticing his occasional grimacing, his unsteady walk and slightly spasmodic speech, but I attributed it to the peculiarity of adults, especially those who lived in New York, instead of the most wonderful place in the world, Topeka, Kansas. My father never liked my mother's brothers, except for Seymour. He called them mama's boys, and he blamed Sabina's "domineering" ways. I thought that might also explain their odd behavior.

Growing up among small-time merchants and musicians, Mom somehow acquired an early interest in biology, perhaps from her visits to the American Museum of Natural History, where she had wandered as a child among the dinosaurs and fading dioramas. She had always loved the place, and she would take Nancy and me there whenever we visited New York. Perhaps her father's mysterious illness also stimulated her curiosity about science. By the early 1930s certain fields in science were opening to women. A few women were earning Ph.D.s in zoology and botany, including my mother's friend Rose, but Mom was not among them. "Can you believe," said Rose many years later, "that the parents of nice Jewish girls generally did not encourage the pursuit of graduate studies?" Sabina worried that her daughter would not marry if she pursued a doctorate. So now, in the middle of the Great Depression, Mom chose a less ambitious route. She ranked high in the examinations for her high school teaching credential and was endorsed "with enthusiasm" by the examiners, who noted that she made her students love her subjects. Too young at first for a permanent position, she served several years as a substitute teacher in a tough Harlem high school and looked so much like her pupils that the other teachers would sometimes order her to the principal's office for violating student rules.

Dad liked to tell how his mother, vacationing with the family at Miami Beach in the winter of 1936, had caught sight of an attractive young girl staying with her mother at a nearby hotel. My grandmother urged him to introduce himself. "But Mom," he protested after striking up a conversation, "she's not a young girl, she's a scientist and a teacher." Actually, they had met before, and in other versions of the story Dad had been driving in Miami when a car pulled over to ask directions. Looking inside the car, Dad recognized a young woman he had met back in New York. When they returned from vacation, Mom invited Dad to a party, and soon they were keeping company. They made a handsome couple, Mom with her graceful figure and bright smile and my tall, lanky father. Dad had the lean, muscular build of a runner, with sandy brown hair and light blue eyes, though he was slightly self-conscious about his nose, which was large but not unattractive; for a while he adopted the middle initial "B," after his great literary hero Cyrano de Bergerac. In her Woods Hole photo album with the Miami Beach palm trees embossed on the cover, Mom mounted snapshots of herself in her bathing suit, beaming up at my father on the beach, and pictures of the two of them camping at Lake George the following summer, before they were married.

Years later my father recalled how Mom had become ill shortly before the wedding, so that they had had to postpone it first one week, then another. During this time, Sabina had telephoned him with a strange request. She urged him to call Dorian Feigenbaum, a famous psychoanalyst who was supposedly a distant cousin of hers. She said Feigenbaum could give him information that might be useful. Dad was puzzled, suspecting that perhaps Mom's father, who he knew had died many years earlier, had once been a patient of Feigenbaum's and that Sabina wanted Dad to know about it. He made the telephone call, but Feigenbaum declined to give any information. Dad did not pursue the matter and forgot about it for almost fifty years, when it suddenly occurred to him that perhaps both Sabina and Mom had been trying to tell him something that neither one could bring herself to acknowledge.

At the time he met my mother, my father, Milton Wexler, was twenty-eight years old and practicing law, a profession he hated, in a small office at Broadway and Forty-second Street in midtown Manhattan. Like Abraham Sabin, Dad's grandparents, Moishe (later Morris) and Rose Wexler, had come to the United States from Russia as part of the great wave of east European Jewish immigration. In 1884, my great-grandparents left the town near Kiev, in the Ukraine, where they had been small landowners and shopkeepers. They traveled to Brooklyn, carrying with them three-year-old Nathan, who grew up to become a real estate salesman of wildly fluctuating fortunes— "like Willy Loman," my father said later. My grandfather was a big, affable, gregarious man who smoked cigars and dressed sharply when he could afford it, a very simple man with a concrete, practical mind, according to my father, who rarely heard him discuss anything deeper than pot roast or real estate. He had no interest in politics or literature, but he was a generous father, Dad always said, and he liked women, especially one woman with whom he carried on a long-term relationship through much of his marriage. Dad recalled later that his father—whom he used to call "Governor"—had delegated him to visit the woman and end the affair, since he could not bring himself to do it. But that failure of nerve cost him a lot, because after that my father lost a certain respect for him, though he still treated him with great affection.

No doubt that affair also contributed to my grandmother Mollie's chronic depression, which turned toward the end of her long life into extreme paranoia and a fear that everyone around her was trying to poison her. Dad always said his mother was "smarter by far" than his father, though she had never gone beyond the third grade. Hers was the more intellectual side of the family, and it was she who encouraged her children's education. Mollie Skolnick too had come as a child from Russia, the daughter of Moishe and Golda Skolnick, whose keen psychological insight, evident in her underlinings in the family Bible, my father noted as part of the family legacy. The Skolnicks, a large, close-knit tribe that counted among its members the famous Yiddish actor Boris Thomashevsky, formed a mutual aid organization of which my father, as a young lawyer, became the president. But despite her family's warmth and sociability, Mollie's nature was melancholy and puritanical, according to her sons. That and my grandfather's migraines probably helped account for the fact that all three of their sons became psychologists, two of them psychoanalysts.

When he was still quite young, Dad began to build radio sets, which astonished his parents. "I'd let them listen in on the headphones once in a while and they'd be flabbergasted," he recalled. In high school he joined the debating team, which in those days, he said, had great prestige. Debaters traveled, and debating events were like boxing matches, attracting big crowds and much excitement. He always insisted he was not a natural speaker, immediately relaxed and comfortable in front of an audience. But he performed well with preparation and hard work. The anxiety of public speaking attracted him, too; it posed a challenge that he found exciting. "I would try any contest," he said years later. His senior class at Alexander Hamilton High School in Brooklyn elected him president, and he was also class valedictorian and winner of the Benjamin Franklin Award for "general excellence." When he graduated, the New York Forensic League awarded him a one-year fellowship to the university of his choice. Though he initially chose

Harvard, he ended up at Syracuse University, where his elder brother, Henry, was enrolled and where Dad dashed through the three-year prelaw program in two years.

Law school at New York University quickly chilled his enthusiasm. He took Freud and Dostoyevsky to class to read behind his lawbooks and studied just enough to pass the exams. The excitement of competition changed to disgust as he saw issues of rights and justice giving way before skillful courtroom manipulation. "I was good at writing briefs," he said, "because I could pick out weak spots in other people's arguments. But I was never proud of it because it always seemed to me a trick. I could write a brief without any conviction whatever about the justice of the case. I had no passion about it." His law practice increasingly disturbed him, especially since he knew that many of his clients were crooks and he was aiding and abetting them. The injustices, the boredom, the aggression needed to fight these cases "just wiped me out and I was no damned good."

In the middle of the Depression, with young lawyers flocking to Washington, D.C., to work in the New Deal administration of Franklin D. Roosevelt, my father might have found some outlet for his idealism even as a lawyer. But he felt drawn to an entirely different field. As a boy, he had helped care for his younger brother, Murray, who had undergone a serious ear operation. Carting Murray around on his back in the Catskills one summer, taking him to picnics and parties, had inspired strong rescue fantasies in my father and stirred an interest in becoming a therapist. Later, while he was still in law school, he had worked one summer in a sanitarium caring for a boy with schizophrenia. Dad had shared a room with this boy, whom he later learned had impulses toward violence. These experiences intensified Dad's fascination with the vagaries of human character and his desire to help people in emotional distress.

With Mom's salary as a teacher, and an income from a small apartment building he purchased with a cash wedding present given him by his father, Dad left his law practice and enrolled in the clinical psychology program at Columbia University, where he eventually earned a Ph.D. What really excited him, though, was psychoanalysis, which was given great impetus in the United States by the arrival in New York of European analysts fleeing the Nazis. Although Freud's 1909 visit to the United States had sparked a growing interest in his ideas—they had become almost fashionable during the 1920s—psychoanalysis was considered suspect by most academic psychologists. In Europe during the early years, the field attracted the more adventurous characters, mavericks and bohemians drawn to its utopian dimension and excited by the belief that freeing people from their repressions and inhibitions could lead to a freer, fairer world. My father was probably motivated less by a reforming zeal than by an endless fascination with human character. He was drawn to rebels and outlaws even if he himself was reserved and somewhat conventional. He jumped at the chance to begin an analysis with Theodor Reik, formerly a close associate of Freud's in Vienna. Since Reik had just arrived in the United States, he was charging five dollars an hour, a price my father could afford. Soon Dad was attending Reik's seminars on psychoanalytic theory and starting to treat patients of his own. His professors at Columbia, who scorned psychoanalysis in their classes, were full of curiosity in the corridors and begged him to get them admitted to the seminars. Dad recalled that, though he was a lowly graduate student, he had suddenly acquired a certain prestige. At the age of thirty, a beginning student all over again, he knew he had found the world he was seeking.

In an influential essay, historian Joan Kelly described how a historical moment viewed from a man's perspective may look very different from a woman's point of view.[1] Something of this difference may have distinguished my parents' experience of

Topeka, Kansas, where we moved after the war so Dad could work at Menninger's. World War II, with its high rate of psychological casualties, had dramatized the need for trained mental health workers. Shortly after the war, the Menninger Clinic and hospital (later Foundation), founded by Dr. Charles Menninger and his sons Karl and William in 1919, began a large-scale program to train not only psychiatrists but also psychologists, psychoanalysts, social workers, and nurses. Designed as a pilot project for the Veterans Administration, by the late 1940s this program would become the most prestigious psychiatric training and research center in the country. In 1946, Dad had just completed a wartime stint in Washington, D.C., at the U.S. Navy Department. There, he had designed a study to measure the effectiveness of psychological testing of naval recruits, a stupid study, he said later, but Columbia accepted it as his doctoral thesis. He had not yet received his Ph.D. when Karl Menninger invited him to Topeka.

My father always referred to his five years in Topeka as a kind of heaven. "We were so preoccupied with learning and experimenting," he told me later, "digging, being excited about this monumental educational program, trying to see new ways of doing things, that everything else became highly secondary, and we were deeply invested in debates, arguments, the clash of ideas, friendships, etc., etc. And life seemed very rich and very rewarding in those days." He became chief of psychological services at the Winter Veterans Administration Hospital while working part-time, and later he worked full-time as a senior staff psychologist at Menninger's. Here he joined the high-powered group around the brilliant analyst David Rappaport, head of the Research Department of the Menninger School of Clinical Psychology, where Dad also taught. Dad was especially proud of the research grant he received because the Menningers had trusted him to do whatever he liked: he could sit under a tree and dream, if he wished. In fact, he began intensive psychotherapy with a patient with schizophrenia who would change his life even as he changed hers.

Those years at Menninger's, with their intellectual intensity, missionary fervor, and close personal relationships, strongly influenced Dad's development as an analyst. He worked there with some of the most distinguished men and women in his field, and though he was critical in some respects of the "family spirit" cultivated in particular by Karl Menninger, he felt himself among the favored sons of "Dr. Karl." He loved the combination of a tight-knit intellectual community, interdisciplinary work, collaborative projects, and indeed the Menninger tradition of support for research. Dad's association with Menninger's became, I think, an important part of his professional identity, for he would often refer back to this exciting period and many years later would draw on these experiences in developing his own research foundation.[2]

To my mother, however, a young wife with two small daughters and a marriage that had already unraveled more than she knew, the joys of Topeka must have been considerably more muted. She shared some of the closeness of the community, and she was a wonderful mother to my sister and me when we were small, always making us feel valued and wanted. But she longed for her family and friends in New York, and especially her beloved friend Alene Mintz (née Lowenstein), whom she had known since the age of seven and who was like a sister to her. "You have no idea how I miss you and how much I think of you," she had written to Alene several years earlier from Knoxville, Tennessee, where Dad had taught for a year at the University of Tennessee, just before the war. "We have always been so accustomed to each other, to talking and seeing each other, that I really feel a gap somewhere. It will soon be over and then we'll talk and talk and talk."[3]

But it never was over, and in Topeka Mom found herself once again far away, a full-time housewife and mother to boot.

She complained to Alene that she had no time to read books and that she had forgotten how to recognize the birds she once had known. "By now I can't even identify them stuffed and handed to me on a platter," she wrote.[4] These were the post–World War II years of strenuous domesticity and Cold War "containment"—of women as well as of Communists and other dissenters—and I never heard Mom voice regrets about abandoning either science or teaching. The professional women at Menninger's were mainly single, and most of them held traditionally female jobs as dietitians and nurses, though there were a number of powerful women analysts and psychologists as well. For all her superior education, Mom was no rebel. Like most of the women she knew, she cheerfully centered her life around her family, joined the Winter Wives, planned dances and socials, hauled her children to piano lessons and parties. Dad taught Mom to drive during those years, and she got great satisfaction out of being able to go "when and where I please. It makes me so independent." In her few free moments, she also managed to take painting classes, which she loved, "altho I hide my masterpieces in the basement."[5] One painting especially stands out in memory, of a small red sailboat floating near a blue beach. There were no beaches near Topeka, and I always wondered what she had been dreaming of when she painted that picture and whether she longed to sail away across the ocean, to a place where we could not follow.

Nancy, born in 1945 in a Washington, D.C., naval hospital just before we moved to Topeka, was changing from a fat, bald, wrinkled baby into a skinny golden angel. She soon developed a powerful will. When she could barely stand up, she insisted on dressing herself. At the age of four, determined to button herself into her fat blue snowsuit without assistance, she toppled over and landed on her chin, bloodying her face and leaving a permanent scar. At six, she was so maternal that she would tuck her small army of dolls and stuffed animals into her bed each night, leaving only a tiny, uncomfortable corner for herself. "Nancy is still an imp," Mom reported to Alene in the spring of 1951. "She loves kindergarten and loves her teacher, although there are 55 kids in the class. Her teacher told me Nancy greets her every morning with a big smile. That's Nancy. Everyone is her friend."[6] I was envious of my sister's charm and plotted to make her my slave. But Nancy soon saw through my schemes. In retaliation, she turned her skinniness and dilatory nature into weapons and used them skillfully. Meals with Nancy lasted for hours as she mounded her meat loaf into castles, sculpted her potatoes into moats, and posted string beans as sentries, exhausting even our extremely patient mother. "Sitting in a restaurant waiting for Nancy to finish a meal is slow, delicate torture," Mom wrote Alene on one occasion.[7] Looking at Nancy's angelic smiles, it was hard to believe how stubborn she could be.

Still, from an early age we were allies and coconspirators. I loved teaching her how to tie her shoes, and holding her as we went bellywhopping on a fat innertube tied with a rope to the back of our car, which drove slowly through the icy Topeka streets, bouncing us up and down while we shrieked with pleasure. We were, it seemed to me then, a perfect family, especially when my father, whom I adored, would explain to us the orbits of the planets as he moved oranges around a large grapefruit in the middle of the dinner table, or would try to explain Einstein's theory of relativity. Or on Sundays in the blazing Kansas summers, when we would pile into our pretty blue Oldsmobile and drive out through the flat countryside to the swimming pool at St. Mary's. My sister and I would jump onto our father's back and swim with him for hours, our arms clasped tightly around his neck. Afterward I always felt at home in the water, as if I could still feel my father's strong body holding me up, still hear him laughing and splashing in the sunlight.

I remember one winter night, when I was seven or eight, gazing out our bedroom window and watching our parents skating on the ice-glazed lawn, looking on excitedly as Dad casually lighted Mom's cigarette and the two of them swirled about with graceful ease, their cigarettes burning bright holes in the darkness. I remember thinking how splendid they looked and how fortunate we were to be their children. I wanted to stay forever in this house, with this mother, this father, this sister, our beloved dog, Lucky, here in Topeka, Kansas, the center of the universe. I was Dorothy in the Land of Oz, and the Wicked Witch was nowhere in sight.

Two

SILENT SUBJECTS

Is your wife going the same way as her mother, and all knowing it?

—JEAN RHYS
Wide Sargasso Sea

There is not one but many silences . . .

—MICHEL FOUCAULT
History of Sexuality

At the age of eight, I did not know of the letter our parents received, in September 1950, from a New York neurologist, describing his examination of Mom's three older brothers. For some time, the eldest brother, Jesse, who was forty-eight, had noticed "jerkings" in his feet and "cracking" sensations in his toes. He tripped on stairs, dropped things, and had difficulty walking in a straight line. He complained of "nervous reflexes" and thought his memory was going bad. His wife, Lucy, was worried and took him to see a neurologist, who then asked to see the two other brothers.

Paul, who was forty-four, told the doctor he had been "nervous" for about ten years. He often stuttered or had difficulty finding words to express his thoughts, and he suffered from feelings of inferiority. He felt as if he were not balanced properly while walking, and his memory was so bad he had to make notes of everything he wished to remember. Seymour too came in for an examination. At the age of forty-three, he showed the fewest signs of anything wrong, but he too admitted he had felt "fidgety and restless" for the past four years and suffered a tendency "to forget little things."

The doctor wrote a long report of his findings. The eldest brother had a "generalized chorea with a well advanced organic mental syndrome." The second one, Paul, also showed "distinct choreiform movements" in the hands, feet, and tongue. The third brother, Seymour, had the mildest symptoms, but he too showed slight but definite choreiform movements when tense. "It is obvious," concluded the doctor, "that the Sabin brothers have a neurologic disorder which is characterized by chorea, mental changes, familial and probably hereditary factors." Their father had died of "nervous trouble" in a state hospital on Long Island, they said, but they believed his condition had been caused by business reverses and was not hereditary. The doctor thought otherwise. "The exact etiology is unknown," he wrote, "but it is believed to be a heredo-familial process in which there is a slow but progressive degeneration of the brain. The prognosis is not good," he added, "but I presume that there have been cases in which some members of the family are not affected."[1]

My father asked the doctors at Menninger's about this illness. They gave it a name: Huntington's chorea, a name all too familiar to my mother. Dad now learned that Abraham Sabin had died of Huntington's chorea, a fact Mom had not told him before. Since she thought only men could get this disease, she had not spoken of it. At least that is what she explained to Dad at the time and told us later, after she herself developed the same symptoms, though she also said she *had* told Dad, only he didn't remember. The idea that Huntington's was exclusive to one sex or another was common among affected families, who constructed different theories depending upon who among them had the disease. Some physicians also spread similar misinformation. Still, I can't help wondering how Mom, a genetics student, could have relied for her knowledge on one erroneous neurology text, as she said, unaware of the considerable medical literature on the subject. Had she managed to persuade herself she was not at risk, despite what she had read? Had she conjured up this idea much later as a way of explaining her silence in the past? What was certain is that at the age of thirty-six our mother learned that all her brothers were ill with Huntington's. And if she had not already known her own risk, she discovered it now. Not only she, but her daughters as well, were at risk for her father's disease.

I scan the snapshots for traces of the avalanche that had come crashing into our mother's future. What was she thinking, that autumn afternoon, when the letter from New York arrived in Topeka? In whom did she confide? With whom did she weep? With our father, who did his weeping elsewhere, though we did not know it at the time? In a passport photo from the summer of 1951, Mom and Nancy and I gaze into the camera, our three serious heads nestled together as if for warmth. Someone photographed our family on the deck of the Stavangerfjord *before we sailed from New York to Oslo, where Dad was treating a patient for the summer. Dad looks irritated, Mom is exhausted and smiles wanly, Nancy and I are bashful and hot in the summer sun. In a trunk full of photographs from that summer in Norway, I find Mom's green diary, where she wrote about our travels and the hospitality of our hosts. There is no mention of chorea.*

I have no memory, nor does Nancy, of any emotional scenes at that time, nor any recollections of Mom's shock or grief, though it is difficult to believe she could have wholly hidden these feelings from Nancy and me. We were five and eight at the time, old enough to notice. What I do recall is a scene of myself seated in front of the large radio console in the dining room of our house in Topeka, waiting for my favorite program. But instead, a man's voice came on the air announcing that there would be no *Baby Snooks* because Fanny Brice was dead and there would be a program of classical music instead. I did not want classical music, I wanted *Baby Snooks,* and I felt angry and abandoned. Today, though, I wonder if that memory of mourning for *Baby Snooks* might disguise a deeper memory of Mom's grief for her brothers, which she tried very hard to hide from us. For Dad told us later how devastated Mom had been at the news about her brothers, how fearful of what lay ahead for them and for herself. And how guilty she felt that she might have passed on the illness to her children. What did she see when she looked at us now, her daughters, frightening memories of her father still lingering from her childhood? What did we see when we looked at her, our young mother, her eyes filled with sorrow?

Dad decided he must leave Topeka and Menninger's for private practice elsewhere. Mom's brothers did not have much income, and he felt a sense of financial responsibility; he worried that someday he might have to care for Mom too. Although he loved Menninger's, he had dreamed of moving to California, perhaps to San Francisco, where he had been born. His parents had gone to San Francisco from New York shortly after the 1906 earthquake, hoping to cash in on construction opportunities. But the West had disappointed them, and soon after Dad's birth in 1908 they had gone home to Brooklyn, dreaming of an eventual return. For my father in 1951, the time seemed right. He immediately began scouting out possible locations.

Mom, however, felt ambivalent about leaving a community where she had finally made friends and begun to feel comfortable. Her letters to Alene in the spring of 1951 were unusually cryptic. "I suppose you know that we are making decisions about leaving here," she wrote. "The reason is financial. We are going to need quite a bit more money." She would explain when they came to New York that summer. She did not mention chorea, but she did mention how hard it was to move again "even further from our family and from you." She wished they could live close enough together to enjoy each other's kids. "It just doesn't seem right that we should be so far apart just now." Mom ended the letter with intimations of disaster. "The world situation certainly stinks," she wrote. "I felt quite hesitant about making a move now when things are so uncertain, but Milt says we must live as we want while we can and so I am just hoping we can do it."[2]

Soon after our arrival in Los Angeles in the fall of 1951, we moved into a big, raw, ranch-style house on hills overlooking the Riviera golf course and the Pacific Ocean in the distance. Our parents joined the circle around another analyst and his wife, Ralph (Romi) and Hildi Greenson, who had a kind of salon at their Santa Monica home. Actors and analysts, dentists and writers and musicians gathered every weekend at the Greensons', where there were string quartets, readings of Eugene O'Neill, and always lots of warmth and laughter. Dad and Romi became close friends, sharing an office together in Beverly Hills for the next twenty-five years. Mom too began making friends among the wives of the analysts and the mothers of our friends. "Of course the physical aspect of our living is delightful," Mom wrote Alene soon after we arrived, "if only our friends and family were here, it would be ideal. We feel so damned far." She longed for Alene more than ever. "I have made many friends here," she once wrote, "but there has never been anyone who could quite take your place."[3]

Mom spoke little about her brothers, who were far away in New York, though she visited them every year. Nancy and I knew vaguely that something was wrong with our uncles, especially after Seymour came to visit and we could see his strange, stumbling gait, his constant grimacing and slurred speech. But these uncles seemed to me a shadowy presence, more names and faces in photographs than real people. None of them had any children, so there were no first cousins to make the connection, though we later discovered more distant cousins. Mom didn't explain, and I guess we didn't ask.

Grandma Sabina died suddenly a few years after we moved to Los Angeles—like everything else in Mom's family, this death felt vague, faraway, slightly unreal. We had not known our grandmother well, except that Mom always spoke of her adoringly and would tell us how strong and vivacious she was. She had raised Mom essentially as a single mother when her husband became ill and had remained an emotional mainstay of her daughter's life. Mom flew to New York for the funeral but didn't say much about it afterward. She mourned her mother's death as she had her brothers' diagnosis, quietly, privately, and out of sight of her children.

What we saw in our mother in the mid-1950s was not a grief whose origins we could grasp but a sadness and shyness that seemed part of her nature. Although she could still muster moments of gaiety with friends, she struck them as frightened and amazingly insecure. At home she grew quieter, more timid and unsure. She had been unable to choose furniture for our new house, so Dad hired an interior decorator to come up with colors and designs. A dinner party required weeks of anxious effort and elaborate preparations. Even our own friends were not always welcome unless the house was immaculate. Once, when I invited my sixth-grade class to a graduation party, Dad, in a spectacular tour de force, hypnotized Mom in front of the entire group. Sitting there watching with my friends, I was proud of my father, yet irritated with him for calling everyone's attention to himself. And I was ashamed of my mother, and it occurred to me that she seemed hypnotized much of the time anyway, even without Dad's machinations. I wondered in my diary if she was very intelligent, because "she never says much during more profound conversations, nor has any ideas."

Nancy and I tried to get Mom to talk to us about the past, but she told the same stories, over and over, about her summer at Woods Hole and teaching in Harlem. Finally we stopped asking. When we went to her for advice, she would always say, "Ask your father," until we gave up in despair. Her passivity was maddening, yet every time I got angry with her I felt like a monster. I hated the way she played the martyr, always sacrificing herself for others, never asserting her own wishes, always apologizing just for existing. I envied my friends with loud, bossy mothers who punished them when they disobeyed and knew how to stand their ground.

Now in her early forties, our mother seemed increasingly spectral, like one of the shades in Virgil's *Aeneid* whose laments we translated in my high school Latin class. I remember once sitting with her at the breakfast table, watching her as she smoked a cigarette and gazed out the window dreamily, looking past the rosebushes in the backyard and out toward Catalina Island in the distance. I asked her whether she and Dad would ever get a divorce, since they spoke so rarely to each other. Smiling sadly, she assured me that they wouldn't, that they were happy, that they loved each other. I think I believed her. But I couldn't help wondering why Dad never looked at her when he came home for dinner, preoccupied and irritable, and why he always shut himself up in his study at night to dictate letters on his new Dictaphone, while Mom sat alone in the living room, reading or watching television. For a long time I thought the natural relationship between two married people was silence.

Years later, Dad would tell us how much Mom had changed from the lively, witty, vivacious woman he had married in 1936. By the late 1950s, she had become obsessed with household chores and domestic routines. Her checkbook baffled her. Although she read books and followed the news, she feared to voice an opinion and would always defer to my father. She began to seem more like another child in the family than a mother. Certainly she had long since ceased to be a wife. As we grew older, she mined her past with a certain urgency, seeking memories to bolster her self-esteem. She began turning increasingly to her daughters as proof of her own self-worth. "All in all, taken all together, I could not have been such a bad mother to have produced wonders like you," she wrote plaintively to Nancy and me.[4] I hated it when she talked like that. If she could not have her own life, how could we have ours? I felt vaguely guilty, as if we had somehow stolen hers away.

A gigantic black hole yawned at the center of our family, but no one named it or acknowledged its existence. This was just the way things were, though Nancy recalls sensing that something was actually wrong with our mother. My sister and I did not discuss these feelings, and I am not at all certain we could have, since we really did not know what else to expect. The idea that our mother was seriously depressed and needed help never occurred to me. If Mom was more passive than most women were, she was merely an extreme version of the ideal American wife. Could we have known something was awry and yet not known, all at the same time? Did our minds work hard not to know, not to interpret the signs all around us? The diaries I kept make no mention of anything gone wrong in our family, only in myself. These were the 1950s, after all, and in many ways we fit the ideal of a successful American family, with all the trappings of affluent domesticity. If I felt unhappy or distressed, the problem was mine.

Yet what were the fifties but an attitude of denial, that peculiar Cold War state of mind in which painful stories were carefully buried while we composed cheerful ones to take their place? As a child I had been exceptionally happy, my life a series of exciting adventures crafted with my sister and various friends. I was Nancy Drew solving murder mysteries in the empty lots and chaparral-covered hillsides of our neighborhood. I was Brenda Starr, girl reporter, editor of our fifth-grade newspaper at UES (the experimental University Elementary School at UCLA, for training teachers). After our class toured the *Los Angeles Times* and I got to interview Aline Mosby, the first woman United Press International correspondent in Moscow, I decided I would become a correspondent too. Besides writing stories, I loved playing the piano, a skill I acquired at the age of six. Discovering that I had perfect pitch and could play by ear, like her musician brothers, Mom carted me off to lessons and I became quite a proficient pianist. I always felt most myself while playing the piano.

Around the time Elvis Presley appeared on *The Ed Sullivan Show,* I noticed I was not happy anymore. While my friends began having boyfriends and dates, I had none, convinced I was doomed to be ugly and unpopular. From the ranks of successful children, I was becoming a junior high school outcast. True, I did well in school and was always dashing off to some meeting or other of the clubs and committees to which I belonged. But forever awkward in braces and glasses, I felt increasingly like a ghost, completely lacking in looks and personality. Clearly I did not look like any of the 1950s versions of a beautiful girl, like the star of *Gidget,* Sandra Dee, for instance, who graduated from my high school the same year I did. In my shyness and anxiety, I was terrified of becoming just like Mom. I looked like her—everyone said so—despite my red hair and freckles. With her blond hair and blue eyes, Nancy resembled our father, and as we grew older the family lines were drawn. I kept a diary to document my misery, noting unrequited love for boys who never acknowledged my existence and fierce contempt for those who did. There was certainly something wrong with me, I felt, but I never could figure out just what it was.

For a while in the midst of that Cold War decade, dimly aware of the Bomb and Joseph McCarthy, I was obsessed with death, cremation, and mortuaries. Dying fish jumped out of my dreams, flapping on floors and gasping through torn gills. I walked along the beach looking for death, transfixed by dead seals that had drifted onto the shore, dead jellyfish melting in the sun, dead gulls with broken necks and matted feathers. Dad said I was morbid and should try to think of more cheerful things. I thought about sex, which I studied in his books. The complete works of Freud marched across the shelves of my father's study, along with my favorite text, that lurid 1950s classic by Edmund Bergler, *Neurotic Counterfeit—Sex,* which Dad had warned us not to read. I was especially intrigued by Bergler's exciting descriptions of "perversions" such as homosexuality and exotic forms of masturbation, which I practiced at night beneath the sheets while imagining various scenes from these thrilling books.

Dad said I was unhappy because I was preoccupied with being popular, a teenage disease, and he regaled me with stories of his own teenage shyness, as if to assure me that my peculiar state of mind was merely a stage of normal adolescence. My one undisputed talent, playing the piano, linked me with Mom's strange musician brothers, and I certainly did not want to be like them. I wasn't sure what I wanted to be like, though I knew I liked writing—poetry, journalism, stories, diaries, anything that involved putting words on paper. Entering Stanford in 1959, I signed up as a psychology major, vaguely intending to follow in my father's footsteps. But the classes bored me and I had no talent for them. Nor did the honors program, into which I was invited, arouse much enthusiasm.

Fidel Castro and the Cuban revolution excited me more than my dull psych classes or my honors seminars. So after spending a semester abroad at Stanford-in-France, I changed my major to Latin American Studies and landed a position writing for *The Hispanic American Report,* a monthly journal staffed mostly by radical graduate students. The sixties had not yet reached Palo Alto, and I knew only vaguely of the Beats in San Francisco and the Free Speech movement across the Bay in Berkeley. But hanging out at Bolívar House, practicing my Spanish and using my newly acquired French to write the sections on Haiti in the *Report,* I felt I had found my milieu.

Nancy, meanwhile, had blossomed in high school and even began attending classes at UCLA before she graduated. She won first place in a contest sponsored by the Pacific Palisades Junior Women's Club, and afterward her beaming photograph with our parents appeared in the *Los Angeles Times.* When she graduated among the highest in her class, her English teacher, one of those rare individuals for whom teaching was a genuine calling, wrote in her yearbook that students like her made it all worthwhile.

Yet Nancy bore the brunt of our parents' deteriorating marriage, particularly after I left home for college and she found herself, while still in high school, playing the role of confidante to each of them. She and I did not speak much about the events transpiring at home. I did not want to think about the family situation and pretty much left my sister to face it alone. Later she admitted how difficult it had been and how frustrating she had found Mom's growing withdrawal. She told how once, at a friend's house, she had started "sobbing and shaking in despair, crying that I no longer had a mother, that my mother had escaped somewhere and left a shell, that I didn't want only my father's voice, my father and a shadow, but I wanted two parents." But Mom steadily grew more distant and depressed, as if she had retired to a land beyond our reach.

Mom told me the news of Dad's decision to divorce in the summer of 1962. She had come to Paris where I was staying after the session at Stanford-in-France had ended. Feeling very independent, I was not pleased to have my mother arrive to take me on a vacation of her own, particularly now, when I felt I had to console her in her deep distress. Nancy and Dad were off in Mexico City at a psychoanalytic congress, no doubt having adventures. I felt bereft, jealous too, since they were together while I was stuck with my depressed mom. For all my doubts about our parents' marriage, the news of the divorce came as a bitter revelation. Part of me really had idealized our family, accepting a kind of family romance in which we were superior to other families with their messy fights and delinquent kids. Besides, our father was a psychoanalyst whose business it was to treat other people's problems. He was not supposed to have problems of his own. But there it was, a divorce after twenty-five years of marriage, years when I had struggled hard not to see what was going on around me, training myself not to know, not to question, not to trust my own perceptions.

Dad always traced the beginning of our hostilities, his and mine, back to the divorce, and perhaps he was right. No doubt he received a double dose of anger, the anger that could not be expressed so directly toward our more vulnerable mother. All of a sudden I could barely talk to my father, raging at him not for divorcing Mom but for the many years in which we had watched his daily, obvious dislike of her. Mostly, though, I was furious with him for the sense of betrayal I felt when we found out that the woman whom we knew as his professional colleague, a clinical psychologist, was also his lover and had been for many years, since Nancy and I were both small children in Topeka. Dad and Maryline Barnard had met at Menninger's in 1946, and she too had moved in 1951 to Los Angeles, where she shared the office with my father and Romi Greenson. We knew her also as a trusted family friend, especially after Dad bought a summer house at Lake Tahoe and he and Maryline bought another one down the road from us to use as an office (and as Maryline's home) and we all spent several summers there together when Nancy and I were teenagers. Some of their most severely disturbed patients would go to Tahoe to continue their therapy—as part of Dad's intensive approach to treating schizophrenia—and he and Maryline would see these patients several hours every day. Sometimes Nancy and I helped care for them.

No one spoke about the relationship between Dad and Maryline, neither Nancy nor I, not our mother, not any of their friends, at least not to us. It simply *was*: a fact of nature, a relationship that had existed for as long as either my sister or I could remember. Dad always referred to Maryline as his associate, and that was that. It was as if a powerful taboo surrounded these adult relationships, akin to the confidentiality associated with patients in psychoanalysis, so that we did not even dare to question their relationship in our heads, much less speak of it aloud. To do so would have been far too frightening, since it would probably have brought our parents' marriage to an end much sooner. Dad's relationship with Maryline, highly visible yet hidden, remained like a tight knot at the center of our family, a firmly closed book. Even after the divorce, we did not really discuss it. To raise questions about it, even many years after it ended, seemed to them an attack, a brutal invasion of privacy, an expression of my hostility and anger, which was always lurking under the surface, ready to explode. Knowledge and the taboo against knowledge competed for legitimacy in our family, and there were strict borders around that country of curiosity that all adolescents inhabit. Nancy and I could, I suppose, have broken up the family by posing questions early on, forcing the issue on all concerned. "And would that have been better?" Maryline asks me now. "What would have been a better alternative?"

Nancy did not share this rage I felt toward my father and Maryline, nor the sense of betrayal at discovering this family secret, perhaps because it came as less of a shock to her. Nancy pointed out that Mom too had colluded in the fiction of the marriage, had pitied Maryline even, as a single woman with no children of her own, a difficult life in the 1950s. And Dad had not abandoned our mother, had not walked off and left us on our own, as so many men left their children. He had stayed with us, making sure Mom was well taken care of, materially at least. Should we blame him for wanting to stay with his children even after his marriage had become a desert? He had played the role of husband so well their friends had believed they were happily married. He thought of himself as an angel of endurance.

By the time Nancy entered Radcliffe, in the fall of 1963, the civil rights movement was in full swing, *The Feminine Mystique* had just appeared, and the Kennedy era was about to end in a blast of gunfire on a Dallas street. She felt relieved, I think, to leave the gloomy atmosphere at home and sent us all long, ecstatic letters in triplicate describing her classes and recounting her discoveries of Thomas Aquinas and the Russian folklorist Vladimir Propp. After much hesitation, she finally chose a major in social relations in order to work with the psychoanalyst Erik Erikson and wrote an honors thesis on George Eliot, a psychological literary study I always thought was as much about her own struggle for independence as about that of Marian Evans. She also acquired a boyfriend, a handsome fellow student who lived for a time in Boston's South End, where Nancy spent days, even weeks, at a time.

We wrote letters back and forth between Cambridge and Caracas, where I had gone to study on a Fulbright after graduating from Stanford in 1964. Nancy came to visit me at Christmas, and we traveled to Margarita, a pearl-fishing island where we ate fresh oysters and lolled on the beach. Ostensibly studying "social change" at the Central University in Caracas, I spent much of that year traveling around the country with my boyfriend, an anthropology student and aspiring *político*. Together we went on field trips through the *llanos* of southern Venezuela and around the shores of Lake Maracaibo, though I had no idea about Huntington's then, no notion that Maracaibo would play such a major role in the life of our family.

Uncle Paul died that year, the second of Mom's brothers to go. While Mom was in New York for the funeral, Dad took Nancy out to dinner and briefly explained the disease. Our mother, he said, was not in danger. I had not yet returned from Venezuela, and neither of them wanted to convey this news long distance. When I came back, the need for discussion seemed to have passed.

If, however, we did not discuss the past, we did talk about the future in great detail. I don't know how our father, whose ideas about women were quite conventional, so readily accepted the professional aspirations of his daughters, but he did, with much encouragement and even enthusiasm. For several years he wrote Nancy and me long, thoughtful letters, urging us to think beyond the search for a man and to consider work we would really like, spelling out the drudgeries and advantages of graduate school as he had experienced it. He talked me out of journalism school on the grounds that a graduate degree in an academic field would be better preparation. Ultimately he talked me out of journalism altogether. Or perhaps I was beginning to have doubts about my desire to live in Latin America and whether I was assertive enough for this career. I decided to pursue a Ph.D. in history, specializing in Latin America. At least, I thought, I would have stories to write, even if they came from the archives rather than the streets. After completing the course requirements at Indiana University, I started to work on a dissertation about the tango and popular culture in turn-of-the-century Buenos Aires, while spending as much time as possible in bed with a blond midwestern fellow student, trying to make up for my lost years as a virgin. After exams, I would finally get down to the business of being a real historian—and a writer.

Nancy had still not decided on a profession even after she graduated from Radcliffe in 1967, although she was considering psychiatric anthropology, "the common thread through many of my interests," she wrote home to Dad that summer. Like me, she received a Fulbright fellowship, and she spent half a year in Jamaica, at the University of the West Indies in Kingston, trying to put together a research project that might be "the kernel of a Ph.D. dissertation." Just as Nancy had visited me in Caracas, I went to see her in Kingston, taking with me a copy of Ernest Jones's biography of Freud, which I had never read. Both of us, I suppose, were trying to find ways to build on the family legacy of psychoanalysis while creating a separate identity for ourselves. But while I approached psychoanalysis gingerly, perhaps not wanting such intimacy with my father, Nancy embraced it with considerable, if critical, enthusiasm. After six months in Jamaica, feeling frustrated with the slow progress of her research at the university, she decided to leave for London, where Dad had arranged for her to study at Anna Freud's clinic for child psychoanalysis in Hampstead. Nancy spent the next six months observing "Miss Freud," as everyone called her, and sending us amusing descriptions of the "hot air" and "drips" and "tight, unexpansive spinsterish people" she encountered, including a medical student who blushed whenever anyone mentioned sex.[5]

It was during this period of immersion in psychoanalysis that my sister finally decided to pursue graduate work in psychology at the University of Michigan, one of the few clinically and psychoanalytically oriented programs in the country. She and Dad had been corresponding extensively, and Nancy felt grateful for his encouragement. "Much much love and the fatherly tone of your letter was fantastic," she wrote him in the spring of 1968. "I still get scared and need to learn temperance and moderation." Psychology, she felt, was "something I would have to come to terms with sometime or other, anyway. It's funny that now when I've decided on a Ph.D. in psych. and am even looking forward to ploughing [through it], I feel more than ever that I don't need to stick to psychology. . . . I don't know what branch I will go into, teaching or therapy, or what, but I don't care. It will work itself out."[6]

Our parents' separation in 1962 had released all sorts of energies and enthusiasms in our father. He traveled in Europe in the summers, studied French at the Alliance Française, took a boat to Greece and toured the ruins and the islands. He wrote us exuberant accounts of his adventures, and when he returned home he became more involved professionally with a group of emerging Los Angeles artists, whose work he came to know and admire. His associations with artists such as John Altoon, Ed Moses, Larry Bell, and Billy Al Bengston—who were beginning to gain national recognition—would later deeply influence his approach to science.

Our mother too seemed to flourish, at least for a while. She took up the painting she had begun back in Topeka, had dinner parties and went out with her friends. After an absence of twenty-five years, she returned to school, to UCLA, earning A's and B's in the graduate courses required for a junior college teaching credential in biology. Living in an apartment on Sunset Boulevard in Brentwood, alone for the first time in her life at the age of forty-eight, she spoke about finding a job, though Dad continued to support her financially. He still watched her for symptoms of Huntington's. But he detected no signs of incipient illness and was beginning to feel confident that she had escaped.

The year after the separation, in the summer of 1963, Mom stopped in Mexico City on her way to visit Nancy and me in

Guadalajara, where we were studying Spanish. Early one evening, on the Paseo de la Reforma, four young thugs stopped her taxi, shoved the driver out of the car, seized her wallet, pulled off her earrings and wedding ring, blindfolded her, and drove her high into the Lomas de Chapultepec, where they dragged her out onto the ground, beat her severely, and raped her, each one sitting on her head while another took his turn. Then they left her there, alone in the cold Mexican night and knowing no Spanish. Dazed and bloodied, she went from house to house, knocking on closed doors and pleading for help, until finally someone phoned an ambulance and she was taken to a hospital, terrified and swollen and covered with bruises. Dad flew to Mexico City and took her back with him to Los Angeles, returning angrier than I had ever seen him at the indifference of the U.S. consul, who had blithely informed him that such things happened every day and that nothing could be done, not even a protest, because it would be bad for tourism.

Mom spoke little about the rape, at least to me. But she took a year's leave of absence from her courses at UCLA, and for months afterward she locked and relocked all the doors of any car she was riding in, and she suffered severe anxiety attacks. Yet somehow she mustered the energy to return to her classes in 1964 in order to complete the requirements for teaching. She received her credential in 1967.

She was volunteering now in a genetics lab, where she helped prepare slides for the microscope. Huntington's was clearly on her mind, and despite her active social life, she felt lonely, writing us letters full of painful longing. "It's funny," she wrote once, "last night I had 3 drinks, I could not even be gay. I think having you both here this summer was so wonderful but now it is quieter than ever and I seem to mind it more." When I sent her a poem I had written, in the summer of 1964, she wrote me a poignant reply, telling me that my "beautiful poem" had made her cry and that she had never understood me. She hinted at the inner life that she had never been able to share with us. "I have always felt that my writing could not begin to touch any of you in the family," she began, "so I was always content to send off the happy little on-the-surface letter describing the externals of my life." She wished "we could start over again, without the mistakes, but we can't." She blamed herself for the abyss between us. "I know there were so many times when I was hurried by lots of small things and couldn't take the time to listen. Now, I have the ears, the time and the inclination, and no one at all is here." And then, everyone was "so wrapped up in their own inner voices that it is hard to look around at others. Your father never really talked to me for such a long time, and I suppose I in turn was battling so much inside of me that I couldn't hear you." She was not sure she was making sense, "because I know I am feeling so sorry for much time we had together that was not only not meaningful but painful."[7]

Mom's letters to us were written in a neat, upright hand, on pink notepaper. Gradually they came less frequently, then not at all. In the late summer of 1967, returning from a trip to Buenos Aires, where I had begun doing research for my dissertation, I was painfully impressed by Mom's lack of initiative. I noted in my diary the great distance between the accomplished young woman she once had been and the passive, depressed, childlike creature she was now, at the age of fifty-three. Her aimlessness also struck Nancy when Mom visited her in Jamaica that autumn. As they went to sleep at night, sharing one bed, Mom seemed unusually restless and twitchy, as if she simply could not get comfortable. Still no one spoke of Huntington's, not even when Uncle Seymour died later that year, the last of the Sabin brothers to go.

Now Mom seemed to have abandoned all her earlier projects. Her plans for teaching, for finding a job, were no longer discussed. She seemed to be waiting for something to happen. "I know something just right for me will turn up," she would say and drop the subject. Her attention span had grown shorter, and she became querulous, upset over trifles. She seemed nervous and fearful, ready to jump at any unexpected noise. Although she loved music, she would not turn on the expensive hi-fi that Dad had installed in her living room; the dials distressed her. Shopping had turned into a compulsion. She filled her closets with Italian wool suits from Saks, pastel-colored linen dresses, and expensive silk evening outfits for events she would never attend. She talked obsessively of food, and her loneliness hung about her like a shroud. "She is alone, looking into space with big sad eyes," I wrote unkindly in my journal, "not comprehending, like a child beaten by an invisible ogre, who silently cries for mercy from the unseen monster." She did comprehend, but she could not speak the name.

Three

1968

It is either the beginning or the end
of the world, and the choice is ourselves
or nothing.

—CAROLYN FORCHE
"Ourselves or Nothing"

Even now, the diagnosis of Huntington's melds in memory
with all the other apocalyptic moments of that spring and summer of 1968—Russian tanks smashing into Prague, Martin
Luther King, Jr., dead of a bullet in Memphis, Robert Kennedy
shot in Los Angeles as he campaigns for president at the
Ambassador Hotel. Nancy is off in London, doing fieldwork
among the psychoanalysts at the Hampstead Clinic. She writes
home that she fears she has shocked Anna Freud with her
short skirts and freewheeling ways. I am in Bloomington,
preparing for doctoral exams, watching Eugene McCarthy's fal-
tering campaign, and trying to break up with my hippie
boyfriend, who has decided to go to work for the railroad after
finishing his M.A. in history.

One day Dad telephones Nancy in London, and then he also
calls me. He urges each of us to return to Los Angeles for our
annual summer visit somewhat earlier than we had planned,
proposing that the three of us take a vacation together. We
could drive across the country, he says, through Yellowstone

and Jackson Hole and the Dakota Badlands, while we make our way back to Indiana and Michigan for the fall semester. His sixtieth birthday is in August, and he would love to spend it with us in this way. We both agree to come. By chance, a few weeks later, my sister and I arrive in Los Angeles within a few minutes of each other. Dad meets us—unusual since Mom generally picks us up at the airport—and we drive to his apartment in Westwood. We go into the bedroom and sit on the beds, perhaps—as my father says later—to recall our childhood days when my sister and I would climb into our parents' bed. Words are spoken, but I no longer remember them. I recall the whiteness of that apartment, our three frozen forms like a George Segal sculpture, my sister and I sitting with our arms around each other staring at my father's ten-foot-high Mike Olodort painting of a huge upside-down Humpty-Dumpty with tiny arms and legs waving in the air and an enormous, sinister smile on his face. There are no tears, no welling floods of grief or anger, but for me only a numb, anesthetized feeling, like being shot full of novocaine. In an instant I shut out my father's words, which I have never been able to remember, as if denial could undo the event.

Years later, I ask Dad just what he said that afternoon. "I told you your mother had Huntington's chorea," he says, "that it was a progressive, degenerative, neurological illness, that it often caused madness, that it was always fatal, and that both you and your sister each have a fifty-fifty chance of inheriting the illness yourselves. You know what you both said?" he asks. " 'Fifty-fifty? That's not so bad.' That took a terrific load off my mind." "But of course it wasn't true," I tell him. "I was scared to death." "Maybe," he replies. "But I was awfully glad to hear it just the same."

Dad, Nancy, and I head out along Highway 99, driving east through Las Vegas and Salt Lake City and then north along the

Snake River into the Grand Tetons and Yellowstone. I do not re-
member much about the trip except feeling miserable. But there
are snapshots of my sister smiling out of the mist at Old Faithful
and seated on the ground cross-legged with her camera raised,
squinting up at the strange granite faces of Mount Rushmore, and
my father posing like a boxer on the rim of the Dakota Badlands.
Dad is already full of plans for fighting this illness, mobilizing sci-
entists to engage in research to find a cure, or at least a treat-
ment. He is going to save Mom, save us, save everyone else who is
at risk for Huntington's. The genetic revolution has begun, he
says, and everything is possible. Nancy catches his enthusiasm
and excitement. They are like two kids spinning out fantastic pro-
posals, already on a crusade to "lick this thing," as Dad would
later put it. I am feeling extremely sorry for myself, and their op-
timism and energy annoy me. Why do they have to be so damn
cheerful, I ask myself morosely, even though I know they too are
in pain. The highway stretches through endless empty wastes,
cracked and barren like a Frida Kahlo landscape. As we drive we
listen to battle reports on the radio from the Democratic National
Convention in Chicago, hear police smashing the heads of stu-
dents. Later we see pictures of Russian tanks rolling into Prague,
a fitting metaphor, I think bitterly, for the crushing of our own
hopes and dreams. Our Prague Spring has ended, too—will there
ever be another?

I had never heard of Huntington's chorea until that afternoon in our father's apartment, and at first I did not want to
learn too much, as if knowledge of the symptoms would bring
them on. Mom's experience was not unusual. One morning in
May, a policeman had seen her weaving her way across a parking lot in downtown Los Angeles, heading for jury duty in the
Federal Building. "Hey, lady," he had called out, "aren't you
ashamed of being drunk so early in the morning?" But she had
not been drinking—in fact, she drank very little—and she

must have known instantly what the words really meant. In a panic she had called Dad, who had told Romi Greenson, who in turn had called a neurologist he knew who agreed to come by his office later that afternoon to take a look at Mom when she came back from jury duty. Dad said later that after seeing her and hearing the family history, the neurologist knew at once. There was never any doubt.

I dreamed that a friend was going to be hanged. The event took place in a large school auditorium that looked out onto a hallway, like a hospital corridor, very cold, damp, and grim. The auditorium was filling up with people. I wandered off into the corridor. When I returned, it was over. His body was lying on one of the balconies where he had been hanged. I went up to see him. He was fully clothed, lying as if asleep on some benches. But his face was all black and blue and terribly distorted. He began to twitch, to jerk around, to throw his arms about. And then he actually began to get up. His eyes opened. The girl watching over him said this was normal, that dead people often got up and jumped around like that. But I wasn't so sure he was really dead.

George Huntington once attributed his interest in medicine to an accidental childhood encounter with the illness that later came to bear his name. "Driving with my father through a wooded road leading from East Hampton to Amagansett [Long Island], we suddenly came upon two women, mother and daughter, both tall, thin, almost cadaverous, both bowing, twisting, grimacing. I stared in wonderment, almost in fear. What could it mean?"[1]

What it meant, he learned later, was a condition that had existed for many years on Long Island. Evidently it had existed for many more years in western Europe, where it has been traced back genealogically to the mid–sixteenth century in Norway and to the early seventeenth century in France and

England. It is unclear, however, if people at that time thought in terms of an inherited family disorder or even if they considered the symptoms as a disease. The later designation of certain "megrims" or "magrums" families suggests that these behaviors may have been popularly regarded as a peculiarity or a defect of particular families, rather than a definite illness.[2] As they often were even in the twentieth century, these families may have been regarded as "queer" rather than sick, and affected individuals as mean and malicious rather than ill.

Still, some descendants of the English colonists who settled in Massachusetts, Connecticut, and New York, especially on Long Island, in the 1630s, used names more indicative of disease, including "that disorder" and "Saint Vitus' dance" (a name that technically referred to the temporary chorea often striking children in the aftermath of rheumatic fever). Sometimes they spoke of the shakes or the fidgets or, more colorfully, the jerks, or simply, nervous trouble. Some said it had begun as a curse on those who had persecuted the religious dissident Roger Williams, while others traced it back to their English ancestors.[3] Though the disease evidently first arrived in New England from England, immigrants from other parts of Europe took the condition to different parts of the United States, while European and North American immigrants and travelers to Africa, Asia, Australia, and Latin America established further outposts of the illness; the history of chorea is also the history of European emigration and colonial expansion.

Medical accounts of involuntary, excessive, and uncoordinated movement began with the great Renaissance physician Paracelsus, who introduced the term "chorea" in the sixteenth century and described some varieties of chorea as the product of organic disease. He and others after him, especially Thomas Sydenham, an eminent seventeenth-century physician in England, attempted to classify different types of chorea and to describe their causes, whether organic or psychological, temporary or chronic, coming on in youth or striking in middle age. None of these early accounts mentioned heredity as a cause. Still, there were so many theories about the origins and varieties of chorea that the famous American physician William Osler once compared it to the classic Spanish "rotten pot" meal of boiled meats and vegetables. "In the whole range of medical terminology," he wrote, "there is no such *olla podrida* as chorea."[4]

Not until the early nineteenth century did considerations of heredity enter the medical accounts of chorea. In the 1840s, several physicians, in the United States and England and also in Norway, began writing about people with involuntary movements and mental disturbances inherited from a similarly affected parent, an illness they called chronic hereditary chorea. Just why a disorder that seems to have existed for several centuries was not described unequivocally in the medical literature until 1841 is unclear. Possibly physicians did not regard inheritance as a differentiating factor until the emergence of evolutionary theory and hereditarian social thought in the nineteenth century.[5] At any rate, a number of neurological diseases, such as Tourette's syndrome, were also first described by doctors in the mid–nineteenth century, and the growing social emphasis on heredity certainly helped focus attention on inherited mental disorders. The increasing professionalization of medicine in the United States may also have motivated more physicians to publish their observations in the medical journals: all three of the earliest American accounts of the illness were by young clinicians just out of medical school.[6]

George Huntington was only twenty-two when he delivered his paper in 1872. Though not the first, his was the most accurate and eloquent description of hereditary chorea put forth until that time. It also accorded more importance to "the tendency to insanity, and sometimes that form of insanity that leads to suicide." Indeed, clinicians today place increasing emphasis on the cognitive decline and severe emotional disturbance that accompanies the physical disorder, especially depression, irritability, out-of-control angers, obsessions, and compulsions. Subtle personality changes sometimes precede the involuntary choreic movements by many years, so much so that doctors now refer to a zone of onset rather than an age of onset. Although people with Huntington's retain their sense of orientation through most of the illness (unlike with Alzheimer's, for example), dementia is common toward the very end, which might be ten to twenty years after the onset of the earliest symptoms. As one neurologist later wrote, "In the final stages of dementia, the patient presents the pitiful picture of the complete ruin of a human being."[7]

George Huntington's account won immediate recognition, prompting a spate of publications on the disease by some of the most eminent turn-of-the-century neurologists and psychiatrists, including William Osler, perhaps the most famous physician in late-nineteenth-century America.[8] (Indeed, the period from about 1900 to 1917 constituted something of a high point of interest in Huntington's, with a surge of publications in the medical literature emphasizing the genetic dimension; not until the 1950s, with growing interest in human genetics prompted by the discovery of the double helix and concerns over the genetic impact of the Bomb would Huntington's again attract growing medical attention.) In the decades prior to World War I, the impetus was as much social and cultural as medical or scientific. In an era of mass immigration from southern and eastern Europe, with the tremendous growth of cities and the spread of urban slums, eugenic ideas flourished, particularly among the white, native-born, Protestant population fearful of "race suicide" and their own loss of status. The popularity of eugenics no doubt helped call medical attention to this obviously inherited physical and mental disease.

One of the most enthusiastic eugenicists, the biologist Charles B. Davenport, discovered in Huntington's a powerful ammunition for his eugenic ideas. Davenport had founded Cold Spring Harbor Biological Laboratory on Long Island, near where some of the earliest families with the disease had settled. In 1910 he also established a Eugenics Record Office which sponsored studies of families with allegedly inherited disorders. He believed Huntington's was "one of the most dreadful diseases man is liable to," though he did not have much sympathy for those who had it. In his view, the state that understood the dangers of chorea and did not "do the obvious thing to prevent the spread of this dire inheritable disease is impotent, stupid and blind and invites disaster."[9] The "obvious thing" was compulsory sterilization and immigration restriction, to keep people with Huntington's and those at risk out of the United States. But despite Davenport's repressive agenda, he usefully documented certain characteristics, such as the autosomal dominant inheritance pattern of the disease—which means that only one parent, of either sex, need have it to pass it on to a child. He also sponsored the largest study until recently of families with Huntington's, sending out a young physician, Dr. Elizabeth Muncey, to interview hundreds of individuals in the New York–New England area. The chorea stories she gathered offered powerful testimony to the emotional horrors of the disease, as well as the resilience and courage some people mustered in dealing with it.

With all the increasing attention, however, recommendations for therapy remained almost nil. Some physicians told of favorable results with arsenic. Others recommended potassium of bromide, quinine, chloral, or hyoscine for sedative effect. Belladonna alkaloids were used into the mid–twentieth century, along with recommendations for rest, isolation, exercise, and a regular life. William Osler even suggested a water bed to avoid bedsores. The most poetic prescription lauded the music of a violin, which the keeper of a county almshouse reported had had wonderfully soothing effects on one of his patients

DOMINANT INHERITANCE

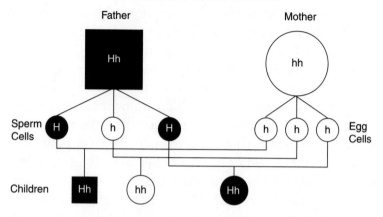

Parental genes come in pairs, except in the egg and sperm cells that have only one copy of each gene. In this family, the fate of each child depended upon whether the father's normal gene (h) or the Huntington's gene (H) was present in the sperm at conception.

with chorea, allowing him to eat his meals and go to sleep at night. After all, observed Clarence King, a physician with a particular interest in Huntington's, "The soothing strains of music have been known to appease the wrath of demons and quiet the fury of beasts. . . . Why, then, should we be skeptical as to the influence of music upon the brain centres in other directions?" But despite King's enthusiastic call for music therapy, none of the treatments slowed the progression of the disease, nor did they reliably ease the symptoms. William Osler's despairing observation in 1894 would remain relevant for decades to come. "Unhappily," he wrote, "the treatment of chronic progressive chorea is futile."[10]

If eugenic ideas and the rediscovery of Mendelian genetics stimulated interest in Huntington's disease at the turn of the century, so too did advances in neurophysiology and neurology. Although some researchers argued that chorea resulted from inflammation related to encephalitis or meningitis, a few investigators had begun to theorize a correlation between involuntary physical movements such as those seen in Huntington's chorea and damage to that part of the brain known as the basal ganglia. This structure, buried deep inside the brain, was known to have some control over movement, as well as over cognition and emotion. It consists of several distinct knots of neurons (hence the name "ganglia," or knots). At the center of the basal ganglia is a lens-shaped knot made up of two parts, the globus pallidus and the putamen. These structures nestle next to a larger elongated structure called the caudate nucleus, which curves over and around them like a tail or a tongue, thicker in front and thinning out toward the back. (Because of their streaked appearance, the caudate, putamen, and globus pallidus are called collectively the striatum.) Physically separated from the striatum but intricately connected to it through a series of neuronal pathways is the substantia nigra, consisting of two small knots of neurons on either side of the striatum.

By the early twentieth century, investigators had identified the caudate nucleus as a central target of destruction in Huntington's chorea. They noted too that the brains of people who had died of Huntington's had shrunk drastically, especially in the region of the caudate nucleus, whose weight had sometimes decreased by a third. But what caused the brain to wither and die? And why did specific types of cells in the caudate nucleus die more rapidly than others? Were they victims of a murderous toxin produced in the brain? Were they dying for lack of some crucial nutrient? Did they somehow commit suicide, following the timetable of genetically programmed cell death? Or was this destruction in the brain a by-product of a disease process taking place in some other part of the body?

There were other peculiarities that researchers had noted earlier. While symptoms generally began in the fourth or fifth decade of life (Huntington had described a slightly earlier onset), about 10 percent of the cases involved children. And of these, most had a father with the disease, rather than a mother. Moreover, though the ill parent of a child with Huntington's might have the characteristic uncontrollable choreic movements, children who developed the juvenile form of the illness showed quite a different picture. They usually grew rigid and stiff, slowing down dramatically both physically and mentally. Moreover, they usually deteriorated more rapidly than the stricken adults, often dying within seven or eight years rather than the characteristic ten to twenty. Clearly the same gene was capable of causing a surprisingly wide range of symptoms.

There was also the mysterious fact that when people with Huntington's fell asleep, their movements ceased and they looked like anyone else. Yet when they awoke the insidious movements immediately started up again. Not surprisingly, people with these movements usually grew thin and often emaciated, unless they were able to maintain a high-calorie diet, which was hard since eating and swallowing became progressively more difficult as muscle control weakened. Researchers were uncertain whether the constant movement of chorea consumed enormous numbers of calories and led to weight loss or if there were metabolic changes that might also account for the physical wasting.

What made Huntington's especially cruel was that everyone who developed the disease had usually seen what happened to an affected parent or other relative. They had often grown up in a severely disrupted family, especially if they were relatively young when a parent began to show symptoms. Frequently they did not know the parent had a specific illness, since relatives often suppressed this information. Misdiagnosis was also prevalent—people with Huntington's were often told they suffered from alcoholism, schizophrenia, or assorted other maladies. Whether diagnosed or not, Huntington's involved

behavioral changes that usually carried serious social consequences, and children frequently suffered both the loss of a
parent and the stigma and shame of social isolation, of feeling
different and abnormal. Huntington's could make a parent
abusive or turn a young child into a caregiver for a sick parent.
And since adults had usually had their families by the time
they became symptomatic, they also suffered the guilt of knowing that they might have passed on their illness to their
children.

It was this possibility of transmission that persuaded Dad
not to tell Mom right away that she had Huntington's. He
feared the consequences of hitting her with this double blow—
a death sentence for herself and a 50 percent risk to her children. So instead of telling Mom the truth, he and the
neurologist told her that she suffered from demyelenation of
the nerves, a condition not unlike multiple sclerosis, which
was causing her to weave and stumble. The condition was progressive, they said, but not hereditary. She would not pass it on
to her daughters.

I doubt that Mom believed this story, knowing what she
knew about her father and brothers. But she did not question
it, and perhaps for a while she tried to accept it. To Nancy and
me, she did not appear much different than she had before the
diagnosis, but we paid more attention now to the tiny twitches
of her fingers and toes and the way she swayed slightly as she
walked beside us, especially as she climbed the stairs to her
apartment, leaning into us from time to time. The slight movements of her body could have passed for ordinary restlessness,
the faintly grimacing smile a forced effort at pleasantry. But we
knew now that they weren't, and we found ourselves watching
her more closely, as if our own mother had suddenly turned
into a stranger.

After a while, Nancy and I began to feel quite uncomfortable
with the false diagnosis she had been given. We thought she

had probably guessed the truth, even if she did not say any-thing to us, and we felt as if we were somehow conspiring against her. One day, Nancy took her to see the Arlo Guthrie movie *Alice's Restaurant*. Nancy thought that seeing the charac-ter of Woody Guthrie in the film might help Mom to talk about her own condition. In the movie, Arlo goes to the hospital to visit his father, who is bedridden and far advanced in his ill-ness, though he still manages to smoke a cigarette. At that point in the film, Mom became very agitated, turning to Nancy and insisting that they leave the theater. Once they were out-side, Mom refused to talk about what had upset her. Nancy said later she felt like a murderer, since she gone to see the film knowing it might mention Huntington's.

Sometime later, we were all over at Maryline's house in Brentwood, sitting outside by the oval-shaped swimming pool in the backyard. Maryline still shared an office with Dad and worked closely with him, though their relationship was now more professional than personal. She remained a family friend, and Nancy and I usually stayed at her home when we came to Los Angeles to visit; we all occasionally had dinner together. Whatever our mother may have thought about this situation— she never told us; nor did we ask—it was not unusual for us to be at Maryline's house with Mom.

At fifty-three, Mom was still slender and attractive, with smooth, soft skin and short, carefully coiffed brown hair barely streaked with gray at the front and sides. She appeared so youthful that the three of us could almost have passed as sis-ters, sprawled on our beach towels in the southern California sun. Nancy began telling Mom about some of the fund-raising activities that Dad had begun at that time on behalf of Huntington's disease.

"I know," Mom said, "I read about it in the newspapers."

"So she does know!" we both thought. "Isn't that great!"

Nancy said, "There's really beginning to be a lot of interest in this illness." She launched into a detailed account of new research and fund-raising projects that were under way.

"Yes, it's terrific," Mom agreed. We both breathed a sigh of relief, thinking we wouldn't have to pretend any longer. "But I don't have Huntington's disease."

Nancy and I looked at each other, startled. Mom was seated between the two of us, facing Nancy. I sat slightly behind Mom at the edge of the pool, where she could not see me, dangling my feet in the water. Fearing to upset Mom, I started motioning to Nancy not to continue. But Nancy was too distressed by the games we were playing to stop now and felt it would be better to come out with the facts. "Mom," she said gently, taking a deep breath, "you do have Huntington's. At first we thought you didn't, that it was some other illness that was causing your unsteadiness. But now the neurologist is certain. That's why Dad has become so active in doing something for Huntington's. It's because of you."

Mom accepted the information bravely, and we were even more certain that she had already known. How could she not have known, a biologist trained in genetics who had watched the illnesses of her father and all three of her brothers, all dead of the disease? Afterward I felt ashamed that we had played this game, hiding a truth that must have been obvious all along. At least now, on account of Nancy's courage, there were no more secrets and it was better because we could talk about Huntington's without having to dissemble and pretend. We could let her know that we were not going to abandon her on account of this illness or hold her responsible for our own fate. Dad too made it clear that he was going to take care of her, even fight on her behalf.

Mom had never spoken much about her feelings, and now we continued to talk with her mostly about practical things—the apartment, clothes she needed, medication, subscriptions to magazines, doctors' appointments. But her eyes were full of a fear that never really left her, and she was rapidly losing whatever strength and initiative she had mustered following her divorce. She complained mostly of her loneliness. She continued to live in her apartment on Sunset Boulevard, with a live-in nurse whom Dad hired to take care of her. Helen was a wiry, chain-smoking woman from Boston, an Irish Catholic turned Buddhist who wore a white nurse's uniform and had Mom chanting mantras all day long until she finally protested and we persuaded Helen to call off her campaign. Eventually we moved her into a house in the San Fernando Valley with a nurse and several other people in need of care, and she stayed there until the nurse and my father had an argument. Then we moved her into a nursing home on San Vicente, the first of many. Since Mom and Dad were divorced, Medi-Cal paid some of the bills and Dad took care of the rest. Dad also turned to his physician friends, especially Bernard Salick, who cared for Mom faithfully through all the crises. The San Vicente place was not unattractive, and she had a pleasant room with a small patio and plenty of light, but she knew what lay ahead of her and exactly what to expect.

I dreamed I was leaving Mom's apartment with a friend, about to drive downtown, when I remembered I had not brought my lunch. As it was too expensive to buy lunch, I rushed back inside to make a quick sandwich. I opened the refrigerator to find that Mom had neatly laid out, in a plastic bag, a skinned snake, split open like a cleaned fish. I shuddered in disgust.

In Ann Arbor and in Bloomington, Nancy and I struggled to come to grips with our mother's illness and our own new identity—a "spoiled identity," as the sociologist Irving Goffman might have described it. I did not, of course, think of it that way at the time. Rather, Mom's diagnosis plunged me into a crisis of self-confidence. Once again my beliefs about our family had been overturned with the revelation not only of Mom's illness but of her knowledge, and Dad's, about Huntington's in the family, which she and Dad had not disclosed. I marked a new notebook "Vol. I, No. 1," as if unconsciously recognizing this new phase of my life, though I did not write anything about the disease. Instead I filled pages with obsessive self-criticism and endless worry, especially about my resemblance to Mom. Was I going to become just like her? Perhaps I already was. The thought of seeing a therapist put me off even though I knew needed help, because "wouldn't that be essentially seeking out a father surrogate?" I did not need another analyst/father. Ending the relationship with my boyfriend that was spluttering to a halt, I resolved to give up men and sex, as if this sacrifice of pleasure could restore Mom to health. The words "Huntington's disease" did not appear in my diary at all.

Five months later, I fell in love.

It was in January, and I had gone to retrieve some blue book exams from the house of a fellow graduate student; we were teaching a course together at Indiana University, and the exams had gotten mixed up. Doug wasn't home, but his roommate was. John had just bought a Melitta coffeemaker, and he invited me in for a cup of espresso. He was getting his doctorate in medieval English, he told me. With his dark, curly hair, startling blue eyes, and full lips, I assumed he was Jewish but soon found out that he was Syrian American. Later we used to joke that he looked Jewish but wasn't, while I didn't look it but was.

Within a few weeks I knew this was the man I wanted to marry. Beginning his career as a medievalist, John Ganim had already won distinction as a critic and writer. He was also an inventive cook, whose wonderful meals were famous all over Bloomington. His father was a pharmacist and his parents ran a drugstore near Weehawken, New Jersey. Growing up just across the Hudson River from Manhattan gave him, I thought, a wonderfully original sensibility, as if he were always looking from off center. He had spent much of his adolescence and his years as a Rutgers undergraduate in the cafés and experimental theaters of Greenwich Village, and he introduced me to avant-garde art, to underground films, writers and theater. He especially had a passion for architecture, and he educated me not only about buildings but about cities, and how to see them and live in them. I later felt that I learned more from John than from all the formal education I had ever had. In addition, he was affectionate and very funny and made me laugh. If he was also a little emotionally distant, I tried not to let it bother me. I felt ecstatic that I had found this man, who I was certain was the great love of my life, "the one and only. And I've never believed in such things before." Just a year after Mom's diagnosis, and about five months after John and I met, I noted in my diary "the end of an incredibly happy year."

But in fact, for much of that year, and for a long time afterward, I was overcome by terrible feelings of inadequacy. It was only a matter of time until John realized his mistake. True, I had told John about Huntington's soon after we met, and he had assured me that he accepted the risk and that he wanted me anyhow. We had even discussed the likelihood that we would never have children of our own, and that, too, John was willing to accept. Nonetheless, in the midst of this new love, I was often seized with an overwhelming anxiety, as if something terrible were about to happen. I remember, in the lush green of our first Indiana springtime, wandering the campus feeling barren and empty, as if nature were somehow mocking my own lost possibilities.

On the weekend of my twenty-seventh birthday, May 31, 1969, I hit a new low. John and I had traveled to New Jersey to visit his family in Weehawken. Despite their warm welcome, I felt increasingly awkward, tongue-tied, and depressed. Meeting John's friends, I felt even worse, "so inadequate, so boring and dull, couldn't think of anything to say," I wrote miserably. John asked if I were tired and sad. "You look sad," he kept saying all through the weekend. But I had no answer. Huntington's did not seem an adequate reason for feeling so unhappy, since it still seemed distant, Mom's illness, not mine. One night, after a party with John's friends where I had felt utterly miserable, I broke down in tears, sobbing that I did not deserve his love, that I feared disappointing him by not being more lively and interesting. John was genuinely surprised, reassuring me that this was totally absurd and that I seemed to think he was not very perceptive. Neither of us, as far as I remember, ever said a word about Huntington's that weekend. I too had learned habits of denial and displacement, determined not to let the illness—or my consciousness of the illness—intrude on my life, though I realized "it's almost as if I'm trying to *prove* to John I'm not worthy of his love. As if I *want* to destroy our relationship to prove that I'm right—that I really am no good." John's love, I thought, might be able to save me. I clung passionately to that love even while fighting crazily against it.

Mom's diagnosis had shattered my plans to return to Argentina for a year of research. Going so far away from home felt like abandoning the family, although no one ever suggested it was. Besides, a murderous right-wing military dictatorship had come to power in 1966, and I wasn't sure I wanted to return anyway. Nor did I want to leave John for so long. All I wanted was to finish my degree as quickly as possible. Instead of Buenos Aires, I went to Washington, D.C., to research a historiographical dissertation on Spanish, Cuban, and U.S. narratives of the 1898 war in Cuba—a topic that interested me much less than the tango. These were the years of the huge anti–Vietnam War marches and the Washington Area Free University, and I became active with both for a while, especially with *The Tin Drum*, the WAFU paper. Struggling with my thesis at the Library of Congress, and then later back in

Bloomington, I felt thrilled to be living with John yet tormented by anxiety and bouts of depression whose origins I still could not fathom. Here I was, twenty-eight years old, achieving everything I wanted—graduate school success, a dissertation almost done, a boyfriend whom I loved very much—and I felt "old, ugly, useless, out of fashion, out of step with everyone and everything." John too was haunted by "some terrible huge thing with which he must come to grips" and a fear of "some secret unknown terror, like a feeling of guilt or sin." Except for brief moments, Huntington's simply did not enter into the conscious emotional landscape of our lives, which were either beginning or ending—I could not decide which.

How do I piece together the shards of memory from that time after the diagnosis, when we were trying to get on with lives that could never really be the same? How to construct my sister's thoughts and feelings from the conversations, letters, snatches of dialogue over the phone late at night or on walks through Ann Arbor in the middle of winter, when we would stop at a playground and swing on the swings, laughing hysterically like kids, then go back to her apartment on Hill Street, where we would down a quart of ice cream in half an hour, listening to Vivaldi and Woody Guthrie and the Rolling Stones? She too tried at first to live as if nothing had changed, not talking to friends or professors about being at risk. Yet how long was it possible to live divided, concealing what was becoming the real center of her life?

Even before Mom's diagnosis in 1968, Nancy had heard about our uncles' disease, when Paul died. But Dad had assured her that Mom would not get it, and she had felt a sense of shock and unreality when she heard that Mom had not escaped. Her immediate response was that here was a story from someone else's life. "What did a *goyishe* [non-Jewish] name like Huntington have to do with us?" she wondered. Afterward, two images lingered from that afternoon. "What I remember most taking away from that day was that our mother was dying and that I had decided I shouldn't have children."

She liked her new life as a psychology graduate student. Already in her second year she had patients of her own. She was rushing around among classes, supervisions, patients, T-groups, drug outreach programs, and case presentations. She was camping, cooking, going to parties, movies, and concerts, taking trips to Detroit, Toledo, Upper Michigan, New York. Perhaps we had only imagined this disease running in our family, this new way of thinking about our lives. Perhaps we were just at risk for life, like everyone else. She did not speak much about Huntington's to her friends. It was hard enough being a new graduate student, living this new existence. She was just starting her professional career, and she wanted to think of beginnings, not endings.

She wrote us wonderful letters, apologizing for not writing sooner even if she had written the week before. "Dear Mom," began one letter. "Sorry it's been so long since I've written. I've been fantastically busy since we last talked." But things had been exciting "and I'm happy with my work and my friends. Life is very active but I enjoy running around."[11] A friend, John Weisman, a music critic for the *Detroit Free Press*, took her to concerts, including a Rolling Stones concert, where they sat close to the stage. "I could see the sweat flying in every direction and every leer and goggle and fish mouth of my dirty idol," she wrote ecstatically. The next night they hiked up to Keith Richards' hotel room to see tapes of the show—"Keith looks like a real Soho hooligan," she wrote, "streaked cyclonic hair, missing tooth. What a phenomenon!"[12]

The suicide rate for people with Huntington's is seven times higher than the average, especially for those in the early stages of the illness. Even before we told her the truth about her illness and

before the idea ever entered our heads, Mom had insisted pro-
fusely to Nancy and me that she would not try to commit suicide,
perhaps to let us know she was really considering it. One night,
about a year after the diagnosis, Helen, the nurse, happened to
awaken toward 3 A.M. and noticed the bedroom light on in Mom's
room. She went in to look and found Mom sleeping deeply, an
empty bottle of pills next to the bed. When Mom could not be
awakened, Helen called Dad, who called an ambulance and
rushed over with Romi Greenson, who gave her a shot to stimu-
late her heart. Then they went with her in the ambulance to the
hospital where her stomach was pumped out and she was revived.
But afterward she worried that she had done further damage to
her brain, and there were many occasions when she considered
making another attempt and even talked about it with Dad and
with us. Years later Dad said he thought he had made a terrible
mistake that night when Helen called. He'd acted stupidly, he felt,
on reflex. Mom knew what lay ahead from having seen her broth-
ers, and she might have been spared the awful, miserable years
ahead. He hoped that if he were sufficiently disabled we would
"help him across" as well.

Nancy said later that Mom's suicide attempt had marked a
watershed in her life. It had brought home to her for the first
time, in a very concrete way, how desperate Mom felt. She decided she wanted to do something on behalf of those with the
disease, "to feel as if I was taking some mastery over this
calamity that had befallen us," she wrote later. She had always
described herself as a "doer-freak," attracted to things that
made her feel slightly anxious. Just because Huntington's disease was so threatening, she wanted to find out all about it, to
try to do something about it. As Nancy put it later, "My way of
handling things is to be as counter-phobic as I possibly can. If
I'm afraid of something, I want to know the best and the worst
about it, rather than live with an unnamed dread." If her dis-

covery of Mom's illness just when she was entering graduate school had struck a hard emotional blow, it also came when she was still considering her professional options, before she had specialized. Now, very gradually, she was beginning to see Huntington's not only as a curse but as a challenge. Dad summed up the feelings of both of them. "Activity, fighting the devil, was our only hope for survival," he wrote years later. "As long as we were in motion we could maintain some hope."[13]

From the start of Mom's illness, and especially after the suicide attempt, Nancy and I constituted ourselves as Mom's personal cheering section.

October 28, 1971: "Dear Momele, Como está? Life has been quite hectic but on the whole I enjoy my work. The HD committee is growing by leaps and bounds. We're really getting it together and I expect a breakthrough soon!!!!! Much love doll. I miss you. love N." November 5, 1971: "Dear Momaligula, I've just skipped class and am taking a little break—dreaming out my window on a chill, windy day. Thank God it's Friday. What a week! Working every night. Went out to dinner and got lobster on Weds. Yum!!! The HD stuff is going great guns and is all I'm interested in doing. School work is for the birds." "It was terrific to hear from you again!" Nancy wrote to Mom in March 1972. "You and your phoney balony about handwriting! You know, your HD isn't going to disappear if you don't write letters. Maybe that's harsh but it's true—your handwriting isn't going to get better or worse if you don't write—in fact, it probably benefits from practice (look who's talking—old letter writing kid herself!). Anyway, your handwriting is very legible and hasn't changed at all as far as I can see." And again, "Much much much love and *many many* thanks for writing. I think you don't realize how much it pleases me." Most of the time she was so busy "I can't keep track of myself!" a refrain heard more and more over the years.

Mom sometimes returned to the subject of suicide, and Nancy and I would plead with her not to try again. Nancy especially wrote her long letters trying to cheer her and urging her to keep on with the struggle. "Dear Momele," she wrote in 1973, close to five years after Mom had been diagnosed. "I hope you are feeling somewhat cheerier these days. When I said it was OK to feel depressed I really meant it. But there is a big difference, Ma, between feeling depressed and trying to kill yourself. Dad said you were looking for some medications to overdose again. I *know* this is a scary disease, Mom, and I *know* you get very discouraged, but you are very far away from the way you last remember your brothers. You are clear in your speech and make very much sense when you talk. As a clinician, I can guarantee you that you are in no way, shape, or form crazy and you can communicate very well. . . . You know, there is no telling how much functioning may come back when they find a cure." Nancy emphasized that Mom could help the struggle. "You've got to be part of the fight too," she urged Mom. "The most important reason to keep on fighting, though, is that Aly and I love you very much and you mean a lot to us. You talk about changes which are happening to you but doesn't it occur to you that we love you however you are? Why do you think we want to move to Calif? . . . Don't rush it. You are still our Mother. . . . HANG-ON-IN-THERE, MA!!!!!" Nancy urged. "I know it is rotten and miserable, and frightening and infuriating and all the rest, but that little 94-lb. body of yours has got the answer in it and WE ARE CLOSE!!! You were a pioneer in your family, in your teaching, in your genetic research. It's not easy, it's tough and painful, but you've got to be a pioneer for us all now once again. And I think you can do it! Love and love and love and love, Nancy."[14]

We must have convinced her, for she never made another suicide attempt, and she was always eager to participate in research efforts, even when they involved painful spinal taps or foul-tasting food. Aware of her steady decline, she faced her illness with dignity and grace, though we did not always see it that way at the time. She was the last of her family to develop Huntington's—after all of her brothers—and the first, we hoped against hope, who was not going to die of the disease.

Four

DREAMING CHOREA

I look like you, you look like me. I look at myself in you,
you look at yourself in me.

> —LUCE IRIGARAY
>   "And the One Doesn't Stir Without the Other"

In individual emotional development, the precursor of the
mirror is the mother's face.

> —D. W. WINNICOTT
>   *Playing and Reality*

Mothers and death haunted my dreams. The nights were
filled with terrors and rescues, with landscapes threatening
danger and disgust. I dreamed of a hospital ship, with long
white corridors, crushed by a huge wave, bodies drifting everywhere, and me rescuing them all and earning their gratitude.
And then I was flying through ancient hillside ruins, a man behind me in hot pursuit through all the crumbling rooms and
rock piles. Hiking through wildflowers, I spotted a girl whose
skull was ripped off and bloody at the top. Inside, her head
was almost empty, except for the brain stem, which stuck up
like a stalk of celery. We carried her to the hospital, too late.
Much later I dreamed of a broken doll, the limbs all withered
and falling off the body. It was the remnant of a baby, my baby,
that I had allowed to die through my own negligence. I had
forgotten all about her for several days.

*I was staying in a large house, like a villa. The lady of the house
was petite, trim, feminine in a traditional way, like Mom.*

Suddenly a catastrophe struck. It might have been an earth-quake, but the ground didn't shake. Outside I saw my car melted away, only the burned top was visible. The other cars too were piles of ashes. I was with John. I said to him, "No matter what happens, I'll always love you." We stood waiting to see what would happen. Later I discovered a piano in the spare room of the house. I had wanted a piano so much but hadn't even bothered to explore the house fully to see what was there. It had been there all the time.

I watched myself for signs and symptoms. Sitting in the library or playing the piano, I would inspect my fingers for jerks and twitches. After a while I stopped the piano lessons I had resumed in graduate school, since playing reminded me of my musician uncles, all dead of Huntington's. Besides, the piano now seemed less a pleasure than a test of coordination and steadiness. (In my dreams, though, the piano reminded me of my childhood, the sign of a skill that no one else in the family possessed.) When I lost my checkbook, could not find a word to express my meaning, when my thoughts refused to organize themselves on the page or a minor mishap sent me into a fury, when I stumbled across a parking lot or fidgeted through a lecture and couldn't remember anything that was said, I would get extremely anxious, wondering if the process had begun. Like many people at risk, I worried most about a mental decline, fearing that my brain might be going to ruin and that I could no longer trust my thoughts. These fears led an underground existence, unacknowledged except occasionally in conversations with Nancy. I never wrote about Huntington's in my journals at all.

Though I had done very well in graduate school up to now, the fact that I had changed my dissertation topic troubled my adviser. He felt that I had abandoned not only Latin American history but him as a mentor, and he questioned the seriousness of my commitment as a scholar. I had not, of course, told him that I had just learned of Huntington's chorea in my family. Switching advisers, I managed to complete my dissertation and land a job as assistant professor in the history department at Sonoma State College (later University), an hour north of San Francisco. Mom was thrilled, "The first Ph.D. in my family and very exciting news," she wrote to me in her shaky scrawl. In this small, liberal arts college, the department wanted not only a Latin Americanist but someone to teach classes in the history of women in the United States. I did, and found I enjoyed it and wanted to continue. For a conference in 1973, my students and I created a multimedia slide show on women's history, which they took out into the community, as far away as Mexico City and Washington, D.C., where they persuaded Congress to mandate a National Women's History Week. I felt proud when the collective they formed around the slide show became the foundation of a National Women's History Project, bringing a feminist, multicultural history of women into the secondary schools.[1]

I dreamed I was taking care of a baby chicken—only it was almost like a baby. It was wearing a diaper—when I brought it back to the nurses taking care of it, they took off its diaper and there was an enormous steaming pile of shit on the plate—almost as big as the chick itself. Later the chick was in a casserole in the oven. I took it out and pulled off the pastry and celery leaves covering up its head. It looked up at me sadly. It realized it was going to die. They were going to bake it. I couldn't figure out if this was a baby or a chicken.

One day David Schickele, a filmmaker friend, announced that he had fallen in love with Emma Goldman, or rather with her 1931 autobiography, *Living My Life*. David suggested we make a film about this militant early-twentieth-century anarchist and feminist. In the process of researching the proposal, I fell in love with her too. Or perhaps not exactly in love, for Goldman inspired admiration and respect more than love. "Her name was enough in those days to produce a shudder," wrote a friend. "She was considered a monster, an exponent of free love and bombs."[2] That was probably why I liked her. I too felt a bit like a monster. And except for the fact that they were both Jewish, Goldman was about as unlike my mother as any woman I could imagine, strong, expressive, and fiercely present. David and I eventually had to drop the film project, but I was hooked on Emma Goldman, especially since her passionate inner life and sexuality seemed so accessible—unusual in a public figure. I taught a class on her life and soon began to think about writing her biography.

All this activity helped ease the pain of watching Mom's decline, but it could not stop the inexorable progression of the disease, which was becoming all too real and palpable. My sorrow for my mother was all mixed up with sorrow for myself and for my sister, for our blighted futures, for the children we would never have. I summoned that common fantasy of daughters, of some infinitely healing conversation in which Mom would confide all her hopes and fears, her own history of this illness that had rampaged through her life, which she had known of but never told us about. She would break through my lifelong disappointment with her passivity, and we would console each other for all our losses.

But there was to be no real talk between us, not then or ever, and the occasions when she did tell us a little about her childhood and her life were so special that I always noted them in my diary. Much later, my sister and I would try to reconstruct the history of her illness, to date the onset of her symptoms. We would ask ourselves, over and over, what in Mom's behavior was due to chorea? what to character? what to the Cold War culture of the 1950s, with its celebration of the feminine mystique? How much was grief over the long dying of her brothers? the loneliness of an unloved wife? anxiety about her future and ours? What if she had remained a scientist, still studying those *Drosophila* she had started to investigate back in Thomas Hunt Morgan's fly room at Columbia in the 1930s? Most of all, we wanted to know, why, why, had she not told us about Huntington's long ago, so that at least we could have shared her sorrow?

I sometimes thought of my mother as Gertrude Stein thought of Oakland—"there's no there there"—and yet her physical loss seemed to awaken all sorts of longings and confusions and angers I could not understand. New fantasies entered my imagination, of watching women making love or making love myself with a woman while in reality I was making love with John. These new images both excited and frightened me, seeming like a barrier between us that could not be scaled. I did not then consider pursuing these fantasies in real life, yet there they were in my imagination, and sometimes in my dreams as well.

John and I were living in Cotati, an idyllic little town near the college and close to the wine country of the Napa and Sonoma valleys, where he finished writing his dissertation. When he was hired by the English Department at the University of California at Riverside, not far from Los Angeles, I moved to San Francisco. This arrangement made commuting easier, and we also both preferred the city to the sleepy charms of Sonoma County. We commuted on weekends, we struggled, fought, were lonely, were loving, and missed each other terribly. Sometimes I felt angry at John for not being the mother I had never had, and sometimes I felt angry at him for being too much like her in his emotional reserve. I wanted him to engage more with me, fight with me, even, while he, who had always had too much of fighting in his family, longed for peace and a kind of acceptance he felt I could not give. My at-risk status made him feel anxious and paralyzed; how could he get angry at me if my moodiness and withdrawals were the first, early signs of Huntington's? How could I get angry at him, who had given up the possibility of children to be with me, who had chosen to live with this horrible threat?

I came home and found all my books missing from the bookshelves, and all my clothes gone from the closet. I had an awful sinking feeling of having lost something irreplaceable.

Five years after we first heard about Huntington's, I was feeling alternately hopeful and desperate, full of a longing I could not name, yet also blocked, as if an ice field were growing inside me. John and I separated, then came back together. Our shared sorrow over the absence of children in our lives helped bring us closer. I began really to think about being at risk, admitting to myself that perhaps "I was trying completely to deny the whole thing by pretending it wasn't there." I knew I had not come to terms with the illness because "even now, to discuss HD or genetic illness is very disturbing and makes me feel very depressed." In a diary obsessed with self-analysis, the word "Huntington's" had rarely appeared, and only in connection with Mom. I decided to enter therapy in San Francisco, to sort out the strands of my confusion and depression. Dad's fierce determination to "fight the devil" certainly helped me, but I think, in the beginning, it also made me feel as if I too must be stoic and heroic, as if sadness were a feeling that must be fought rather than an appropriate response to the disclosure of Huntington's in the family. For a long time I felt ashamed that I was not as active as my father or my sister, who was writing her dissertation on the disease. Yet before I could do that I needed to grieve for the mother who was dying and the mother who had never been, as well as for the loss of my own previous identity, before I became a person at risk. My therapist, Alan Z.

Skolnikoff, helped turn depression into mourning: "He suggested realizing that there *was* something to be depressed about, me being thirty-five, fear of getting the disease, onset between 35–40 etc. could indeed account for depression." Slowly, very slowly, I began to feel I could untangle my depression "from me, that my being, my essence, was not depression."

Nancy and I spoke often on the phone, running up huge bills as we tried to sort out the symbolic meanings of this disease. For both of us, the diagnosis of HD struck at the heart of being a woman. In the sexual economy of our family, the facts of genetics were inescapably entangled with those of gender. Dad was strong, healthy, independent, while Mom was weak, dependent, and sick, an unloved and rejected wife to boot. It was hard not to feel that being a woman carried unbearable risks and dangers, that femininity itself was a disease. Not so different from other families, perhaps, except that, apart from Maryline—whose ambiguous status in the family complicated the connection we felt with her—there were no strong grandmothers, aunts, neighbors, or substitute mothers who might have taken Mom's place. Since the risk of Huntington's seemed to foreclose any possibility of bearing children, Mom's diagnosis meant a double blow to our identities as women. As Nancy wrote me several years later, "When I decided not to have children of my own I felt much more masculine and barren—as if the knowledge that I could have kids was an integral part of my feminine identity. I felt infertile—not that I had made a voluntary choice—and also damaged and less attractive as a woman. I also felt," she added, "that to be identified with Dad—to be masculine—was not to get sick with HD. I don't know if any of this applies [to you]," she wrote me, "but I do know that when I first found out about HD I felt much less of a woman."

But what exactly was a "woman"? The feminist movement

that blossomed in the late 1960s and early 1970s moved this question to the center of debate among the young women of our generation. Everyone was struggling to redefine what it meant and to throw off the repressive legacy of the 1950s—those long years of watching Debbie Reynolds and Doris Day and Marilyn Monroe at the movies or seeing our own mother, with her advanced biology degree, spending her days shopping and cooking. Huntington's merely gave palpable form, a powerful biological twist, to the fear many of us felt of becoming our mothers or, worse, of becoming the body out of control, joining that long line of monstrous female bodies our culture held up as the very figure of disgust—the witch, the hag, the hysteric, the whore,[3] and now, in our own private imaginary, the woman with Huntington's. At least Nancy and I had a special kind of sisterhood, and my attraction to feminism no doubt drew as much on the powerful bond between us as it did on our experiences of injustice as women. Just being able to compare reactions offered some consolation for the isolation of being at risk. But it was also true that within the family, accepted wisdom held that I looked more like Mom while Nancy resembled Dad, though she and I probably looked more like each other than like either of our parents. With Nancy following in Dad's footsteps by becoming a psychologist, I felt half consciously as if it were my fate to follow my mother by becoming ill, even if, by becoming a historian, I was taking a path unlike that of anyone else in the family.

There were other issues to explore as well. Were my lesbian dreams and fantasies, as my therapist suggested, representations of the bargain I had made with fate when Mom was diagnosed: that I would give up (hetero)sexuality as the price of her life, and of Nancy's and my own? Were they perhaps an unconscious effort to bring my mother back to life, to elicit the responsiveness that had been so missing in her, to make her come (back)? Or were they simply an expression of desires that could not be acknowledged more directly, and had nothing to do with Huntington's?

Nancy and I were walking home at dusk. A man stopped his car in the road to ask us directions. Then he got out of the car and started chasing us. We climbed down an embankment and ran into a little club at the bottom that turned out to be a gay bar. The man got distracted, so Nancy and I left. We were again walking along the road. We passed a parked car. Inside was a woman with a machine gun. We started running. Everywhere, it seemed, there were cars with people holding guns aiming at us.

Nancy and I tried to connect Mom's history with ours, to trace our common legacy of "a slow but progressive degeneration of the brain," the habits of secrecy and knowledge of stigma, the denials handed down from generation to generation. Years would pass before I could see a link between my own adolescent depression and my mother's deep sadness; years before I could recognize the sorrowing mother whom I carried inside me for so long. Had I perhaps taken into myself her sense of having something wrong with her, her worry that there might be something wrong with me, the daughter she had named after her father (Abraham), who looked like her and played music like her brothers, with their same fat thumb? Perhaps I was trying to prove her right, identifying with her anxiety and fear, modeling myself on an image of femininity that already bore the traces of Huntington's disease.

I dreamed of swimming in an old swimming hole with Nancy. Suddenly the water level started to go down and I could feel the muddy bottom and all sorts of huge, monsterlike fish burrowing around in the mud. They were horrible: enormous, ugly, slimy things. We ran out of the pond and back to the cabin where we were staying, trying to forget.

Mom's illness was turning all of us, but especially me, into historians, or Dostoyevskian grand inquisitors, as my father claimed when he felt I was tormenting him with my endless questions. For a second time, issues of knowing and not knowing, of secrecy and silence, suddenly grew charged. Once again what my sister and I thought we knew about our family suddenly shifted, and everything had to be rethought, reinterpreted. Who we were had suddenly been called into question and everything had to be reconfigured taking into account the presence of the disease. It was as if we had been experiencing fallout from some unseen bomb for all these years, and suddenly the great mushroom cloud had come into view and we could see the source of all that radiation. Struggles over Huntington's became the vehicle for expressing anger and guilt about that other family secret. Certainly my arguments with Dad recalled our earlier fights over Maryline and Mom, as if all our unresolved rages and resentments got displaced in a heap onto Huntington's.

"Did you know then?"

"No, I didn't know."

"But when did you know?"

"I told you. I didn't know."

"But when did you find out?"

"Not until Jesse was diagnosed."

"But didn't she ever say anything before that time?"

"No."

"Didn't she ever tell you about her father?"

"She just said that he had died."

"Did she tell you what he died of?"

"No."

"Did you ask?"

"No, I didn't ask. Why must you always accuse me?"

"I'm not accusing you."

"Why can you never believe what I say?"

"I do believe you. I just want to know. Would you have had children if you had known?"

"No . . . yes . . . I don't know."

These discussions always ended in tears and recriminations. "You're not interested in the truth!" my father would shout at me. "You just want to judge!" At one point, Dad's brother Henry wrote me a letter claiming that Dad had told him about Huntington's before my sister and I were born, not after, though later Henry decided his chronology was mistaken. But when I told Dad, one night in an ice cream parlor on Santa Monica Boulevard, what Henry had said, he flew into a rage. I had always done this to him, he said, I was so angry and judgmental. My question about whether he knew of Huntington's before having children was outrageous. "You didn't ask me innocently," he said. "How could you ask about a decision like that, about exposing children to such a terrible risk? How could you ever think I could do that knowingly?" He insisted he felt no guilt because he hadn't known about HD at the time. Why should I feel guilt? he asked. I never could persuade him that I was not blaming him but was asking these questions because I too wanted children and was trying to think through all the choices people might make if they already knew. When I allowed as how I was glad to be alive, even if he had known about the illness before Nancy and I were born, he got even angrier and we stopped speaking for a month.

On another occasion I called Dad on the phone to ask him when he would have told Nancy and me about Huntington's in the family if Mom had been killed in Mexico, before she was diagnosed. He wouldn't have told us, he said, he wasn't thinking about it then. He said he had probably deluded himself about it, he was convinced we were in no danger. He and Mom had never talked about it—"We didn't talk much about anything," he said—and he didn't think about telling us until after her diagnosis. I was shocked, so I didn't say anything. After I'd been silent for a minute or so, he started yelling at me about how Nancy and I were inquisitors, putting him on the rack, and so on. About how I was so goddamned self-righteous, so contemptuous, that I never believed what he said, that everything was an open question with me, there was never any closure, and so on and so on. He didn't want to be reminded of all his mistakes, and he thought my questions about Huntington's were just an excuse to express my hostility. "And I'm not the only one who thinks so!" he shouted. The other one was Maryline, of course, who thinks that if you ask her about the weather you are being a Sherlock Holmes. Dad said I was acting just like a lawyer or, worse, an investigative reporter, whose business it was to seek out wrongdoing. That I couldn't just accept an answer but asked the same question over and over, after he'd already answered it. All he wanted was a little peace and quiet, he wanted to think about the future, he'd earned that, he thought, and here I was always asking him, what were you thinking on such and such a day, when he didn't remember. "I think he's always had this attitude," I wrote in my journal, "don't ask questions, about Maryline, about Huntington's."

I'm in a house trying to pack up from a visit, but there are little fish everywhere, even in the toilet—when you flush, instead of one fish there are two—like little goldfish, but grey and ugly. They are all over the room, on the floor, in the suitcases, multiplying rapidly . . .

For a few years after her diagnosis in 1968, Mom wrote us letters, watched television, and played bingo with the other people in the convalescent hospitals that had become her home. Her old friends came to visit, taking her out for movies and walks. She read *Newsweek* and the *Los Angeles Times* and voted by absentee ballot for George McGovern in the 1972 presidential election. A lifelong Democrat, Mom observed wryly that "Most of the people here, the patients, are for Nixon. Can you imagine that!" For a while her involuntary movements were barely noticeable, just slight twitches in her fingers and toes, a tendency to lean to one side as she walked, an occasional stumble, frequent shifting of postures.

And then slowly Mom began to get worse, her depression more severe, her movements more noticeable. Her smile seemed forced, more like a grimace. She spoke more in short bursts, as if hurrying the sentences to get out the words, which were no longer clear. Previously a graceful person, she moved now in a jerky manner, especially when eating, an activity no longer to be taken for granted. Bringing a fork to her mouth required intense concentration. It would often land on a cheek or nose or anywhere but her mouth, smearing food over her face. She spent more and more time just sitting in a chair, her head flopping to one side or the other, then jerking upright, like a person fighting against sleep. An arm would suddenly extend itself at the elbow, only to be brought back down abruptly, and then after a moment of pause repeat the motion. Instead of resting quietly on the floor, her legs would continually shift and stretch, changing position in a perpetual silent dance. Mom's most passionate activity was smoking, which itself grew increasingly difficult and exhausting. As her chorea increased, she took higher doses of Prolixin, which calmed her body but, she feared, dulled her mind. "So I have to settle for being in good condition, but quiet," she wrote me. "Anyway," she added, "your father has not noticed my being quiet." During nine years, she was in five different nursing homes and two hospitals, losing friends to moves and, more often, to death. The frequent sirens from ambulances arriving at the convalescent home frightened her. "This place is making me sicker," she would whisper plaintively, like a terrified child. As it grew harder for her to talk and walk, and as her thinking narrowed, conversation grew exhausting and then almost impossible. She knew her words were barely intelligible and grew frustrated and angry at her inability to communicate. She would shout at her friends to go away and then complain bitterly of her loneliness.

One person whom she did not shut out was Maryline, who also visited her and helped Dad with some of the responsibility for her care. I could never decide whether Maryline's role as caregiver was the ultimate insult or an act of incredible generosity on Maryline's part, or even Maryline's way of staying close to Dad. Perhaps it was all of these. In any case, as Nancy reminded me, Mom accepted Maryline's help and did not scream at her or tell her to leave, comfortable, perhaps, with their long familiarity. During these years, Nancy grew closer to Maryline and even came to regard her as a second mother, a strong woman who could take care of herself and took the place of the mother who was fast fading from our lives. With me it was the reverse, since friendship with Maryline always felt like a betrayal of Mom. For a long time I oscillated between gratitude for Maryline's help and anger, not only about the past but about Maryline's sense that my anger was somehow illegitimate and inappropriate. Later, this book opened an abyss that could not be crossed. Maryline demanded that I leave her out, while I did not see how I could write it without her; she had been an integral part of our family, a part of my story as well as her own. She did not wish to discuss the situation or perhaps was no longer capable of doing so after having suffered a stroke in 1987. By the time she gave me "permission" to write what I wished, it was already too late, and we remained estranged.

Because Nancy and I lived so far from Los Angeles, it was Dad who bore the brunt of taking care of Mom, Dad who visited her every Sunday for ten years and often on weekdays, Dad, and sometimes Maryline, who fielded the emergencies and crises that always arise in the life of a person with Huntington's disease. As Mom grew worse, our family life ironically improved for a while, as if the seriousness of her situation overshadowed our various grievances and the need to fight against the disease overwhelmed our battles with each other. If many of our fights were never resolved but simply abandoned, at least we were learning how to put our disagreements aside and move on.

For all my anger at my father, I loved him deeply and knew our fights caused him pain. I knew that he had tried his best to protect us and that the knowledge of our risk was almost more than he could bear. I admired his courage and his lack of self-pity about what fate had handed him. I never once heard him complain about the burdens he had taken on after Mom's diagnosis. Nor did he complain about her failure to tell him the truth at the time of their marriage, although he must have felt deceived and perhaps angry at himself for not pursuing the hints thrown his way. He never asked Nancy or me to return home to take care of our mother, nor did he reproach us for pursuing our own lives far away from Los Angeles. He was incredibly generous, both emotionally and financially. Had our father not been so strong and so present—so much a mother as well as a father—I'm not sure how Nancy and I would have coped. As it was, for all our furious fights and shouting matches, we knew deep down that we were in this together, that love, at least, was on our side.

The question of probabilities haunted our lives. Nancy and I each had a fifty-fifty chance of inheriting our mother's illness, although whether one of us developed symptoms had no bearing on whether the other would as well. And yet we could not help thinking that somehow, if one of us were free, the other must be cursed. Magical, tormented thinking: if I wished to be free of the Huntington's gene, I felt as if I were cursing my sister. If I wished her free, then I felt doomed myself. Would we, if we could, find out about the future? Nancy thought she would; I was not so sure. Yet how else could we escape the ambiguity that seemed at times an unbearable tension? Whatever we did, we would do it together. Of that much we felt absolutely certain.

When I was sixteen Mom gave me a beautiful gold ring with an apple-jade setting. I loved that ring and wore it everywhere, but it was loose on my finger, so I took it off to type or to play the piano and one day it was lost. Ten years later, movers brought the family piano from my father's apartment to our house. They tilted the piano in order to bring it into the living room. "Hey, lady," called out one of the movers, "do you know there's a ring stuck in this piano?" With the end of a hanger he fished it out from between the strings. I remember thinking for just an instant that I hoped this gift from my mother was the only one she had left behind. I wear that ring now every day, as a kind of amulet, and no longer play the piano without it.

CHOREA
STORIES

Five years after her diagnosis with Huntington's in the spring of 1968, Mom's smile had begun to resemble a grimace.

Five

NEDDA AND HOPE

I said I would not be a tragedy,
I said to myself: Life, life . . .

—Minnie Bruce Pratt
"Seven Times Going, Seven Coming Back"

I always thought Nedda had a lot to do with what happened later in our family, that her getting better made a great impression on my father and persuaded him that even hopeless diseases might yield to research.

We had met Nedda back in Topeka, when Dad invited her over for dinner one night. She had been very sick, he told us, and he was taking care of her at the hospital. She was a grown-up woman, but she liked dolls and Nancy and I could give her one for Christmas if we wished. Nedda turned out to be a tall, muscular woman in her early forties, with bright red smudges of lipstick on her mouth and cheeks. At the hospital she tied her hair up in hundreds of tiny toilet paper bows, though when she came to visit the bows were missing. She carried the doll my sister and I gave her around with her and smiled and giggled throughout the evening. I don't remember her saying much, but sometimes Dad would put his arm around her shoulders and tell her how nice and sweet she was.

Most of the time, back at the Veterans Hospital, Nedda was

not sweet but stormy and voracious. Much later we learned that she had a severe case of schizophrenia, spent much of her time masturbating openly on the ward, and spoke only a gar-bled "word salad"—one of my favorite phrases as a child. An uneducated woman from the plains of east Texas, of an in-tensely religious and conservative background, she had been discharged from the Women's Army Corps on psychological grounds. She was not bright, not attractive, not talented, not appealing in any way. She was destined, surely, to spend her life on the locked back ward of a state mental institution. The hopelessness of her situation and the chance to challenge the theories of a famous psychiatrist named John Rosen, who boasted easy cures for schizophrenia, motivated my father to take on this patient. Dad began a grueling process of treatment with her, trying all the approaches he could think of, to no avail. Then one day, in the midst of an argument, she lunged at him and kicked him hard in the testicles. Without thinking, he slapped her face. Suddenly she straightened up and said, "Why'd you do that?"—the first rational sentence she had spo-ken in years. That sentence led to others. Gradually Dad devel-oped an active, directive, and very intensive mode of therapy, spending hours with Nedda each day and setting rules and limits that seemed to afford her some relief from the chaotic terrors of schizophrenia.

Out of the years he spent with Nedda, Dad elaborated on Freud's hypotheses about schizophrenia as an illness of deficit rather than conflict, akin to the loss of memory traces in the mind, like erasing the lines on a map. His first published pa-pers were about Nedda. Indeed, Nedda helped establish his reputation as a promising—and controversial—young analyst who, in part because he had a Ph.D. instead of an M.D., would always remain something of a maverick within the profession.

Nedda eventually got well enough to leave the V.A. hospital in Topeka and go back to Texas—a great triumph, not only for her but also for my father, and indeed for the Menninger Clinic and for Karl Menninger, who had been interested in the psychoanalytically informed treatment of schizophrenia since the 1930s. Nedda showed that even the most seemingly intransigent illnesses might yield to determined, intelligent effort. By the time Mom was diagnosed with Huntington's disease in 1968, Dad had not seen Nedda in many years, though they continued to exchange letters, and he had had many other fascinating patients. But in some way she had entered his life at a time when he needed her just as she had needed him, and I think her memory remained with him as a source of hope when all our own dreams for the future seemed smashed forever.[1]

The first physicians in Los Angeles whom Dad approached knew little about Huntington's, or else they described it as "the most diabolical affliction man is heir to." But in certain respects, the timing of Mom's diagnosis was fortuitous in that it coincided both with a revolutionary expansion of molecular biology and with an awakening of interest and activism focused on the disease. As Dad would soon learn, he had entered the Huntington's world just at the moment when several other people with the illness in their families had begun major fundraising initiatives. Moreover, biomedical interest in Huntington's had also started to revive, at least among a small group of neurologists and geneticists. That year, George W. Bruyn, a Dutch neurologist, published the first notable compendium of knowledge about Huntington's in the authoritative *Handbook of Clinical Neurology*. Two years earlier, a medical geneticist at the National Institutes of Health (NIH), Ntinos C. Myrianthopoulos, had also published an influential review of the literature on Huntington's, stressing the urgency of "integrated team work in the field, the clinic, and the laboratory" to address this seemingly hopeless disease with its "sobering probability figure of one in two."[2]

Dad was determined to respond to the challenge. First, though, he had to learn some basic science. Although he had no formal background in biology, Dad began studying genetics on his own. He studied the work of Gregor Mendel, whose ideas about heredity had established the foundations of classical genetics. The mathematical ratios for the inheritance of traits worked out by Mendel in the mid–nineteenth century—and still referred to today as Mendelian inheritance—would become the basis of much genetic research, including the research on Huntington's disease.

Mendel, an Austrian scientist, had studied the reproductive patterns of flowering pea plants in the monastery garden where he lived as a monk. By counting the characteristics, such as color and pod size, of different generations of pea plants, Mendel came up with what have been known ever since as Mendel's laws. He showed that traits are transmitted from generation to generation in discrete units of heredity that he called elements (later called genes). These are inherited in an all-or-nothing fashion; the genetic elements do not blend or combine, as they had previously been thought to do. Second, for a single trait (color of flowers, shape of the pod, and texture of its skin), an organism possesses two separate elements, one inherited from each parent. Only one of these traits is actually expressed. The ability of purple-flowering plants to produce offspring with white flowers showed that the genetic elements could be present but not expressed in one generation, only to show up in the subsequent generation. Mendel called those traits recessive that could disappear from view and then reappear in a later generation. Those traits that were always expressed without skipping any generations were called dominant.

The phenomenon of dominant and recessive traits, moreover, suggested a possible difference between the physical appearance of an organism—the phenotype—and the units of inheritance inside it that could transmit physical traits to the next generation—the genotype. A purple plant might carry two elements for producing purple-flowered offspring and thus be homozygous for the color purple. Or it might carry one element for purple, which is dominant and therefore expressed, and another for white, which is recessive and hence not expressed in the company of a dominant. In this case the plant would be heterozygous for color, since it carries two different forms, or alleles, of the genetic element for color. There is no way of knowing which is the case just from looking at the appearance of the parent plant. Only the characteristics of the offspring it produces will reveal, retrospectively, the genotype of the parent.

By tracking several different sets of traits through a number of generations, Mendel came up with the law of independent assortment, another foundation of modern genetics. This law holds that the inheritance of one trait or traits from a parent has no bearing on the inheritance of others. Mendel based this law on his finding that a parent plant with round yellow pods (both dominant traits) will produce the expected proportion of similar offspring when crossed with another parent plant with wrinkled green pods (recessive traits). However, a significant proportion of the offspring will bear no resemblance to either parent plant. That is, they may have round green pods or wrinkled yellow ones, unlike either of the parent plants. Mendel concluded from these experiments that the elements of heredity assort independently during meiosis, that is, when the gametes, or sex cells (egg and sperm), are formed. A child might inherit brown eyes from his father but not his father's dark hair or tall stature; instead the brown-eyed son might be short and fair like his mother and thus look significantly different from both his parents.

There are, however, some important exceptions to this principle. Although early investigators noticed the tendency of certain pairs of genes to travel together from parent to offspring, they had no explanation for why this occurred. Thomas Hunt Morgan began studying this question in the common fruit fly, *Drosophila melanogaster,* which he bred in his "fly room" at Columbia University. Tracking the inheritance of eye color in *Drosophila,* Morgan formulated the idea of sex-linked traits. He confirmed the prediction of other geneticists that genes are located on chromosomes—threadlike, dark-staining, paired bodies inside the nucleus of every cell except the sex cells, egg and sperm, which contain a single set. Each organism inherits one set from the mother and one from the father. *Drosophila* possess four pairs of chromosomes, while humans possess twenty-three pairs, including the two chromosomes that determine sex, X and Y. Morgan further theorized that each gene occupies a specific place, or locus, on one particular chromosome and that genes are arrayed in a precise linear order along the chromosome. He also explained the exceptions to Mendel's law of independent assortment by theorizing that genes that are often inherited together are likely to be located near one another on the same chromosome. Morgan called this important phenomenon linkage.

Occasionally, though, the expected linkage does not occur; genes presumably located in close proximity on the same chromosome are sometimes not transmitted together to the next generation. Morgan inferred that in these cases, the two linked genes had somehow gotten separated. This separation might occur when one segment of a chromosome switches places with a stretch of its corresponding (paired) chromosome during meiosis. That is, a small stretch of a chromosome inherited from the mother might separate and change places with a stretch of the corresponding chromosome from the father. Morgan referred to this event as crossing over, or recombination.

A student of Morgan's, Alfred H. Sturtevant, later postulated that one can estimate the relative distance between two linked

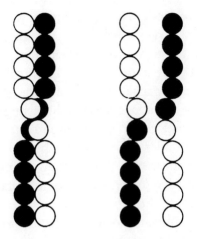

Crossing over takes place during the formation of the egg and sperm cells (meiosis), when a stretch of one chromosome changes places with a segment of its corresponding (homologous) chromosome; also called recombination.

(From Horace Freeland Judson, "A History of the Science and Technology Behind Gene Mapping and Sequencing," in Daniel Kevles and Leroy Hood, eds., *The Code of Codes* [Cambridge: Harvard University Press, 1992], 46.)

genes by observing how often they are separated by recombination when they are transmitted from parent to child. Genes that often become separated are probably a greater distance apart on the chromosome than those that tend to remain together. Measuring the frequencies of recombination events between any two genes is a way of approximating the physical distance between them. Maps that track the frequency of recombination are called linkage maps, and they would play a critical role in later Huntington's disease research.

Of course, at that time a linkage map measured only the relative positions of different genes on a chromosome, because there was no way to measure the physical distances. In fact, there was no way to look directly at genes at all. No one even knew what a gene was. All measurements of linkage were based on the observation of an identifiable trait—the phenotype—such as wing length or eye color, for which a single gene presumably existed. Nonetheless, by tracking the transmission of such traits through several generations, Sturtevant had drawn the first gene map in 1913. Later, other investigators began using X rays to make mutations in the genes of fruit flies and tracing these mutations through different generations. And by the 1930s, giant chromosomes from certain species could be distinguished under the microscope by their distinctive pattern of bands made visible through new staining methods. It thus became possible to correlate genetic mutations with visible changes in these chromosomes.

Unfortunately, humans possess no giant chromosomes. (Not until 1970 did new staining techniques facilitate the identification of individual human chromosomes.) Nor do people lend themselves to experimental mutations or to breeding for the purpose of tracking inheritance. Human genetics had to be done retrospectively by tracing back the inheritance of traits through family pedigrees. Moreover, by the 1930s, human genetics had become tainted by its association with eugenics and by the cooperation of some human geneticists in Germany with the Nazis' compulsory sterilization and eventual extermination of those with genetic disorders. Besides, finding large, multigenerational human families to study was always difficult. After World War II, however, human genetics began to expand with the development of molecular biology and concern over the genetic impact of radiation from the atom bomb. In the United States, growing numbers of physicians entered the field, which increasingly became defined as medical genetics.

By that time, scientists had begun to elucidate the chemical makeup of the gene. They had also determined that genetic information is coded in deoxyribonucleic acid, or DNA, a molecule found inside the nucleus of each cell, although just how DNA functions remained a mystery. For a long time DNA had been considered boring, far less interesting than protein, a much more complicated substance that for many years had been thought to contain the genetic information. DNA is made up of subunits called nucleotides. Each nucleotide, in turn, is composed of a sugar, a phosphate, and one of four chemicals called bases—cytosine, guanine, thymine, and adenine, usually referred to by their initials, C, G, T, and A. Experiments in the 1940s had shown definitively that this dull compound does indeed contain the genetic information. And in some mysterious manner, the linear order in which these nucleotides are assembled along the chromosome manages to spell out the incredibly complex instructions for an entire organism. But how can such a simple structure direct such a complicated operation as a human being?

The climax of a long series of efforts to answer this question came in 1953, when James Watson, an American biologist in his early twenties, and Francis Crick, a British biophysicist in his thirties, formulated the structure of DNA. Aided by the collaboration of Maurice Wilkins and especially by the elegant crystallographic X-ray photographs of Rosalind Franklin, whose work they appropriated, Watson and Crick theorized the form of DNA as a double helix—that is, a double-stranded molecule that winds around itself in seemingly endless spirals, like a twisted ladder. They determined that the four different bases pair themselves to form the rungs of the ladder joining the two sugar-phosphate sidepieces: adenine with thymine, cytosine with guanine. These four nucleotides, distinguished by the particular base they contain—A, T, C, and G—make up (almost) the entire alphabet of the genetic language. (Ribonucleic acid, another class of nucleic acid, contains a different form of sugar and substitutes uracil for thymine.) There are some three billion pairs of these nucleotides inside the nucleus of every human cell, arranged in sequences that manage to write the directions for an entire organism, like letters in an alphabet spelling out the words of an unknown language.

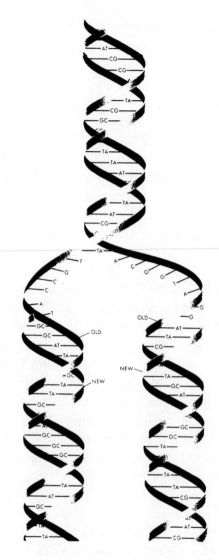

Each strand of the DNA double helix unwinds to form a template for the formation of two new strands, each one complementary to the original.
(From James D. Watson, John Toozer, and David T. Kurtz, *Recombinant DNA Short Course* [New York: W. H. Freeman, 1983], 20.)

What made the work of Watson and Crick so powerful was that in theorizing the form of the DNA molecule, they also demonstrated how DNA might reproduce (or replicate) itself. They showed how the molecule of double-stranded DNA "unzips" itself, with the paired bases separating in the middle to form two distinct strands. Each old strand, then, forms a template, or guide, for the production of a complementary strand. From the original strand of DNA two new double-stranded copies are thus produced. Moreover, if a double-stranded stretch of DNA is separated artificially into two single strands, by heat or chemical means, for example, the two complementary strands seek each other out and recombine, or hybridize, precisely as before. It does not matter if each single strand comes from a different species, say a human being and a mouse; as long as they are complementary, they will combine with each other. That attribute of DNA would later prove immensely valuable in the construction of what came to be called recombinant DNA.

By 1966, other researchers had cracked the genetic code, determining that the four different bases, A, C, T, and G, make up three-letter "words," each of which denotes one of the twenty amino acids that in turn form the basic building blocks of proteins. The precise order of these "words" along the chromosome indicates the order of amino acids making up a particular protein. A gene, then, is a sequence of thousands, sometimes tens of thousands, of these nucleotides located at a specific point, called a locus, on a chromosome and (usually) spelling out directions for making a particular protein. Researchers also began to determine the way in which the information coded in the DNA directs the complex process of protein synthesis in the cell, a process known as translation. And, in 1968, the first non-sex-linked gene was mapped to a particular chromosome. Apart from illuminating normal genetic function, these developments opened new vistas for studying at the molecular level the mechanism of genetic mutations—errors in the genetic code that sometimes have catastrophic consequences, such as Huntington's and other diseases, sometimes merely minor effects, like the fat thumb of my own right hand.

Reviewing all these advances, Dad was completely caught up with the romance of the new genetics, perhaps because it offered him hope at a moment when he feared his entire family might be obliterated. Even before he had grasped its fundamentals, he was organizing educational seminars for people who might fund genetic research. But he was not alone in his enthusiasm. As one historian of science wrote, "no other science, not nuclear physics, has ever expanded as biology did in North America and Europe from the mid fifties to the mid sixties." Even many scientists felt that a golden age of biology had just begun.[3]

Along with molecular biology, the neurosciences also expanded enormously, in ways significant for Huntington's research. Harvard formed the first multidisciplinary Department of Neurobiology in the country in 1966, and many universities followed Harvard's example; in 1968, the year Mom was diagnosed, an international Society for Neuroscience was organized. As researchers elucidated the ways in which nerve cells send electrical and chemical messages to one another to communicate impulses to distant destinations, they also articulated different ways of thinking about brain function and opened new possibilities for treating malfunctions. A particular source of scientific excitement was the study of neurotransmitters, the chemical substances released from a nerve cell to its neighbor that spark the continued electrical firing of cells—an action called excitatory—or slow down the cells' activity—an effect described as inhibitory.

But what got a number of neurologists specifically interested in Huntington's was a finding relating to Parkinson's disease, another movement disorder of which Huntington's was sometimes described as the "mirror image." While people with advanced Huntington's move around wildly, people with severe Parkinson's can hardly move at all. The illness usually begins with a tremor, accompanied by a growing stiffness and difficulty in initiating movement. People with Parkinson's acquire a slow, shuffling walk and an impassive, masklike expression. Eventually they lose the ability to talk or to walk or eat unassisted; toward the end many become paralyzed and bedridden. Parkinson's generally strikes people over fifty. It is a fairly common illness with devastating consequences, although it is not thought to be hereditary.

In the late 1950s, two researchers in Europe made a crucial discovery about the brains of people who had died of Parkinson's. Arvid Carlsson, of the University of Göteborg, and Oleh Hornykiewicz, of the University of Vienna, ascertained that, in these brains, certain neuronal pathways had been destroyed or damaged. The most devastated pathways were those that used the chemical neurotransmitter dopamine to send their messages from one neuron to another. Because so many of these dopaminergic neurons, as they are called, were gone, the level of dopamine in these particular brains was far below that of the normal brain. Dopamine was known to be a neurotransmitter capable of producing excitatory effects (though it had many other properties as well). So it seemed logical that someone lacking in dopamine would have difficulty walking or, apart from the tremor, even moving at all.

This finding was purely serendipitous, according to the researchers, since they had not been specifically studying Parkinson's disease or looking for medical applications for their work. As a result of their discovery, however, other investigators were able to develop a treatment to replace the missing dopamine. They could not use dopamine itself, since it does not pass through the blood-brain barrier, the membrane that separates brain tissue from the blood. Instead they used a chemical precursor of dopamine called L-dopa, which the body then converts to dopamine and absorbs into the brain. If the L-dopa is administered in high enough doses, it can lead to a dramatic reduction of the symptoms. From a catastrophic illness that is seriously debilitating and often fatal, Parkinson's became an illness that can be partially controlled, even if it cannot be cured.

Some of the neurologists who treated patients with Parkinson's also saw people with Huntington's disease. They had noticed for some time that the most effective drugs for treating the choreic movements in Huntington's are those that reduce the actions of dopamine in the brain. They also noticed that giving too much L-dopa to their patients with Parkinson's could produce chorea-like movements. There seemed to be some correlation between the activity of dopamine in the brain and involuntary, choreic movements of the body.[4] Some researchers began investigating the possibility that the chorea associated with Huntington's disease is caused by too much dopamine in the basal ganglia. Or perhaps the chorea arises from some overactivity or oversensitivity of the dopamine receptors, the protein molecules, lodged in the surface membranes of neurons, that regulate the entry into the neuron of dopamine from neighboring neurons. Perhaps the receptors overreact to normal levels of dopamine, or maybe there are too many of them, which could also intensify the action of dopamine. All in all, dopamine seemed implicated in the chorea of Huntington's—but how? The mystery lay in the absence of any discernible dopamine-related abnormality in the autopsied brains of people who had died of Huntington's. Some other biochemical abnormality must be producing these dramatic symptoms.

Though he had no answers, André Barbeau persisted with questions. A neurologist at the University of Montreal, Barbeau had been among those who had discovered the usefulness of

L-dopa for treating Parkinson's in 1961. He also treated people with Huntington's and had helped compile a register of families with the disease in French-speaking Canada, all of whom traced their ancestry back to a single person in France in the mid–seventeenth century. Barbeau had been impressed by Myrianthopoulos's 1966 review article decrying the lack of knowledge about Huntington's. As an organizer of the Second International Congress of Neurogenetics and Neuro-Ophthalmology in Montreal in September 1967, held under the auspices of the World Federation of Neurology, Barbeau decided to invite all the people who were working on Huntington's and had published papers on the subject to present their research. But, he told me later, he could find only twelve researchers from the entire world.

Actually, there had been a considerable upsurge of publications on Huntington's since the mid-1950s. At least sixty papers appeared in 1966 alone. Responding to Myrianthopoulos's call for "integrated team work," the researchers who attended the congress in Montreal—including Myrianthopoulos—decided to form an international research group on Huntington's that would meet every eighteen months or two years. At first the group consisted of only fourteen or fifteen individuals. But for the first time, a continuing nucleus of investigators was actively committed to studying this disease.

The scientists may also have been responding to the efforts of nonscientists, who had begun to organize prior to the Montreal congress. It so happened that Marjorie Guthrie, ex-wife of songwriter Woody Guthrie, had begun to organize families with the disease to raise funds and lobby Congress for more research. Woody, certainly the most famous American with Huntington's, was in the last stages of the illness at Creedmoor State Hospital in Queens, New York, where his neurologist, John Whittier, was studying the disease. Whittier put Marjorie Guthrie in touch with Myrianthopoulos, who in turn asked Barbeau if he could invite her to Montreal. By the time of the meeting, she had formed the Committee to Combat Huntington's Disease, or CCHD). Another woman, Alice Pratt, had formed the Huntington's Chorea Foundation in Texas to fund basic research on the disease. Two lay organizations were already in place when the neurologists decided to establish their own group.

Marjorie Guthrie had been a dancer with the Martha Graham Dance Company and had later taught dance at her own school in New York. She was strong in a way that belied her delicate appearance and bubbly manner. Perhaps from her experience as a performer and her long involvement with the Left cultural scene in New York, she also had a great sense of showmanship and a powerful public presence that she would put to good use with doctors and congressmen. Although she had already divorced Woody Guthrie by the time of his diagnosis in the early 1950s, she had taken responsibility for his care throughout his long illness, managing somehow to keep the family together—there were four small children when he got sick. Soon Woody would be gone—he would die in October 1967—but there were children at risk, and Marjorie wanted to do something for their future. The neurologists in Montreal strongly encouraged Guthrie's efforts, particularly since access to people with the disease and those at risk was essential to researchers. Although later Barbeau would recall that the neurologists had inspired Marjorie to organize, it may have been the other way around.

That summer of 1968, Dad was still reeling from the impact of Mom's diagnosis, wondering how he was going to cope. He had dreaded telling Nancy and me, he said later, convinced we would drop out of school and throw our lives to the winds. When we apparently took the news in stride, he felt heartened and able to move ahead. He confided often in his brother

Henry, who was assembling a bibliography on the disease at the library of the Yale Medical School, with which he was affiliated. Dad and Henry were not especially close, but, in times of crisis they supported each other. It was Henry, in fact, who urged Dad to contact not only clinicians but basic scientists as well. "I wish a Linus Pauling, a Watson etc. could get interested in this problem," he told Dad. "These men who are experimenting on basics are worth knowing, talking to about the situation if they can be reached, if only to get their ideas." He thought some scientists might be fired up by the challenge of this strange disease.[5]

Meanwhile, in early August, even before he had told Nancy and me the news, Dad and Maryline organized two meetings, in Los Angeles, of people from families with Huntington's who might be interested in fund-raising. In the fall, Dad flew to New York to meet with Marjorie Guthrie, who urged him to start a California chapter of CCHD. Feeling greatly encouraged, he drew on his contacts in the Los Angeles arts and entertainment communities to mobilize a group of supporters to help organize fund-raising events; they agreed to underwrite the administrative expenses of the chapter so that all the other money raised could be used to support research. Dad also recruited a group of science advisers, mostly clinicians at this point—neurologists and even a couple of psychoanalysts, since these were the people he knew. Maryline proved a key ally in these efforts, his trusted associate in all the Huntington's work. She acted as official treasurer of the California CCHD chapter and later of the Hereditary Disease Foundation, though she preferred to play a low-key role in public, more Dad's assistant than his equal. But the scientists and the families all loved her, and her financial and personnel skills were critical to the success of the chapter and the foundation.

It was clear from the start that the California group would have a great deal of financial clout. It was not clear how this group, which would be subordinate to the national office in New York, would relate to the larger organization, or how my father and Marjorie, both strong-minded characters, would get along with each other in the long run. For the moment, however Dad was blissfully happy to have found an ally for the long struggle ahead.

Six

"TAINTED BY SMOG AND HOLLYWOOD"

Scientific knowledge, like language, is intrinsically the common property of a group or else nothing at all. To understand it we shall need to know the special characteristics of the groups that create and use it.

—THOMAS S. KUHN
The Structure of Scientific Revolutions

Soon after meeting Marjorie Guthrie in New York, my father came up with three proposals. First, he wanted to build a focused Huntington's research center, "pulling in the best neurologist-biochemist to be found anywhere, setting him up in the best research facility, supporting him with the best technical assistance, providing him with the smartest panel of brainstorming experts, and turning the thing into a Manhattan Project." He was convinced that supporting "miscellaneous projects throughout the world on a grant basis is totally wasteful."[1] He also thought Los Angeles the best location for a center, since the high-profile visibility of such a place would make it an effective focus for fund-raising. Moreover, a major medical center, Cedars-Sinai, was ready to provide space, personnel, and facilities. Dad had recruited Ronald Okun, the chief of pharmacology at Cedars-Sinai, for the California CCHD Scientific Advisory Board, and he would give the group considerable leverage within the institution.

Second, Dad proposed a traveling scientist who would

spend six months or so visiting labs in the United States and Europe talking to all the investigators working on Huntington's and to others whose work might be useful. The California chapter eventually sent Leon Freeman, a biochemist and Scientific Advisory Board member, to France, Germany, and Italy for three months in 1971 to talk to various neurologists and scientists. Freeman visited distinguished researchers such as the Nobel Prize winner François Jacob at the Pasteur Institute, as well as less-known doctors, including a young neurologist in Vicenza, Italy, who had had promising results giving patients a combination of amantadine hydrochloride (Symmetrel) and an Italian semisynthetic penicillin called Suvipen. But despite his travels and the report he wrote about it, Freeman's expedition did not come to much, although for a time Dad was excited about Suvipen and tried to get it into this country.

Third, Dad wanted to invite all HD investigators to a major international symposium on Huntington's. He pushed these ideas during 1969 and 1970 to Marjorie and all his contacts in New York. He was quite chagrined to discover that his proposals met a cool reception from everyone in the HD field. Coming back from a meeting in New York in December 1970, he reported that these ideas "didn't excite, interest, or appeal to any of them." Dad even had the impression in New York that "these assembled doctors felt that California was somehow in the hinterlands, tainted by smog and Hollywood." He found it all quite depressing, since the people he had met with in New York—John Whittier, André Barbeau, Ntinos Myrianthopoulos —were the most influential people in the field.

In general, they argued that adequate channels of communication were already open between researchers, so site visits by a traveling scientist were a waste of time; that productive hypotheses, some of which still lacked funding, were already available; that a research center would be wasteful, duplicative, and expensive; and that an international Centennial Symposium on Huntington's Disease was already being planned for

March 1972, the one hundredth anniversary of George Huntington's original paper. "There was more," Dad added in a letter to Leon Freeman, "but my thoughts then, and at this moment, went more to the psychological atmosphere of negation and rejection than to the particular merits of the arguments advanced."[2]

On one point, though, they agreed. In preparation for the 1972 Centennial Symposium, John Whittier suggested an informal meeting of Huntington's researchers in southern California. Dad and others on his Scientific Advisory Board embraced the idea, adding their own recommendations that this be "a free-swinging kind of meeting or workshop" aimed at brainstorming new ideas as well as proposing guidelines for the California chapter. The meeting was set for March 1971, at the Santa Ynez Inn in Pacific Palisades, in the chaparral- and eucalyptus-covered hills overlooking the Pacific Ocean. Dad invited many of the senior researchers in the HD field to attend—longtime investigators such as Myrianthopoulos, Barbeau, and Whittier along with some basic scientists such as William J. Dreyer, an immunologist from the California Institute of Technology; Julius Axelrod from the NIH, a 1970 Nobel Prize winner for his work on neurotransmitters; and Seymour Benzer, a pioneer in phage genetics, also from Cal Tech. Dad was especially impressed by Benzer's demonstration of what he called a "drop-dead fly"—a *Drosophila* that had been genetically altered so that after a few days it developed chorea-like symptoms, staggering and falling and finally collapsing dead. Slides of the "drop-dead" *Drosophila* brain showed tissue full of big holes, like Swiss cheese, suggesting an image of the shrunken brain of a person who had died in the advanced stages of Huntington's. Here, perhaps, was evidence that an animal model might be developed to accelerate the pace of future Huntington's research.

Dad was ecstatic that so many distinguished scientists were willing to spend a weekend thinking aloud about Huntington's disease. "Just fascinating to see those minds work," he wrote Nancy and me in a burst of enthusiasm. "Terribly sharp and knowledgeable. Miracles being performed in genetics. Couldn't believe stuff. We mixed up old researchers in HD with fellows who never heard the name but knew molecular biology, virology, etc. and did they interact! Many fascinating hypotheses to research." To others he exulted that "This was by far the most stimulating and creative group of scientific minds I have ever encountered."[3]

The workshop came up with a long list of questions that might guide future experiments in relation to Huntington's. Were there biochemical imbalances in the brains of people with Huntington's, comparable to the loss of dopamine in the brains of people with Parkinson's, that might be treated with drugs in the way that Parkinson's could now be treated with L-dopa? Did the genetic defect operate outside the brain in tissues more accessible to researchers—in blood or skin cells for example? What were the characteristics of the homozygote— someone who had inherited the gene from both parents—and could such an individual reveal effects of the disease that were masked in the heterozygote? Why did children who developed the disease inherit it more often from their fathers than their mothers? What triggered the death of brain cells in Huntington's disease? Was cell death programmed from the time of birth, or did the HD gene turn on later in life? Could a virus or other exogenous factor play a role in triggering the disease process? Was the onset of illness affected by trauma or other life events? What were the prospects for an animal model since such a model would be extremely useful both for elucidating the illness and for developing therapies? Finally, could a linkage be found between Huntington's disease and some genetic marker such as blood type? If so, linkage might offer a safe means of predicting who was destined to develop the illness later in life and who was free.[4]

These questions would help set the agenda for much of the

Huntington's research during the next two decades. But what my father remembered most from the Santa Ynez workshop was a conversation with two of the participating scientists. At the end of the first day, a major difference of opinion emerged between those participants, mainly neurologists, who had a longtime involvement in Huntington's research and some of the basic scientists—molecular biologists, biochemists, immunologists, virologists—who had no prior acquaintance with the disease. While the first group wanted to recruit additional clinically experienced, senior investigators, the latter group favored recruitment of younger basic scientists, who they believed would come to the problem with a more open mind.

On Sunday, the second day of the workshop, as the group broke for lunch, Seymour Benzer and William Dreyer pulled Dad aside. Benzer and Dreyer told him the workshop idea was great, but that instead of inviting senior scientists to subsequent gatherings, he should find talented young people, postdocs, who had no biases, nothing to prove, no hypotheses to defend. Even if they lacked clinical experience, these young scientists would be familiar with the newest technologies and more open to the kind of interdisciplinary brainstorming Dad was trying to foster. The workshops could provide the setting for developing hypotheses for targeted research. Benzer and Dreyer also agreed that the limited resources of the California chapter would be better spent funding young people for different projects; this approach would be much more catalytic than spending it all on one person at a research center.

Dad listened carefully to Benzer and Dreyer, whose criticism of his idea for a single research center echoed that of the New York CCHD group. After thinking about their suggestions and conferring with various colleagues, he decided to give up the idea of funding a center. He was increasingly persuaded that offering small awards to individuals in different laboratories would yield more rewards than supporting one large institution. It was characteristic of my father, I think, that while he pushed hard for his own ideas, he could also listen to intelligent criticism and respond to the proposals of people he respected. The California chapter decided to develop a program of postdoctoral fellowships and grants that would provide seed money—around $20,000—for imaginative proposals, particularly high-risk projects that the NIH might not fund.

Interestingly, Dad now looked back on his Menninger experience as the inspiration for this approach, although initially it had been far from his mind. The Menningers had given research fellowships on the basis more of the investigator than the investigation. And Dad, as the recipient of one of these fellowships, felt it had left a deep imprint on him. In an unpublished essay, "It Runs in the Family," Dad described how the Menningers' faith in him at that moment in his career—granting him an award to do whatever he liked—had shaped his later thinking about research. "That was the Menninger way of supporting my research interests," he wrote, "four hours a day to dream, think, work, experiment . . . or whatever. They trusted that something productive would come of the time. There was no point in specifying the product in advance." That research—his work with Nedda—had proven immensely rewarding, as had the confidence the Menningers had shown in him. Dad too recruited researchers for the Huntington's workshops who he thought would be imaginative thinkers. But he was far more cautious when it came to grants. Certainly the California chapter and the foundation carefully scrutinized all project proposals submitted for grants, often returning them to promising investigators for further development and explanation. Yet the mystique of Menninger's continued to animate my father's thinking for years to come.

When the Scientific Advisory Board met at the end of January 1972, it supported the recommendation of Dreyer and Benzer and agreed to canvass heads of departments and laboratories for potential postdoctoral workshop invitees. Meanwhile, Dreyer and Benzer had recruited an iconoclastic young graduate student in Benzer's lab, Ronald J. Konopka, to help organize the workshops. A tall, thin, laconic man with a dry, ironic sense of humor, Konopka looked even younger than his twenty-four years, particularly in the plaid shirts and Columbo-style trench coat he wore everywhere. He had been deeply influenced by Bill Dreyer's freewheeling, speculative evening seminars at Cal Tech. Moreover, Konopka credits Dreyer for conveying to him the importance of neurobiology when the field had not yet exploded.[5] Konopka's own research had had little to do with Huntington's disease, but he was attracted to the interdisciplinary approach of the proposed workshops. And Konopka's unconventional outlook and maverick stance were exactly what my father was looking for.

After talking to Dad, Konopka set off on a whirlwind ten-day recruiting tour to university labs around the country. Explaining to the postdocs the aims of the California CCHD chapter, he was surprised at how many young scientists with no involvement in disease research were interested in attending a workshop on Huntington's. After that exploratory trip, Konopka and Dad invited thirteen of these postdocs, along with several senior scientists, to attend a workshop in January 1972. They came from places such as Harvard, Cal Tech, Stanford, Berkeley, Johns Hopkins, Michigan, and the University of British Columbia, and this time there were women among them.

Dad had very specific ideas about running workshops. They grew in large part out of his experience at Menninger's, where open-ended, interdisciplinary dialogue had been de rigueur. Though he did not say so explicitly, I think Dad wanted to create in the workshops the kind of intensity and intellectual excitement he had valued so highly at Menninger's. And, as a psychoanalyst, he believed in free associaton as a strategy for fostering new ideas. Perhaps that was why he had always been fascinated by actors, artists, and writers and had even dreamed of becoming a writer himself.

His contacts with the Los Angeles artists were crucial in this respect. It happened that my father came into contact with the artists at just the time when an important art scene had begun to emerge in Los Angeles, marked by the opening of the Ferus Gallery in the late 1950s and the "light and space" movement spearheaded by artists such as Larry Bell, Robert Irwin, and Ron Davis. After his divorce in the early 1960s, my stiff and rather formal father—at least that was how I thought of him then—moved out of our conventional house on Napoli Drive and into a stark, all-white apartment in Westwood, where he hung the walls with startling work by the L.A. artists he knew, such as John Altoon, Ed Moses, and Mike Olodort. Influenced by his interactions with the artists, Dad was going to gallery openings, reading Susan Sontag and Borges and Machado de Assis, listening to Stockhausen and Pierre Boulez. For a time he worked on a project to start a Foundation for the Generation of Art, which would create a meeting place for artists and the public. "We want to generate new art, not store it," he wrote me. "We're interested in Happenings, group efforts, new music, new poets. Stockhausen wants to put on a 12 day continuous concert—lasting 24 hours daily—come and go as you see fit." He was getting a grant, he added, "to treat artists—for free—so I can study creativity."[6]

Dad eventually started a group for artists that met twice a week, free of charge, for several years. This group mixed intense personal interactions with wide-ranging discussions of art and creativity. Dad felt he learned a great deal, not only about art but about group process and how to get people to speculate and free associate together. Although he had to drop the group after Mom got sick, he kept up his ties to many of the artists, and some of them helped support Huntington's research through donations of their art and participation in fundraising efforts.[7]

Dad's interactions with the artists set the paradigm for his later approach to the scientists. In effect, he wanted to treat the scientists like artists. In the beginning, though, he was so grateful just to have the scientists gathered together talking about Huntington's that he did not interfere much in their usual ways of doing things, which was to give short, formal presentations complete with slides and lots of data. But after a while, and especially with the younger scientists, Dad became more assertive. "Just read these few papers to get some idea of what we're going to do," he would say to them. "And then come without your lectures and prepared ideas, and see what happens." He would explain his faith in the free-association process, encouraging them to let their minds wander into unfamiliar territory. What he most wanted to do was to maintain an open and unconstrained atmosphere. He felt that in an informal setting, where people felt relaxed, even playful, they would be most likely to think creatively.

Each workshop began by introducing to the group a person with Huntington's disease, sometimes accompanied by an entire family—a spouse, siblings, and children, for example. A neurologist participating in the workshop would interview the person with HD, asking about the onset of symptoms, the progression of the illness, the impact on family members, and so forth. A simple neurological exam followed, showing how the disease affected one's ability to count, to recall, to walk across a room or hold one's arms straight out in front. Often spouses or siblings would tell their own stories, giving a powerful portrait of how the disease affected an entire family. These emotional presentations were always very moving and sometimes shocking to the scientists, who often had no clinical experience and had never seen a person with Huntington's. The workshops were the only place where they saw the human consequences of the brain pathology they studied in the lab.

In order to foster the atmosphere of intimacy, Dad insisted that the workshops be kept small—he thought fourteen or fifteen people around a table was best, and at the most seventeen. Personality, as well as scientific expertise, played a part in his choice of invitees. He wanted people who were confident and open, people willing to go out on a limb even, to tread in areas where they were not established experts. Scientists have often said that the best part of a conference or meeting is the informal interaction in the hallways, between sessions, or over meals—"corridor talk," as it has been called; Dad aimed to create "corridor talk" during the actual meeting itself. He also planned a Saturday night dinner or party as part of the workshops, inviting scientists and members of the board of trustees, who included artists, Hollywood and media stars, adding a distinct touch of glamour to these occasions.

"I'm not sure exactly why or how he did it," recalled John D. Minna, then at the National Cancer Institute, "but [Milton] made you feel, like an uncle or a father would, that everything was all right. He would sit there quietly and then when anybody got too judgmental he would always say . . . that it was really okay to let your crazy ideas come out." Most participants found the unstructured openness of the workshops exhilarating. In the view of Ronald McKay, then of Cold Spring Harbor Biological Laboratory, "You were allowed to say what you liked and people thought better of you, not worse. People are able to propose individual and peculiar points of view and they won't throw you out." Minna, too, recalled "the joy in being able to let one's hair down and participate in those discussions in a nonjudgmental fashion. You could say some of your crazy thoughts and you wouldn't get hollered at. Probably THE most important thing that I got out of the workshops was that one could do that. And think and express oneself freely, in a creative fashion. There's a great deal of formalism in science."

Many scientists asserted that the workshops helped them construct hypotheses that they subsequently brought home to test in the lab. Ira Shoulson, a young neurologist at the University of Rochester School of Medicine, spoke for many others when he noted that his research ideas "were percolated through the workshops. That's really where I got most of the ideas. I synthesized and formulated them during the workshop presentations back and forth, either people telling me I'm crazy or my telling them they're crazy. But that process was very effective."

Not all workshop participants agreed. Edward A. Kravitz, a neurobiologist who was studying neurotransmitters in lobsters at the Harvard Medical School, argued the opposition case most eloquently. "When I first came and was told how the workshops operated," Kravitz recalled, "that is, no slides, no data, people just getting up and talking about concepts and ideas and how they might relate to Huntington's disease, I was horrified. It seems to me that scientists work best when they have some data in front of them. If you know the people and you know that the experiments they're talking about are good, reliable experiments, then they can give you the general framework of what they're doing and you'll understand. But if you don't know the people, or if you question the quality of their science, you have no way of evaluating their ideas. This format allows people to just get up and gas." The key, for Kravitz, was the quality of the scientists. Even he felt that the increasing excellence of neuroscience generally, and the neuroscientists at the workshops in particular, made the freewheeling format more successful over the years.

Dad himself attended all these early workshops, held at universities around the country, making a point of getting to know the participants. His involvement impressed many of the senior scientists, who were attracted by his imaginative approach. Certainly his own charisma played a part in enticing people into the work, and for some scientists—not used to meeting Hollywood psychoanalysts in this kind of informal setting—my father himself was a prime attraction. "The most fascinating part of the whole thing for me was interacting with your Dad," Bill Dreyer told me frankly. "I probably wouldn't have spent so much time on it if it hadn't been for that."

There is a photograph of my sister and father, taken at the Twenty-sixth International Psychoanalytical Congress in Rome in the summer of 1969. They stand in a piazza, smiling, at ease with each other in this public setting with assorted analysts milling around behind them, Nancy in her brightly striped minidress, Dad in his dark sport jacket and tie. The photo captures something of their close relationship, though I doubt they thought of themselves as a team, since Nancy had just entered graduate school two years earlier. But the photo foreshadows their alliance, which would unfold over the next twenty-five years as Nancy moved from clinical psychology into an involvement with Huntington's that was very much shaped by Dad's initiatives.

The process was slow and often painful. Nancy felt reluctant to talk to friends or colleagues in Ann Arbor about being at risk, fearing that they would start to scrutinize her for symptoms and perhaps not trust her with difficult patients. She worried that her professors might hesitate to support her, imagining that her future was in jeopardy. Mom's suicide attempt in 1970, however, was a pivotal moment that persuaded her of the absolute necessity of doing something to fight the disease, for Mom's sake but also for her own. She needed to feel she was taking action, not just waiting passively for Mom to die. Through Marjorie Guthrie, she learned about several people with Huntington's in their families who had started meeting in Detroit, about sixty miles away, and she began driving into the city in the evenings to talk over their common problems. In the fall of 1971 they organized a Michigan chapter of CCHD. Soon the chapter was meeting regularly, with Nancy acting as vice president, and later president, masterminding newsletters, fund-raisers, and publicity drives to educate people about the disease.

For a while, Nancy led a double life, doing her academic work in Ann Arbor and commuting to Detroit evenings and weekends to meet with the families. Their overwhelming difficulties sometimes left her feeling so depressed and exhausted that she would almost fall asleep during the long drive home from Detroit to Ann Arbor. She began an analysis, partly because she felt it was a necessary part of her professional training as a therapist but also because of her depression. The therapy helped, but not enough because, as she said later of her therapist, "He really doesn't know what it's like."

As she grew active in the small Huntington's community in Detroit, she began to speak more openly in Ann Arbor about her work, as well as about being at risk. To her great relief, her friends and colleagues were uniformly supportive, providing what she later called "tough nurturance." Some of the doctors at the University of Michigan hospital, where Nancy saw a few of her patients, were fascinated by this strange disease, and several even got involved in research. Eventually Nancy decided to write her doctoral dissertation on the psychology of being at risk. In it she would explore her own situation by interviewing others. I was shocked at first and could not understand how she could immerse herself so completely in Huntington's disease almost to the exclusion of everything else. Dad also expressed doubt, worrying that it would be too depressing. Nancy admitted that the work sometimes lowered her spirits, constantly reminding her of the monumental difficulties posed by the disease. Even in the family she occasionally felt as if all we ever talked about was Huntington's. "ENOUGH HD!!!!!!!!!!" she wrote in 1973 as she was about to embark on her Ph.D. thesis. "I think one of the tragedies our family can run into is that we begin a mini-CCHD and forget that we are people. Disease, especially a disease that Aly and I don't have, shouldn't be the only medium of exchange we have with one another."[8]

But she also felt inspired by the strength and resiliency she saw in the people she interviewed for her thesis. "It is incredible to me what people can live through and survive," she wrote. "I come to appreciate daily what a golden spoon I have been born with." Talking to two young people who were already showing symptoms "really makes me feel like turning myself inside out to cure this thing."[9] With her growing clinical skills, Nancy could offer counseling to desperate families and try to help them find financial and medical assistance. They, in turn, were giving her a heightened feeling of self-worth and sense of mission. Hearing other people at risk talk about Huntington's made it feel less like her individual burden and more like a shared issue, one she could address professionally as well as personally.

Nancy found herself becoming something of a heroine, not only to the families she helped but also to her colleagues. Her two lives began coming together in ways that helped her make sense of both. From her graduate work she wrote two beautiful essays that would become classics in the Huntington's literature. These were "Living Out the Dying: HD, Grief, and Death" and "Genetic 'Russian Roulette': The Experience of Being 'At Risk' for Huntington's Disease."[10] In both these articles, the therapist speaks with the insight of the woman at risk, who understands emotionally as well as intellectually the tremendous costs of this illness.

By the spring of 1972, a more optimistic mood prevailed in the growing Huntington's disease research community, due mainly to increased attention to the disease rather than to any significant findings in the laboratory. Clearly the success in treating Parkinson's disease with L-dopa had boosted hopes for finding an analogous treatment for Huntington's. The Research Group on Huntington's Chorea of the World Federation of Neurology, with the aid of CCHD in New York and the California chapter, had organized the Centennial Symposium in Columbus, Ohio, to commemorate George Huntington's original paper and to assess the current state of knowledge. This was the largest gathering ever devoted to the disease, with 146 researchers from fourteen countries presenting some eighty-five papers. Among them was a Venezuelan psychiatrist, Dr. Ramón Ávila-Girón, who showed a startling twenty-minute, black-and-white film of several communities around the shores of Lake Maracaibo that were ravaged by the disease—a film that would have powerful repercussions in years to come. For the moment, the sheer size and scope of the meeting fueled a kind of euphoria. "We meet in an entirely new atmosphere," announced the chairman, "an atmosphere of optimism which has never before existed in the history of Huntington's disease." [11]

In retrospect, the Centennial Symposium seems as much a symbolic as a scientific event, important for dramatizing the new optimism and for bringing into a dialogue clinicians, basic scientists, members of families affected with Huntington's, and health professionals. It marked another step toward the creation of a Huntington's disease community, in which researchers and people in families with the illness might come together. It made clear the lack of medical progress achieved over the previous hundred years and the urgent need for more research.

The Centennial Symposium also initiated another kind of dialogue between different scientific groups, young and old, neurologists and nonmedical scientists, clinicians and basic researchers, M.D.s and Ph.D.s. Over the course of the weekend in Columbus, it became clear that a new cadre of young scientists was entering the Huntington's field, with different questions and approaches from those of the more established members of the World Federation of Neurology. To a large extent, this was my father's doing.

The California chapter had decided to hold its own workshop in tandem with the symposium so that some of the postdocs could attend the panels and meet together on their own as well. "All the old guard was meeting upstairs and all the young people downstairs, in the basement," recalled Steven Matthysse, a young neurobiologist at Harvard Medical School and at the Harvard-affiliated McLean Hospital. "We noticed that many of the older people wanted to come down and talk to us. But Milton in his wisdom felt that it wouldn't be wise to have too many of them at once because we would be intimidated. You know, you don't really feel that sure of yourself and if an expert comes into the room and starts holding forth, you kind of shut up. So we allowed a few to come down. But it was fascinating, because I think they too sensed that there was a lot of hot talk going on downstairs and they wanted to be in on the action." The established Huntington's disease researchers, who were almost all neurologists, tended to scoff at the notion that geneticists might be crucial to the study of the illness, on the grounds that the genetics of Huntington's was perfectly well understood. They did not necessarily welcome the molecular biologists and biochemists who began showing up at Huntington's meetings and workshops.[12] "In some sense people like Seymour Benzer, Bill Dreyer, Ed Kravitz had no right to say anything about Huntington's disease," said Matthysse. "They're not even doctors. They had no connection with medicine to speak of, they're eminent basic scientists and their life history has been in basic science. Yet some of these people had a tremendous confidence, some might call it arrogance, that they could shortcut the whole procedure. They felt they could see through to the heart of the matter in a way that maybe the echelons of doctors could not."

Dad, of course, was neither a doctor nor a scientist, but he shared some of the confidence and optimism of the scientists. He was excited by men such as Benzer and Dreyer and took seriously their advice to seek out the young postdocs. He also took to heart his brother Henry's advice early on to approach "these men who are experimenting on basics," a Linus Pauling or a James Watson. But there was also the stark reality that the old guard had not yet come up with any solutions, while the younger people were full of new ideas and enthusiasm.

One of the young scientists who won Dad's notice was an earnest assistant professor from Harvard, David Barkley, who already had a theory about Huntington's, although he had been to only one workshop so far. Barkley was a developmental biologist who had discovered the chemical basis of slime mold aggregation. He was now working on multicellular organization in the brain, but he was looking for other research possibilities, and the difficulty of the Huntington's problem intrigued him. He was particularly fascinated by the fact that although Huntington's struck men and women equally, three fourths of those who developed the disease as children inherited it from their affected fathers. Barkley speculated that those who received the gene from the mother might also inherit a partial immune tolerance that delayed the onset of the disease until the middle years, while those who had inherited it from a father had no such immunity. "Since there is no other adequate model for this peculiar observation," Barkley reasoned, "the possibility of autoimmune disease must continue to be considered."[13] Barkley patiently explained his theory to anyone who would listen, including Dad, who liked his enthusiasm and conviction. The intrepid Ron Konopka had been acting as science director for the California chapter, helping Dad select postdocs to invite to the workshops as well as presiding over the review of grant proposals submitted to the Scientific Advisory Board and helping to run the workshops. But it was obvious that a more formal arrangement was needed, with someone who could make this a regular part-time position. Would Dave Barkley be interested in acting as science director, Dad wanted to know, perhaps in the context of a joint appointment with a Los Angeles institution, say UCLA? Indeed he was interested. Dad promised to look into the possibilities.

As the Columbus symposium wound to a close, the rift that had long been developing between the national CCHD office in New York and the California chapter in Los Angeles burst into the open. In part, differences of personal style between my father and Marjorie Guthrie, two powerful, charismatic characters, had made their interaction difficult from the start. Marjorie's effusiveness did not go over well with my patriarchal father, a former debater and lawyer who was blunt and outspoken. Nor was Dad accustomed to working with strong women as equals. Marjorie, for her part, could be maddeningly evasive, avoiding the discussion of serious differences with a smoke screen of vague homilies and exhortations to "togetherness." As Marjorie once put it succinctly in a letter, "This is not just a CCHD problem, but I sense a MILTON-MARJORIE problem."[14]

More problems surfaced in connection with the "Tribute to Woody Guthrie" concert in 1971 at the Hollywood Bowl, all of the profits of which were to go to CCHD, primarily for research. While Marjorie and the New York office of CCHD secured the performers, the New York and California chapters together produced the event. The California chapter had recruited the audience; indeed, it had sold out the entire Hollywood Bowl as a benefit. In addition, Dad had arranged with Warner Bros. to record and film the concert, on the understanding that these productions too would be used to raise further funds for Huntington's research. After the fact, however, Marjorie insisted that since the property rights in the songs belonged to her, as executor of the Woody Guthrie Tribute Fund, the record also belonged to her. CCHD had no jurisdiction in the matter. She would use the profits from the record—although the concert was filmed, a movie was never made—as she saw fit. And that included supporting a Woody Guthrie Memorial in Okemah, Oklahoma, Woody's birthplace. Her success in organizing CCHD had come partly because of the folk revival of the 1960s and the reemergence of Woody Guthrie as a popular hero to young musicians. She felt it vitally important to keep Woody's name before the public, since he was, as she put it, her major currency.[15]

Dad was furious. He, after all, had marshaled all his forces in California solely for the purpose of raising money for research. It was on that basis alone that he had promoted the concert, which had raised some $133,000.[16] If a record was to be made, any profits from that too should be used for research. When Marjorie went ahead with her plan, he felt betrayed. But the battle over the Hollywood Bowl record merely exacerbated a more fundamental philosophical difference between Marjorie and my father. That battle had to do with science.

At the time, Marjorie's group believed that small organizations such as theirs should use their income to push for greater public spending on science; they should not support basic research themselves, though they were interested in funding some clinical research. Marjorie saw herself not as a science activist but as a social force, someone who would lobby Congress and mobilize the medical establishment. Giving money directly for research was, in her view, to fall into the "conventional fund-raising groove, which could actually set back the HD effort instead of advancing it." Sidney Katz, one of Marjorie's main advisers, insisted to Dad that money was being "frittered away in the process of making your grants which are a mere pittance" compared to what the government could do. In his view, the regional chapters of CCHD should use whatever funds they raised (apart from supporting the national office in New York) to interest those "who are capable of generating millions." Prodding the government and the large foundations would be more productive than "the enticing glamour of you yourselves dispensing the money in your possession."[17]

By this time, though, Dad was convinced that Marjorie and her advisers were "piddling at the wrong end of the stick."[18] He was persuaded that even modest sums, used intelligently as seed money, might encourage experimental research approaches that the government might not touch, at least not until they proved successful. A small operation could remain flexible and respond to interesting ideas quickly, without the formality and bureaucracy of larger institutions. Dad definitely wanted more government support for science, but he also thought small research grants from private sources could ultimately yield large benefits. And though he had begun with the thought of funding some patient services and public education as well as research—he and especially Maryline had counseled families at the beginning—he always held out as his highest priority support for basic science.

Tensions increased throughout 1971 and 1972 as New York and California argued back and forth, not only over strategies for supporting science but also about how much of the considerable funds raised by the California chapter should go to the national office, where it would not be spent exclusively on science. This issue was especially critical since the California chapter had considerably greater resources than the national office.[19] Although Dad initially agreed that all the money raised in California would be channeled through New York, he gradually changed his mind as Marjorie and her advisers made clear their priorities about how the money would be spent. After months of arguing in letters and memos, Dad and Marjorie and their advisers decided to meet face to face in Columbus.

Finally, Dad announced his plan to secede from the national CCHD to form an independent foundation. (In 1974, it would become the Foundation for Research in Hereditary Disease and, soon after that, the Hereditary Disease Foundation, or HDF, the name it has kept to this day.) The separation merely confirmed the reality of two distinct sets of priorities: direct versus indirect support of science and funding of basic research almost exclusively versus diversified spending on science, public education, and patient services.[20]

The two organizations differed in structure as well as strategy. The foundation depended financially on a relatively small group of large contributors, many of whom had personal loyalties to my father. Through the workshops, grants, and the fellowship program, Dad sought to build a network among scientists, recruiting young investigators and getting them interested in Huntington's. Annual social events, usually in Los Angeles, helped create a predominantly local network of sponsors, most of whom did not have Huntington's in their families. In contrast, CCHD and its successor organization, the Huntington's Disease Society of America, or HDSA, gradually built a nationwide (and eventually international) network primarily of affected families, caregivers, and health professionals, a more grassroots operation. It had a broader, if more modest, fundraising base and more service- and patient-oriented activities, such as organizing support groups and hiring social workers. CCHD, and later HDSA, did support research, clinical as well as basic, and eventually both organizations found themselves funding many of the same scientists, who often served on the advisory boards of both groups. Annual conventions took place in different cities around the country, though the national office remained in New York. Chapters organized their own activities, and encouraged participation by people with the disease in their families.[21]

Each group, in short, worked on creating different aspects of a Huntington's disease community. Despite the anger on both sides, neither side wanted to lose sight of their common goal. A certain momentum had been created, and everyone wanted to keep it going. "More progress has been made in the past 5 years than in the last 50," wrote Ntinos Myrianthopoulos the year before the Centennial Symposium, "and I venture to predict that the genetic problem in Huntington's chorea will be resolved before the decade is out."[22]

Seven

THE TEST FOR "HD-NESS"

Interpretations do not so much *in*form as *per*form.

—BRUNO LATOUR
Laboratory Life

In telling the story of Huntington's disease research, it is tempting to draw a straight line from failure to success, skipping over the digressions and byways, the ideas that fizzled, the hypotheses that did not pan out. To do so, however, is to impose a misleading order, a linear progression, on what was far more halting and uncertain. Conceptually, the goal of most researchers remained similar for the next two decades—to find a consistent difference, at the biochemical or the molecular (DNA) level, between those with Huntington's and those without it. The difficulty lay in identifying a difference that was clearly a cause rather than an effect of the disease. Finding the basic "HD-ness" of cells in people with Huntington's—for example an excess or a deficiency of some essential substance—could open the way to new drug therapies, as well as offer a means of diagnosis before symptoms began. In the decade of the 1970s, elucidation of the biochemical defect could also offer a promising route toward ultimate identification of the gene.

So first there was the dopamine story, growing out of the work on Parkinson's, which suggested that choreic movements were somehow correlated with the excessive actions of dopamine in the brain. But researchers could find no clear indication of excess dopamine in the brains of people with Huntington's, none at least that corresponded to the dramatic depletion found in Parkinson's.[1]

Then there was the GABA story. GABA, or gamma-aminobutyric acid, was a recently discovered neurotransmitter thought to inhibit the passage of impulses between neurons in the brain. At the 1972 Centennial Symposium in Columbus, a researcher from the University of British Columbia in Vancouver, Thomas L. Perry, announced that he had found significantly lower levels of GABA in the autopsied brains of people who had died of Huntington's. Certainly it made sense that individuals who suffered from excess movement might lack a major inhibitory neurotransmitter. Over the next few years, many investigators tested the functions of GABA and of GABAergic neurons, that is, those neurons that used GABA. They tested GABA levels in cerebrospinal fluid. They studied neurons containing GABA in the striatum, mapping their pathways with increasing precision. But the results of these studies were mixed. Replacing the missing GABA in the striatum turned out to be an extremely difficult proposition, since GABA does not easily penetrate the blood-brain barrier. Getting GABA to its target sites in the basal ganglia was also nearly impossible, since it is taken up by other neurons before it arrives at its intended destination. Nor did administration of a GABA precursor, glutamic acid, offer hope, since the enzyme that converts glutamic acid into GABA—glutamic acid decarboxylate—is also severely lacking in Huntington's brains and essentially not replaceable. In 1976, Ira Shoulson began clinical trials of muscimol, a substance that stimulates GABAergic receptors, with advanced Huntington's patients. But although the excellent research design of this project proved a valuable model for later drug trials, muscimol failed to achieve any real clinical benefit and Shoulson discontinued the test.[2]

Studies of GABA suffered a limitation that afflicted all research on the human brain: brain biopsies caused damage to living individuals, so that researchers were usually limited to postmortem brain tissue. That meant they were studying the disease only in its final stages, which is rather like trying to reconstruct the plot of a movie from viewing only the last few minutes. Some investigators, therefore, aimed to find a measurable difference in more accessible tissue outside the brain. Even though the damage of Huntington's is most visible in the brain, the Huntington's gene is present in the nucleus of all cells of the body and might be expressed in other tissues. Dominant disorders such as Huntington's were thought to involve a mutant structural protein that might show up in abnormal properties of cells all over the body. Theoretically as well as practically, it made sense to look at these tissues for evidence of difference. Finding such differences in skin or blood might point toward treatments aimed at the cellular defect as well as make possible a practical presymptomatic test.

This was the reasoning behind a controversial line of experiments conducted in the 1970s. In 1973, a pediatric neurologist at UCLA named John Menkes suggested that fibroblasts—a type of connective tissue cell—generated from skin biopsies of people with HD and from those without it reproduced in the tissue culture of laboratory dishes at different rates.[3] Specifically, Menkes and his colleague Natalie Stein found that the fibroblasts from people with Huntington's grow less well *in vitro* and had a shorter life span than fibroblasts from individuals without Huntington's did. Menkes and Stein suggested that the decreased life span of the HD cells resulted from a premature aging of the cells that is somehow caused by the Huntington's gene. Subsequently, other investigators found that HD fibroblasts also grow to a higher density than those cultured from normal individuals. These discoveries generated considerable enthusiasm. One investigator wrote that the fibroblast studies appeared to have "opened a new door in HD research." Given the frustrating absence of other definitive differences, the variant growth rates of Huntington's fibroblasts seemed to offer a promising route toward presymptomatic and possibly prenatal testing.

And then, for a while, various cell membrane theories held sway. Far from being a neutral envelope enclosing the cell, the membrane itself is full of intricate parts that regulate the cell's relationship to other cells and to its environment. In the late 1970s, several investigators came up with evidence that Huntington's is a generalized membrane disorder of cells all over the body and not just in the brain. One researcher found differences between the external surface characteristics of erythrocyte membranes (red blood cell "ghosts") from people with Huntington's and those of unaffected individuals. Another researcher found similar differences using fluorescent probes of membranes from fibroblasts. A third investigator found other promising differences after fibroblasts were exposed to concanavalin A, a plant protein. These results impressed many investigators, including the ever-critical Barbeau, who thought research on the cell membrane offered the most promising route to date toward insight into Huntington's.

A quite different avenue of research approached Huntington's as an autoimmune disease. Within a year or two after the Columbus symposium, Dad had hired David Barkley to act as a part-time science director for the foundation, with a half-time appointment at UCLA. Barkley worked with John Menkes on his studies of fibroblasts, but his heart was in the autoimmune thesis. Barkley theorized that Huntington's is caused by a retrovirus—a type of RNA virus—that was accidentally inserted into the genome and thereafter passed down within families in a dominant fashion. The abnormal product of the retrovirus could provoke a response from the immune system. This was a novel idea since, at the time, retroviruses had barely been identified and were not known to exist in humans. Barkley cheerfully acknowledged the arguments against this idea, namely the lack of inflammation caused by lymphocyte infiltration in the diseased brain tissue, a sign often taken as the definitive marker of autoimmune disease. But he was convinced that the disproportionate number of those with the juvenile form of Huntington's who inherit the disease from their fathers pointed strongly toward immune system involvement.

The key question was to find out whether people with Huntington's mount an immune response to whatever it is that causes the disease. If they do, the immune response itself might be detectable even before clinical symptoms appeared and therefore would be useful for presymptomatic testing. More important, antibodies could be used to target the agent responsible for killing off cells in the brain.

Barkley decided to test his hypothesis with a complicated set of experiments.[4] The early results looked encouraging. They seemed to indicate that people with Huntington's do indeed have in their brains an antigen (a substance that provokes the production of antibodies), possibly the lethal HD product, that individuals without the disease do not have. The cellular immune system of the affected individuals might be activated by this antigen, provoking the body to attack its own tissues and thereby causing the death of neurons in the brain.

Unfortunately, the unknown antigen did not appear to be exclusive to Huntington's disease. It also showed up in the brains of people who had died of multiple sclerosis. Moreover, the differences were not consistent, and Barkley's unconventional experimental technique was too cumbersome to be used for diagnostic purposes. Researchers also questioned whether the differences were caused by drug treatments rather than by disease.

By 1978, participants at the workshops were sharply divided on the issue. While some investigators continued to support further efforts to clarify the results, others were impatient with the attention focused on the autoimmune theory.[5] The contradictory results led to a heightened level of acrimony at foundation workshops and other HD meetings, centering not only around the autoimmunity hypothesis but increasingly around the skin fibroblast, cell membrane, and other studies, whose promising early results had begun to unravel. The great numbers of variables in all these studies—differences in culture media, different ways of computing statistical significance, and especially genetic differences between people that were unrelated to Huntington's disease—made replication of the results difficult. At best the reported differences between HD and normal cells contained too much overlap to be useful.[6] Surveying the mass of conflicting evidence accumulated about Huntington's over the years, André Barbeau wrote in January 1978, "It is high time for a coordinated, integrated effort to unravel this mess and to pinpoint which one of these defects has a chance to be primary."[7]

Meanwhile, animal experiments looked more promising. Finding an animal model of Huntington's would immensely aid experimental work, particularly in relation to drug testing, as well as possibly leading toward understanding the basic cause of the disease. The 1972 symposium had devoted a session to animal models. At that time, however, none of the known movement disorders in animals—ranging from dancing mice and acrobatic rabbits to pigs with a congenital tremor—was close enough to Huntington's disease to be a useful model. So researchers were excited when Joseph T. Coyle, at the Johns Hopkins University School of Medicine, announced in 1976 that he had constructed what looked like a model for Huntington's disease in a rat, using a highly toxic substance called kainic acid. Kainic acid is derived from a Japanese seaweed called *Digenea simplex*—the name in Japanese means "ghost [or monster] from the sea." It is related biochemically to a precursor of GABA called glutamate. An excess of glutamate is known to destroy nerve cells. When applied directly to the striatum of adult rats and mice, kainic acid produced a pattern of neuronal destruction that resembled that of advanced Huntington's disease. By destroying the same cells as those that died in Huntington's disease and sparing those the disease left untouched, kainic acid seemed to act much like the unknown substance that might be responsible for cell death in humans. More specifically, kainic acid appeared to work by overstimulating certain cells, exciting them to death, as it were. The fact that there were specific receptors for glutamate in the human brain that kainic acid acted upon, and the possibility that abnormalities in these receptors might be implicated in Huntington's disease, heightened interest in this research. "Minor differences do exist," wrote one enthusiastic author in comparing the effects of kainic acid with those of Huntington's, "but in nearly all respects the similiarities are striking."[8]

But just how striking were they? Although kainic acid mimicked the destructive effects of HD in the brain and rats treated with the substance began to move and behave abnormally, they did not develop chorea, one of the hallmarks of the illness. Joseph Coyle cautioned in 1979 that kainic acid was not simply a neurotoxin that excited cells to death. Rather, it appeared to alter the sensitivity of certain neurons to input from other neurons, so that normally benign neurotransmitters now acquired lethal effects. Possibly people with Huntington's disease produce abnormally high levels of a kainic acid–like substance or accumulate it at inappropriate places. Or perhaps affected individuals inherit a special vulnerability to a substance that, in a normal brain, lacks toxic effects.

Researchers meanwhile discovered another excitotoxin—an excitatory substance with poisonous effects on neurons in the brain—that offered an even closer analogy to the effects of

Huntington's. Like kainic acid, quinolinic acid was chemically related to glutamate. Unlike kainic acid, it occurred naturally in the brain, making it a candidate for the actual agent of neuronal destruction. Injected into the brain cells of rats or mice, quinolinic acid killed neurons by binding to certain glutamate receptors and opening up channels that allowed lethal amounts of calcium to flow into the cells. Even more precisely than kainic acid, quinolinic acid killed neurons in a highly selective way that significantly resembled the pattern of cell death in Huntington's disease. Here, perhaps, was an important therapeutic possibility. If researchers could block the subgroup of glutamate receptors to which quinolinic acid attached itself (called the NMDA receptors), the destructive process within those cells could possibly be halted.[9]

While investigators were testing all these theories, they were increasingly aware that any abnormalities relating to glutamate were secondary to another, more basic, defect that caused the abnormalities to appear in the first place. They also continued to wrestle with the questions of how close an animal model must be to Huntington's disease in humans and how best to study the progression of changes in the brain—that is, which neurons die first, which die later, which manage to escape altogether. In the early 1990s, quinolinic acid remained of great interest, even if clinically relevant results were not immediately forthcoming.

The most romantic theory of the 1970s emerged after Dr. D. Carleton Gajdusek, a Nobel Prize–winning virologist at the NIH, discovered that *kuru,* a lethal neurodegenerative disease found among certain indigenous peoples of New Guinea, is caused by a slow-acting virus. The disease is transmitted through the practice of cannibalism. Subsequently, Gajdusek and others established the similar origins of Creutzfeldt-Jakob disease, another late-onset disorder like Huntington's that causes abnormal movements and dementia. Both *kuru* and

Creutzfeldt-Jakob disease could occasionally be transmitted to primates by injecting them with brain tissue from an affected individual. The question then arose whether Huntington's too might be caused by a virus whose effects were delayed until midlife, when the symptoms gradually emerged.

The slow-virus theory intrigued researchers, as did Gajdusek's stories of his expeditions to New Guinea, but there were many circumstances working against the slow-virus theory as an explanation for Huntington's. Gajdusek's efforts at the NIH to transmit HD to primates by injecting them with brain tissue from humans with Huntington's failed to produce results. Some researchers accepted the possibility that a virus causing the disease somehow enters the genome and is thereafter transmitted in autosomal dominant fashion to successive generations. But that thesis did not reveal much about the etiology of the disease. "My own gut feeling is against this hypothesis," wrote the outspoken André Barbeau in early 1978. He had no objection to the idea that the original mutation may have been a viral insertion. But "so what? we may also have had microbial insertions and why not monkey gene insertions!!!"[10] So far the viral thesis did not hold.

The least glamorous of all these research efforts was a project in genetic linkage, that staple of classical genetics going back to the days when Morgan and Sturtevant had determined linkages in *Drosophila*. We should recall that genes that are located on the same chromosome tend to be inherited together and are said to be linked. But while Morgan and Sturtevant studied linkages between such traits as red eyes and tiny wings, the medical geneticists who followed them tried to link blood type or HLA antigen with diseases in particular families. That is, they used blood type and HLA antigens as *markers*—a marker being any inherited trait that comes in several different versions, much as eyes and hair come in different colors.

If, for example, in a given family, everyone who has Huntington's disease almost always also has blood type A and no one else does, then researchers could infer that the gene for Huntington's and the gene for blood type lie on the same chromosome. Blood type A could then be considered as indicating the presence of the Huntington's gene. The linkage would not mean that blood type A *caused* Huntington's or even *contributed* to causing it: in families without Huntington's, type A blood would have no significance as a marker. Moreover, in some families with Huntington's, type B blood might travel with the Huntington's gene. Linkage would merely mean that the gene for blood-type and the gene for Huntington's happen to be neighbors on the same chromosome, so that, *in affected families,* the disease gene and the gene for a particular blood type are usually passed on together.

The value of genetic linkage for Huntington's was first noted back in the 1930s, specifically for the purpose of prediction. Prediction was also the impetus for the linkage studies undertaken sporadically in the 1950s, and continued more systematically in the early 1970s. Even if you did not know which chromosome contained either the marker or the Huntington's gene or what that gene did biochemically, genetic linkage could offer a means of ascertaining who was destined to develop the disease far in advance of symptoms: the visible presence of a particular version of the marker—for example, blood type A— could indicate the hidden presence of the disease gene. As Myrianthopoulos put it in 1966, the absence of such identification was "downright tragic in such a devastating disease as Huntington's chorea, as anyone who has followed the course of the disease in an individual or in a family will readily admit, especially since onset is usually after reproduction has been completed."[11] By the mid-1970s, as we will see, new techniques for assigning genes to particular human chromosomes had enhanced the potential value of linkage as a step toward localizing the gene as well as identifying its biochemical product.

Several investigators, particularly a population geneticist in the Department of Medical Genetics at Indiana University School of Medicine, P. Michael Conneally, had been interested in linkage for some time.[12] Back in the mid-1960s, he had worked on finding more markers and studying the population genetics of diseases such as cystic fibrosis. One of his graduate students had gotten him interested in Huntington's, and he had helped organize a clinic for people with the disease. He and his colleagues had been the first to document the high percentage of juvenile cases who had inherited the illness from their fathers. When another of his graduate students, Margaret A. Pericak-Vance, was searching for a doctoral project, Conneally suggested she look for a marker linked to Huntington's. He warned her, " 'It's a tough nut to crack. We might be lucky or we might be frustrated because of the nature of the disease [the late onset means that young people, who might still develop the disease, cannot be used for the study].' But she said, 'Fine.' And we became more and more involved with Huntington's by doing this, and getting to know more and more families."

Conneally was especially adept at interacting with the families, for he had had some experience working out in the field. Soon after he had graduated from University College in Dublin in the mid-1950s, he had gone to work as an agent for the Irish Department of Agriculture, teaching highly traditional farmers how to increase their crop yields with fertilizer. But he had found himself less interested in plants and more interested in the people and their problems. He had earned a doctorate in genetics at the University of Wisconsin and had subsequently become a professor of medical genetics at the Indiana University School of Medicine. It was there that he had begun working on Huntington's, shortly after the formation of CCHD.

As it turned out, Conneally and Pericak-Vance were unable to link any known genetic marker with Huntington's, though they did manage to exclude an area of some 20 percent of the genome as being unlikely to contain the Huntington's gene.[13] As Conneally had predicted, the hunt was extremely frustrating. They exhausted all the available markers—some twenty-seven of them by 1978—without finding any linkage with the disease. In the process, however, they collected the pedigrees of many families with Huntington's, including a large family from Iowa who would play a crucial role in the research later on. Most of all, Mike Conneally became hooked on markers. "What was needed—what has always been needed in human genetics," wrote one molecular geneticist in 1991, "was a greater number of *markers*—genetic signposts in the genome. With enough markers, any gene can be tracked down. The race to a gene has always been won by the lab with the most markers."[14] And, he might have added, large families. Huntington's researchers were still searching for both.

By the mid-1970s, Nancy and I were both attending the HD workshops and trying to follow the various hypotheses about the etiology of the disease. But while I attended the workshops on a random basis and tried not to think too much about Huntington's, Nancy took a very different path. In 1974 she completed her Ph.D. and began teaching in the Psychology Department of the New School for Social Research Graduate Faculty in New York. She loved the New School and living in Greenwich Village. She sometimes dreamed of turning to yet another field, such as photography or filmmaking, and she enjoyed her friends who were doing both. Still, she joined the Scientific Advisory Board of the Hereditary Disease Foundation in the summer of 1974 and for a while acted as a liaison between the foundation and CCHD. She was coming to know not only the established authorities in the field of Huntington's research but also many of the younger basic scientists whom Dad and Ron Konopka and David Barkley had recruited. Nancy's intelligence and her keen psychological skills made her increasingly active in the workshop discussions. She liked the scientists, and they liked her. They were moved that this charismatic young woman, who was herself at risk, was so dedicated to solving the mystery of the disease. Her very presence at the workshops served as a constant reminder of why the scientists were there and what was humanly at stake in their research.

Still dreaming of alternative lives, Nancy participated in the early discussions for a Congressional Commission for the Control of Huntington's Disease and Its Consequences. Several families in New Jersey had lobbied for such a commission, which would have a mandate to develop a comprehensive state-of-the-art portrait of the illness in the United States. In the fall and winter of 1975, Nancy took part in interviewing candidates for the position of executive director, commuting down to Washington between her lectures at the New School. She eventually decided to accept the position of deputy director of the commission, since this post would enable her to advance the research on Huntington's more actively and feel she was really helping Mom. But then the newly appointed executive director resigned just as things were getting under way, in the spring of 1976. To Nancy's surprise, Donald B. Tower, director of the National Institute for Neurological and Communicative Disorders and Stroke (NINCDS, later called NINDS), and Thomas N. Chase, who was then head of Intramural Research at NINDS, offered her the vacant position.

The offer thrust her into a state of extreme anxiety. "I had extraordinarily long conversations with myself and panic attacks," she told me later. "I remember lying in bed in New York and thinking, would I destroy the commission?" Just shepherding the proposed commission through the obstacles in Washington to get it approved had taken two years. "The commission could be the best thing that ever happened to Huntington's disease, and I was going to totally destroy it," she worried in her darkest moments. "And I debated with myself whether it was fair to the commission for me to take the job of executive director." Finally, after conferring at length with herself, with Dad, and with Tom Chase, she decided to accept. She credits Chase with helping to give her the confidence to take the position. "Tom Chase was fantastic," she recalls today. "He said, 'You can do it. Go ahead, do it.' I will always be very indebted to him for that." Dad had encouraged her too, but afterward he felt anxious about the implications for her career. "I was worried that perhaps I was pushing her into something that was not only horrendous in itself—that is, the Huntington's picture—but taking her away from an environment [the New School] she had really liked. I felt very ambivalent about what I had done." But Dad, too, rapidly became convinced that Nancy had made the right decision. "It happened very quickly," he told me later. "It was clear in the first meetings with the people on the commission that this was right up her alley. She did it better than I did, or anybody. The minute she got her feet wet she was really at home. I had never seen Nancy like that."

Over the next two years, the commissioners held frequent meetings with one another, other government groups, medical people, service agencies, and the public. They were six health professionals and three laypeople, including the actress Jennifer Jones Simon, along with Nancy, the executive director, and a deputy director, Charles MacKay.[15] As "vice chairperson," Dad was proud to have Nancy as his boss and joked about their role reversal. Marjorie Guthrie chaired the Commission, though she and my father played a more ceremonial role, with Nancy in charge of day-to-day operations. The three of them together made a lively trio, especially at the public hearings, where they took the testimony of doctors, health administrators, public officials, and especially the families directly affected by the illness. "I was amazed at so many horrific stories," Nancy recalled later. "There's no way of going through that ex-

perience and not being immensely impressed by people's resilience and stamina." These hearings often turned into dramatic encounters. "The fact that this was an important project
was therapeutic to people," Nancy said. "Because so many people had been fighting for so long, against ignorance and disin-
terest. Some of them had never talked to anybody. Sometimes
people came to the testimony and they never knew there was
another Huntington's family. That was the first time they met
other Huntington's families. It was like a revival meeting at
times."

The commission also organized working groups to develop
recommendations in specific areas, such as epidemiology,
virology, social management, and genetics. They drew up a series of proposals that they later presented to Congress. From the
start, this commission decided to use a generic approach. They
used Huntington's as a window onto other neurological and genetic diseases, focusing not on the problems unique to HD but
on the broader problems posed by many neurological, hereditary, chronic, and psychiatric illnesses. They kept their proposals simple in order to increase the chances of realization. They
recommended congressional funding for several Centers
Without Walls: combined basic and clinical research centers
drawing in people from different departments and institutions
and perhaps even from different geographical areas. (Two such
centers were funded by the NINDS in 1980, one in Boston, centered at Harvard Medical School and Massachusetts General
Hospital, and the other in Baltimore, at the Johns Hopkins
University School of Medicine.) They urged support for a roster of Huntington's families, in order to facilitate their connections with researchers. (In 1979, Mike Conneally established
the Huntington's Disease Research Roster at the Indiana
University School of Medicine in Indianapolis.) Most intriguing
to Nancy, the commission recommended funding a Venezuela
project to study the communities around Lake Maracaibo where

the prevalence of Huntington's disease was dramatically high. Venezuela had been on the agenda of the foundation ever since 1973, but organizing a research expedition had seemed prohibitively difficult and the idea had languished.[16]

In 1977, while the Commission was in the midst of its deliberations, a development in an entirely different field suddenly made a Venezuela project even more compelling. That year, a pair of researchers at the University of Texas Southwestern Medical School in Dallas, Michael Brown and Joseph Goldstein, identified the fundamental defect in familial hypercholesterolemia, a condition of extremely high cholesterol levels in the blood associated with early heart attacks. They did so by studying children who had inherited the faulty gene from both parents. The effects were much more dramatic when multiplied by two. Perhaps Huntington's would also stand out more starkly in those who had twice the genetic dose. The Brown and Goldstein strategy highlighted the potential value of finding individuals who had two parents suffering from Huntington's; at least some of their children might have inherited the gene from both parents. Only in the small communities around Lake Maracaibo did the likelihood of finding such individuals appear promising. Nancy especially was eager to pursue a project, although any action would have to wait until the conclusion of the commission's deliberations.[17]

Meanwhile, the commissioners also urged the development of a safe presymptomatic test that could inform those at risk of their future prospects. They emphasized, however, the sensitive ethical and psychological issues involved, and pointedly opposed a dangerous experiment performed earlier in Chicago by André Barbeau and another neurologist, Harold L. Klawans. Observing that their Parkinson's patients had developed chorea-like, involuntary movements under the influence of extremely high doses of L-dopa, Klawans and Barbeau had reasoned that administering L-dopa to people at risk for

Huntington's might produce chorea-like symptoms in those who actually carried the gene. Subsequently they had given L-dopa to people at risk, as well as to a group of controls who were not at risk. Of thirty people at risk, none of whom had had any symptoms prior to the experiment, one third developed temporary chorea-like movements after taking the drug, about the number who might be expected to develop Huntington's. None of the twenty-five control subjects was affected. Although the researchers theorized that the responses to L-dopa *might* be correlated with subsequent onset of the disease, only time would actually tell—and that might take twenty years or more. Meanwhile, those who had experienced temporary chorea were left with the terrifying memories of symptoms they might or might not someday suffer. And no one knew whether the experimental L-dopa might even precipitate the onset of the illness.[18] The commission urged caution in the strongest language, while encouraging the construction of an accurate, noninvasive test.

Genetic linkage seemed to offer a more promising route toward predictive testing. The commissioners wholeheartedly endorsed this approach, since subjects would not experience symptoms during the testing process. As a member of the commission's Genetic Linkage Work Group, Mike Conneally helped author its report, which explained the urgency of localizing the gene and the usefulness of linkage studies for doing so. This group especially stressed the importance of developing new markers as a key to future linkage research. Of course, they were thinking of the classical protein and red blood cell markers, but the point was markers, of whatever kind.[19] More important, though, the commission emphasized the value of genetic linkage, not for diagnostic and counseling purposes but for hastening identification of the underlying biochemical abnormality at the heart of the disease. Here was an important shift in thinking about linkage studies that Nancy herself helped to inspire.

Instead of eugenic prevention, therapeutic possibility now moved to the center of thinking about linkage studies, even if presymptomatic diagnosis remained the most immediate potential result.

The commission's ten-volume report offered a bleak picture of the devastation wrought by Huntington's disease and the desperate lack of resources available to the stricken families. Including six volumes of public testimony, the report presented the voices of those who had the disease in their families, allowing people directly affected to describe their needs in public and in print. The result was a powerful indictment of the privatized U.S. health care system, as well as a strong argument for a system of national health insurance, a recommendation also supported by the commission.

For Nancy personally, the commission opened up a totally new world. "The thing that astonished me most about it was the attention being paid to Huntington's, and the sense that something could be done. For the first time there was just a suspicion that something could actually change about Huntington's." In addition, Nancy felt exhilarated to discover "that so many people would actually find this illness interesting and want to work on it, and would spend their time and energy on it. Because I had always felt very embarrassed, even in connection with the foundation, as if I were appealing for myself because I am at risk. But the federal government is saying, this is a disease worth paying attention to. I think there was a genuine sense of hope because other people were saying, yes, this is an important problem, a fascinating scientific project. That made all the difference in the world." It was "like an elixir," she said later, "just like being drunk all the time. It was a very heady experience."

In November 1978, a second International Symposium on Huntington's Disease was held in San Diego to review progress since the 1972 Centennial Symposium. Several hundred clinicians and scientists attended, many more than had been present in Columbus. By 1978, the number of papers published annually on Huntington's disease was more than one hundred (an increase reflecting the institutional expansion of the neurosciences generally as well as a heightened interest in Huntington's specifically). Moreover, the focus of research had shifted from the more descriptive aspects of the illness—the history, epidemiology, differential diagnosis, and clinical description—to the biochemistry, cell biology, immunology, and membrane physiology of the disease. Some people believed the evidence for a generalized defect in the cell membrane was the most promising hypothesis to date.

Clearly Huntington's was no longer the obscure illness of ten years earlier. The amount of research money spent on the disease had increased significantly over the past decade. Growing numbers of people had entered the HD network through CCHD and were actively engaged in fund-raising, lobbying, and forming support groups.[20] Through the Centers Without Walls in Baltimore and Boston, the HD Research Roster in Indianapolis, brain banks in Los Angeles and Boston, and facilities such as the Family Services Center in New Jersey, people with Huntington's had greater access to assistance, while investigators had increased access to research subjects and vital tissues.

Most of all, more basic scientists had begun to think about Huntington's and to work on it in the lab. The foundation workshops had sparked the interest of many talented young investigators and had persuaded those involved in developing new technologies such as positron emission tomography, or PET scan—a method of visualizing metabolic activity in the brain—to apply their techniques to the study of Huntington's. According to John Minna, "There's a whole cadre of people that are interested in the HD problem, even though they're not working on it on a day-to-day basis." At a crucial moment, the workshops had made the difference, "just by bringing the right people together at the right time." In the view of Steve Matthysse, "If you just wanted to study something, would you pick Huntington's? Well, there's good and bad. The good thing is, it's a single dominant gene with an unmistakable pattern of expression. But it has a very late age of onset, and that's hard, because you can't really get the pedigree as well [since people without symptoms could develop them later]. I think I might have been tempted to do something else."

Despite all the heightened attention to Huntington's, the medical situation for those already ill had not really changed. Treatment remained minimal, the progression of the disease inexorable. Watching Mom's steady deterioration, Dad in particular felt a sense of frustration with the lack of any real breakthrough after the tremendous hopes of the early 1970s. In 1980, David E. Comings, a medical geneticist at the City of Hope Medical Center in Los Angeles, highlighted this frustration when the *American Journal of Human Genetics,* of which he was editor, published five papers on HD with negative findings. All the papers disputed previous claims of discovering significant differences between tissue from people with Huntington's and those without it. According to Comings, all the promising findings of the last decade had been strictly random—all the fibroblast growth studies, the autoimmune experiments, the various reports of membrane defects in Huntington's. Comings accompanied these papers with a sharp editorial blasting the investigators who had made the claims and scolding the foundation for sloppy science, though he failed to mention that the foundation itself had funded these studies to sort out the contradictory findings. Why is it, asked Comings, that such erratic results—one step forward, one step back—occur so often in research on diseases, including schizophrenia, manic-depressive psychosis, and cystic fibrosis? He offered several possible explanations: first, the great genetic variability of human beings, who, unlike inbred strains of mice and rats, differ significantly from one individual to the next, making it far more difficult to correlate differences with a specific disease; second, the law of compound interest, which states that the number of false starts in clinical research is directly related to the degree of interest in the disease; and third, what Comings called "blind is beautiful," and the failure of many investigators to do their experiments double blind.[21]

Were there, in the seventies, roads not taken that might have been explored? Did the fascination with finding a predictive test lead investigators down dead-end streets? How did the level of technology during the 1970s limit the questions that could be raised? Did the freewheeling foundation style have its limitations, as Ed Kravitz argued? Or did the constraints of research on human disease, especially inherited disease, inevitably increase the possibilities of confusion? As Nancy pointed out, studying genetic illness in humans was not like studying lobsters in a lab, where you could impose strict controls. Often you had to take what tissues you could get. Still, Kravitz thought that questions such as why cells die—a topic that for some reason had never fascinated my father—should have been pursued more vigorously. After all, the death of neurons was one of the few undisputed facts about Huntington's disease. Certainly the workshops of the 1970s should—and could—have discussed cell death. More studies of cell death could have been funded. As it was, that subject was not broached in depth until Kravitz joined the Scientific Advisory Board in 1980, bringing with him some of the brightest young researchers in the field, such as H. Robert Horvitz of the Massachusetts Institute of Technology, who had studied the famous worm *Caenorhabditis elegans* and who would play a vital role in guiding Huntington's research over the next decade.

Others later emphasized that the genetic dimension had been neglected, that not enough recognition had been given to the need to test for differences between people with and without Huntington's *within the same family.* Certainly it was true that many of the earlier investigators, mostly neurologists, had not grasped the importance of family pedigrees. But it was also the case that it was extremely difficult to find families with Huntington's disease with the right structure for such research, that is, large families with several living generations, including people both with and without the disease. What genetic research there had been during this period—the genetic linkage studies, for example—had failed to turn up significant correlations between HD and any known genetic marker. Although the 1977 commission report had emphasized the value of a linked marker and had even noted the promising increase of available protein markers, the 1978 symposium in San Diego devoted little time to genetics, and the two papers on genetic linkage both presented negative results. By this time, Myrianthopoulos's prediction of a breakthrough within the decade seemed utopian, a fantasy at best. George Bruyn's anguished observation back in 1968 seemed more current. "So many workers have devoted so much time, thought and energy in going up blind alleys," he wrote, "that one might begin to foster doubt whether future efforts will ever be crowned with success."[22]

In science, advances in one field may have dramatic repercussions in seemingly unrelated areas. This was the case during the 1970s, when an array of new techniques transformed all fields of biology. What the recombinant DNA revolution did, essentially, was provide scientists with a variety of tools for manipulating DNA in the laboratory—tools for cutting it apart, putting it together in new ways, combining DNA from humans with DNA from bacteria, getting bacteria to make millions of copies of human DNA so scientists could work with it. Instead of looking merely at the expressed effects of genes—blue eyes, red hair, blood type O, for example—they could look directly at the genes themselves.

One of the key tools in this revolution were certain enzymes from bacteria called restriction enzymes. Restriction enzymes are essentially defenses produced by bacteria to recognize foreign DNA and slice that DNA at a specific nucleotide sequence before it can destroy the host bacteria. Each type of enzyme always cuts DNA at a specific point, like scissors cutting through paper; there are hundreds of different enzymes, each with a different "recognition site." The first such enzyme to be identified, called *Eco*RI, "recognized" the sequence GAATTC in any segment of DNA—whether bacterial or human—and always cut that sequence between the T and the C.

The ability to cut up DNA in precise ways made possible the invention of another basic technology of the recombinant DNA revolution—cloning. In order to work with DNA, researchers need multiple copies of the particular strand they were interested in. Early in the 1970s, two researchers in San Francisco invented a method of inserting fragments of human DNA into a bacterium—not into the bacterium's own genome but into a little circular stretch of DNA inside the bacterial cell called a plasmid. They engineered a fragment of human DNA to combine with that of the plasmid, so that, when the bacterium started to reproduce, it created millions of new copies of itself containing both its own genome and the plasmid with its insert of human DNA. Researchers then used a restriction enzyme to cut out the human (or hamster or mouse or whatever) segment from the bacterial plasmid; the result was millions of copies (or clones) of a specific fragment of human DNA. (In the 1980s, the new technology of polymerase chain reaction, or PCR, greatly simplified this process.) Any specific fragment interesting to investigators could be tagged with a radioactive isotope, causing it to leave traces when exposed to X-ray film. Moreover, if separated into a single strand, this radioactively labeled strand, called a probe, could be used to identify its complementary strand in a mass of DNA fragments, since single-stranded DNA will seek out its complementary segment and reconnect, or hybridize, to it.

Restriction enzymes and probes also made possible a third technique that was developed in 1975. Known as Southern blotting after its Scots inventor, Edwin M. Southern, this method offered a means of identifying and visualizing particular stretches of DNA. To make a Southern blot, blood is drawn and DNA extracted from the nucleus of white blood cells. The DNA is then mixed with a restriction enzyme, which slices it up into a million or so pieces. Placed in small wells at one end of a mold and covered with an agarose gel, the fragments are jolted with an electric current, a procedure known as gel electrophoresis. The current moves the smaller, lighter, more mobile fragments toward the opposite end of the gel, while the larger, heavier fragments, which are more resistant to motion, remain closer to their starting point. The fragments in the gel are then separated into single strands through the use of chemicals or temperature changes, and a nitrocellulose filter is placed over the gel to soak up the DNA fragments, much as blotting paper soaks up ink from a document. A solution containing a radioactively labeled probe is then poured over this filter full of DNA fragments. If DNA complementary to the probe is present on the filter, the single-stranded probe will bind to it. When the filter is exposed to X-ray film, this strand (or strands) will become visible in the form of a dark band or bands. The position of the bands on the developed film (called an autoradiogram) will reveal the size of the fragments complementary to the probe, since the distance traveled by each fragment in the gel is directly proportional to its size: the shorter, hence lighter, the fragment, the lower it will appear on the filter and the film.

Southern blotting would later offer a powerful means of studying the genetic differences of individuals through the comparison of the pattern of bands produced by their DNA, although this use was not at all obvious at first and Southern blotting served other purposes. Additional techniques developed in the late 1960s and early 1970s opened up further possibilities for investigating genes. Somatic cell genetics, for example, enabled researchers to map genes to particular chromosomes through procedures involving the fusion of rodent cells with human cells. Investigators discovered that when the nucleus of a mouse cell was fused with that of a human cell, the mouse chromosomes would gradually drop out, leaving behind only one or a few human chromosomes. If the cell continued to produce a protein associated with a specific gene, the gene producing that protein must reside on the remaining chromosome, whose identity could be determined under the microscope through new chromosome-staining and -banding techniques. Spurred by these new technologies, the first human gene mapping conference took place in 1973, and, by 1977, more than one hundred human genes had been mapped to particular chromosomal locations. Altogether, the development of somatic cell genetics and chromosome staining, and especially the recombinant DNA revolution, would offer those working in human genetics powerful tools for investigating genes at the level of the actual molecules of DNA.

These developments did not go unnoticed at the Huntington's workshops, of course, but their application remained elusive. "If it is possible to test cells for 'HD-ness,' " noted one participant breezily in early 1978, "it should be possible to map the Huntington's gene to a particular chromosome using the techniques of somatic cell genetics." But "HD-ness" was just what no one could yet identify. In pursuit of this goal, the

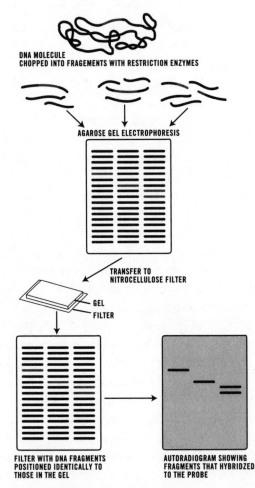

DNA MOLECULE
CHOPPED INTO FRAGEMENTS WITH RESTRICTION ENZYMES

AGAROSE GEL ELECTROPHORESIS

TRANSFER TO
NITROCELLULOSE FILTER

GEL
FILTER

FILTER WITH DNA FRAGMENTS
POSITIONED IDENTICALLY TO
THOSE IN THE GEL

AUTORADIOGRAM SHOWING
FRAGMENTS THAT HYBRIDZED
TO THE PROBE

Making a Southern blot: First DNA is chopped into a million or so fragments with one or more restriction enzymes, each of which cuts the DNA at a specific site. Next the fragments are placed in a gel and exposed to an electric current that separates them by size. The shorter, lighter fragments travel more rapidly through the gel, while the larger heavier fragments, moving more slowly, remain closer to their starting point. Transferred to a nitrocellulose filter paper, the fragments are then exposed to a radioactively labeled single strand of DNA called a probe. The probe hybridizes to any complementary strands of DNA present on the filter. After extraneous DNA is washed away, the filter is exposed to X-ray film. Those strands that have hybridized to the probe will appear as dark bands whose position on the film indicates their relative size.

1979 edition of *Advances in Neurology,* which summed up the research of the 1970s on Huntington's, looked to new findings in cell membrane structure and function as among the most promising developments to date. Just how the new somatic cell genetics and recombinant DNA technologies might advance HD research was a question that had not seriously been asked.[23]

Eight

A DOUBLE DEATH

Finally we're shown the door . . .

—Christa Wolf
The Quest for Christa T.

Mom continued her steady decline. Now each time we came home to visit, she was thinner, her speech thicker, her walk more unsteady, her dark eyes more terrified. She protested that the hospital was making her sicker and grew hysterical at the ambulance sirens blaring at all hours of the day and night. For as long as she was able to go, we would take her out in the car for dinner or for ice cream or for a drive north along the Pacific Coast Highway to Malibu or Zuma Beach. Like most people with Huntington's, she had a tremendous appetite, and, despite the constant danger of choking, she ate voraciously. Nancy and I would bring cookies and candy when we came to visit, and she in turn devoured whatever we brought without ever gaining weight, while we, eating to keep her company, grew plump. We installed a small refrigerator in her room and stocked it with cheese, ice cream, and other fattening foods, which always disappeared between visits. Watching her eat, I was terrified that she would inhale the food and choke to death, which commonly occurs with Huntington's patients.

But although she did sometimes start to choke, she always managed to get the food down without any catastrophes. Walking, too, grew more perilous, as she would lurch unsteadily down the slippery corridors of the nursing homes, aiming for a chair or a couch just ahead and throwing herself into it with tremendous force.

Mom had smoked for many years, and she continued to chain-smoke during her illness, flicking ashes all over her clothes as she struggled to bring the cigarette to her lips. Smoking was one of the few remaining pleasures of her life, and it seemed cruel to try to persuade her to stop, but we worried that she would one day set herself on fire. Always looking for new ways to cope with the illness, Nancy learned about an ingenious contraption called a smoking machine, a small device that resembled a cigarette holder with ashtray attached. For a while she used it, but finally she lacked even the control to place the cigarette in the gadget or to bring it anywhere near her mouth. Almost overnight she stopped smoking, much to the relief of the nursing home personnel and even us, but we also knew she had lost yet another of the small joys of her life. Television had become too difficult to watch, since her eyes could not remain focused on the screen; she asked us to remove it. Even the radio exceeded her abilities. For hours on end she would sit in the chair next to her bed, a strange, twisted figure, her arms flailing, head jerking and falling over onto her chest, legs leaping out from under her. Occasionally she would venture out into the halls to plant herself in the dayroom with the other patients. Once when we moved her to a new nursing home, I walked with her into the day room, where a fellow patient came over to greet her. Without a word he opened his fly, took out his penis, and urinated at her feet. Luckily, Mom appeared not to notice.

Despite her often childish behavior, shouting in frustration if a favorite chair was occupied or screaming at a visitor who entered her room uninvited, Mom never lost an awareness of where she was or the world around her. As the years passed, she could no longer protest in sentences but only in vague, slurred syllables that we struggled, with partial success, to understand. The telephone was especially difficult, though we continued to call even when we could not fully grasp her meaning. At least we could talk to her, tell her we loved her, and almost always we could make out a word or two from her.

By the spring of 1978, Mom's condition had deteriorated alarmingly. Weak and emaciated, she thrashed about uncontrollably, her arms and legs flailing against the rails the nurses raised at the sides of her bed to keep her from falling out. We bought lambswool padding for the rails and an eggcup-foam pad to place on top of the mattress, but her arms and legs were still covered with bruises, and several bedsores had opened on her back. Her speech by now was almost completely unintelligible, her jaw hung loose, her tongue lolled in her mouth. When we walked into her room, she would greet us with a look of recognition for an instant, but then her eyes would wander out of control and she could no longer really acknowledge us. The struggle simply to exist—to breathe, to swallow, to drink, to eat what little she could—consumed all her failing energies.

One Sunday early in March, Dad called me in San Francisco, where I was living while teaching at Sonoma. Dad reported that Mom was in Cedars-Sinai Hospital with pneumonia. She looked very bad. He did not think she could live more than a couple of weeks. I flew to Los Angeles that weekend, as did Nancy, and, with John, we drove to the hospital. As we walked down the hall, strange, inhuman shrieks issued from one of the rooms. We approached, and I realized with a start that those sounds were my mother's voice. Mom was skeletal, yet agitated and upset, flushed with fever. She fought the soft restraints with which the nurses had tied her arms and legs to the side of the bed to keep her from pulling out her IV and injuring herself on the bed rails. But Nancy and I couldn't stand seeing her bound like a prisoner and we untied her, holding her gently when she moved too violently. We fed her slowly, spoonful by spoonful. Finally, sedated by a shot, she slept.

That afternoon we conferred with my father about how to advise Mom's physician. He was now acting according to "no code," which meant that he would keep her as comfortable as possible and treat her for pain but would institute no heroic, life-prolonging measures. We discussed whether to make these instructions more emphatic and whether to specify that antibiotics should not be used in case of further infection. I found that while I longed for her death, I could not bring myself to say the words that might end her life. They would not come. Dad too was haunted by the memory of his own father's agonizing final illness with cancer of the bladder, when he, the son, had had to approve a final shot of morphine for his father, knowing it would probably be the last. Finally we all decided that the "no code" instruction was as far as we could go.

Mom rallied. Within a few days her vital signs had improved, her temperature had returned to normal, her breathing had eased. We had to move her once again from the hospital to a nursing home. But where?

After examining several possible places, Nancy and I found the Patrician Convalescent Hospital, a reasonably decent four-story place on a shady street off Santa Monica Boulevard. The day of the transfer, Nancy traveled with Mom in the ambulance while John and I drove over. When the ambulance arrived, the Patrician nursing personnel took one look at the bruised, emaciated figure on the gurney and announced that they could not accept her because of her bedsores. She would have to leave. But there was absolutely no other place to take her. The hospital would not take her back because she was a patient with a chronic illness, and several other nursing homes had refused even to consider a Huntington's patient. We pleaded and protested, standing there in the entry hall with Mom beside us on the gurney, the ambulance drivers threatening to leave, and the nurses examining Mom's body as if she were a piece of meat. Nancy, furious, insisted that they must take her as promised and called Mom's physician, who threatened a lawsuit if the place did not accept his patient. Finally the staff backed down and took her in.

A few nights later, back in San Francisco, I dreamed that a woman flew in through the window like a New England witch and tried to seduce me, as if I too would be one of the victims of the Salem witches thought to have Huntington's disease. I woke up screaming. Later that night I dreamed that I had returned home to a huge pool of vomit on the front steps of a big house. I wondered who could have been so ill. In my dreams, my mother and I were entangled like the corpses piled up in the mass graves of Auschwitz. She was dying and trying to take me with her; I was living and trying to bring her back from the dead. I longed for her and I hated her, and my dreams were full of miracles and monsters.

Commonly, patients in the last stages of Huntington's disease grow still and quiet. As Mom grew steadily weaker, the chorea began to subside, as if the approach of death granted at least that small reprieve from the curse of continual movement. In her new home, which we knew would be the last, we surrounded her with familiar objects to maintain threads of connection to her family and former life. Nancy placed a photograph of herself and me where Mom could see it on the wall opposite her bed, and we hung one of Mom's own colorful paintings on another wall. Even though her eyes wandered, she could see out the door into the hallway and was alert to the movement of people and of food down the corridor. Although

Mom showed some signs of the dementia common in Huntington's patients toward the end, as well as paranoid fears of other patients, she always knew who we were and maintained a sense of humor far into her illness. On each visit, Nancy would regale her with stories about the Congressional Commission, and when Nancy showed her the dedication in the commission report—"To Woody, Fletcher and Leonore" (Fletcher was the husband of Alice Pratt, who had started her own HD Foundation)—Mom smiled and seemed pleased. Still, it was painful to see our mother's identity as patient subsuming all others. On Palm Sunday the staff passed out palm fronds to all the patients, in commemoration of the holiday, but the sprig of green lying at the foot of Mom's bed seemed to underline her loss of personality in this place, where no one knew who observed Easter and who didn't. "She's Jewish," I thought gloomily. "She doesn't celebrate Easter. What about Passover?" But I didn't say anything, and Mom probably didn't care or even notice.

On a weekend trip to Los Angeles early in May, John and I decided to combine a visit to Mom with an excursion to San Diego to see an exhibit by the Mexican painter Frida Kahlo. We returned late Saturday night to Santa Monica, where we stayed with Maryline for the night. The next morning, at seven, the phone rang. Dad's voice spoke quietly. "The hospital just called," he said. "Your mother died." "When?" I asked with a pang of guilt. "About half an hour ago," he replied. I wanted desperately to see her and thought there might still be time. John and I jumped into the car and raced to the hospital. I dashed up to the second-floor nursing station and inquired impatiently of the nurse on duty as to my mother's whereabouts, since I assumed they had probably already moved her from the room. The nurse gave me a peculiar look and continued with her telephone conversation. I asked her again, but she went on talking, not even looking up. Finally the nurse said, "She's in her room." I thought it strange but raced down the hall and entered. There was a sheet around the bed, but Mom was lying there as before, quietly breathing. "She's dead," I thought to myself, "but she's still breathing!" Visions of Mary Shelley's monster floated before me, the monster Victor Frankenstein had assembled from corpses. For a fraction of a second a doubt crossed my mind—"Is there such a thing as postmortem respiration?"—before I realized with a shock that the nurses had made a grotesque mistake. I stood there aghast, relieved, furious, speechless, feeling slightly faint and nauseated. I dashed back to the nursing station. "She's alive!" I shouted stupidly. "She's breathing, she's not dead!" "Yes, I know," said the nurse calmly, still talking on the telephone. I felt a tremendous desire to bash her head against the wall, but instead I ran down the hall to call my father, who had already notified the physician and several other people of Mom's death. "Dad, she's alive, she's still breathing!" I yelled frantically into the receiver. Dad called her doctor, who came to the hospital immediately. Mom continued to sleep quietly through it all.

Later the head nurse explained that Mom had been breathing so infrequently and shallowly (Cheyne-Stokes breathing) that she appeared to be dead. The nurses, rushed as always, had not checked closely. Now a second grotesque scene ensued. Instead of allowing her to drift into death, the physician felt compelled to enact a rescue. Gently but firmly, he began to awaken her, holding up the frail, gaunt, skeletal shoulders from the pillow, taking her pulse, asking her over and over, "Lee, do you hear me? Lee, can you hear my voice?" until finally, exhausted, with enormous, unwilling effort, she opened her unfocusing eyes and slowly, very slowly, began to wake up. She looked gray, bluish almost, painfully weak, but, more than anything else, utterly exhausted from the bitter struggle of the last agonizing months. Her tremendous weariness filled the room. I stood there in awe, silently holding her thin hand, hoping she would die now, this very moment, yet terrified she might. I felt conscious of my mother's powerful presence as she hovered on the edge of death, as if she had already entered a world far beyond my own. Dying, she had turned fierce, mustering all the strength and fury that had been buried or forgotten for so many years of her life. In the presence of death she seemed dignified, stately, no longer the timid, childlike woman I knew as my mother but some ancient sybil full of wisdom.

But even now she was not allowed to rest. The physician continued his questioning. Instinctively, against all reason, I joined him. "Mom, it's Alice. Can you hear me?" I pleaded for some sign from her. Finally a sound emerged that resembled a "yes," though her speech was almost entirely unintelligible now and only faintly audible. Someone brought in a tray with breakfast—pancakes, hot cereal, juice—as if nothing had happened. I fed her slowly, and she took some food, but wearily, unwillingly, as if just to please. Later, when she fell asleep, I left, walking like a ghost across the street to meet John and my father. I never saw her again.

A week later, on May 14—Mother's Day that year—at 6:30 P.M., I received a long-distance telephone call. A man with an Indian accent asked for me politely, enunciating my name very clearly. "Your mother, Leonore Wexler, died at 6:04 P.M. today," he said softly. (I recalled that Emma Goldman had also died on May 14.) "When the nurses went to feed her dinner, she was cyanotic and there was no pulse." He explained that he had been unable to contact any other family members. I was the first to know.

I remember not wanting to sleep that night. I felt that if only I could stay awake forever, she would not really be dead and I could postpone her death indefinitely. As long as I could stay awake, I could still keep a connection with her, for she had been alive earlier that day, the last day of her life, and a part of me would still be linked with her. I was obsessed with the thought that this night, when I went to sleep, would be the first night in my life that my mother's heart was not beating and that the following day, when I woke up, would be the first day of my life that my mother was no longer alive and breathing. On that day I would be truly motherless and alone. The ten long years of her illness suddenly vanished, and all I could think of was that finally she had crossed into a country I could not enter.

John and I walked for a long time that night through the fog-drenched streets of the Richmond district of San Francisco, past the Chinese restaurants and coffee shops of Clement Street, across California, over to Lake Street and then down past the deserted Veterans Administration Hospital and Mountain Lake Park with its ghostly pines and eucalyptus. An evil-tempered white swan had recently made its home in the pond, harassing the friendly ducks and the dogs that occasionally jumped in for a swim. But that night, I thought I had never seen anything as beautiful as that regal white swan, sketching slow circles on the reflectionless water. We walked, it seemed, for hours. Later, back at the apartment, I sank into a heavy, dreamless sleep, and did not awaken until long after dawn.

More than anything else, I longed to see my sister and to have her with me. I felt sure I could pull myself together if only she were here. At that moment, Nancy was in Washington, D.C., working day and night to finish the report of the Huntington's Disease Commission. She had always come home, instantly, whenever Mom had needed her. But now that Mom was gone, she wasn't certain about taking time off to come to California, since the deadline was so close. "Nancy, please come," I pleaded with her. "I need you here. I want to do something to commemorate Mom's death, and I want you to be here too." She agreed at once and the next morning flew out to Los Angeles, where John and I met her.

We decided to have a service just for ourselves, just Nancy,

John, and me, since Mom had been sick for so long and had not wanted to see her friends. Few of them had stayed in touch. But her childhood friend, Alene Mintz, had sent us copies of the letters Mom had written to her in the 1940s and 1950s, and we decided to read them aloud to each other while we had her body cremated at the cemetery. Sitting on the grass under an enormous spreading oak, we took turns reading the letters, our mother's young and lively voice speaking to us as we had never heard her while she was alive. As we read, Nancy and I both felt strangely at peace, closer to our mother than we had in a long time, and to the vibrant, funny, cheerful young woman she had been, before the tragedies of her life had closed in on her. I was glad I could hold on to these memories, even if they came more from letters than from life.

We scattered Mom's ashes in the Pacific from a boat we hired in the marina near Santa Monica, weeping like abandoned children on the deck as we sailed up the coast to Malibu, throwing handfuls of ash into the waves and saying our final farewells. I remember that, before we docked, the captain of our boat stopped to fill his tank with gas for the next trip, and I was suddenly filled with fury. "Why don't you do that on your own fucking time!" I shouted at him. I was angry at him for saving himself a few extra minutes but angrier still at the terrible injustices of our mother's life and her lingering lonely death, which we had been powerless to prevent.

Later that day, Nancy and I packed a picnic supper and drove up the Pacific Coast Highway to Zuma Beach, where we spread a blanket on the sand. As the waves turned pink and gold under a vast rose-colored sunset, we danced drunkenly at the edge of the waves, crying and shouting over the ocean roar the poems of Edna St. Vincent Millay—my sister's favorite at the time—"I am not resigned, I do not give in!" And then we threw ourselves onto the sand, where we lay sobbing in each other's arms. Hours later, as we got up to leave, I remember feeling as if a suffocating weight had lifted, as if for the first time in many years I no longer had to carry around all that pain, her pain, inside me. We ran toward the car, shivering in the cold, but in my mind's eye, I was diving into the waves, swimming far out to sea until the white dunes of Zuma disappeared over the edge of the earth and all the world lay silent under the stars, drifting in darkness.

MAPS FOR MISREADING

Laguneta in 1983 was an especially desolate *pueblo de agua* built over a lagoon at the southern end of Lake Maracaibo in Venezuela. Almost every house sheltered someone with Huntington's disease, which they called *el mal de San Vito*.

Nine

"LEAPING GAZELLELIKE THROUGH THE GENOME"

In the mountains the shortest way is from peak to peak; but
for that you need long legs.

—FRIEDRICH NIETZSCHE
Thus Spake Zarathustra

A few days after we scattered Mom's ashes, Nancy returned
to Washington to complete work on the Congressional
Commission's report, which had been presented to Congress
the previous October. That summer of 1978, she decided to accept a position as health sciences administrator at the NINDS,
in the program of Demyelinating, Atrophic and Dementing
Disorders, run by Floyd (Jack) Brinley. She would be responsible for administering research grants relating to Alzheimer's,
Parkinson's, and Huntington's diseases. But more important,
she would also help implement the recommendations of the
commission. The report had been enthusiastically received by
Congress and within the NIH, but she felt it imperative to cap-
italize on the momentum and goodwill that had been created,
to ensure that the most important recommendations actually
got translated into action.

That summer John and I visited friends in Hawaii. We hiked
around the volcanoes and went swimming and snorkeling at
Poipu Beach, where I managed to control my fear of fish long

enough to swim close to a school of gorgeous zebra fish. In between expeditions I read books about mothers and daughters, as if seeing Mom's death as an ordinary loss offered solace from the hard drama of Huntington's. Although we had been mourning Mom's loss for many years, her dying, when it came, was unexpectedly painful. "It's as though her death (re)awakened a realization of how much I wanted a mother," I wrote in my journal, "how much I missed having one I could turn to; it's as though I am grieving not only for the mother I lost but also for the one I never had." It helped to recall that my complicated feelings about my mother, including my anxiety about repeating her sad life, were shared by many other daughters, even if Huntington's gave added grounds to these fears.

Now that Mom was really gone, I began to work seriously on a biography of Emma Goldman, as if Mom's death somehow freed me to begin this more ambitious project, or perhaps to fill the absence that was her life by inventing an/other mother to take her place. There were practical considerations too. I felt increasingly that my own time might be limited. If I were to go the way of my mother, I had better start writing now.

For Dad, Mom's death seemed to release memories of an earlier Leonore that Nancy and I had never known, except through the memories of her friends. Dad had never forgiven himself for not allowing her to take her life that night when she had swallowed so many pills, knowing precisely what lay ahead of her. Her death was something of a deliverance. Late in October 1978, he flew to Fishers Island off the coast of Connecticut to stay for two weeks in the empty summer home of a friend. He spent his days trolling offshore for bluefish, swimming, golfing, walking, and, in the solitude of long golden autumn afternoons, filling sheet after sheet of a red spiral notebook in which he was writing a screenplay. He sent me a postcard with a picture of Tintoretto's *Fall of the Manna* from San Georgio Maggiore in Venice, as if to underscore his relief.

On the back he wrote that he was staying in "the most heavenly place on earth. It will be hard," he said, "to return to the realities of normal existence."

The reality that troubled him most was the lack of any real breakthrough in the research on Huntington's. He was dissatisfied, too, with the workshops. "Not that they were bad," he said, "but I felt they could have been better." After David Barkley's resignation in the spring of 1978, Nancy had acted as interim scientific director and both she and Dad had even led a few of the workshops, but they both knew the situation could not continue. When Nancy joined the NINDS that summer, she had had to resign her official foundation post for reasons of potential conflict of interest. It became imperative to find a replacement.

Sometime in the fall of 1978 Dad telephoned Allan Tobin, then a young assistant professor in the Biology Department at UCLA, to ask if he would he interested in working with the foundation and running the workshops. Dad had met Tobin back in 1972, at a workshop in Boston, and had invited him back the following year, and again in 1976, after he had moved out to UCLA. Dad found Allan intelligent and articulate, his assessments of other participants clear-sighted and perceptive. In addition, Tobin was a molecular biologist, a basic laboratory scientist whose work so far was not on disease but rather on the control of hemoglobin synthesis during chick embryo development. Dad had never lost his fascination with molecular biology and the new genetics, although much of the research sponsored by the foundation during the 1970s had been in other fields. He was eager now to exploit the advances that he had been reading about in the science press. Whatever attracted Dad to Allan Tobin—Allan's field as a molecular biologist, his personal warmth and intellectual liveliness, his liking for my father—Dad knew he wanted Tobin to come and work with the foundation.

At the November 1978 International Symposium on Huntington's Disease in San Diego, Dad had courted Allan over coffee and lunches and taken him to dinner at the Hotel Del Coronado. They had gotten along famously. Over the next weeks, Dad and Allan negotiated a part-time salaried position, in which Tobin would spend the equivalent of one day a week at the foundation, organizing workshops, coordinating grant applications, and doing a host of other activities. At the age of thirty-seven, Allan Tobin now became scientific director of the foundation. He immediately submitted a grant proposal to the NIH for $160,000 to support workshops over the next three years, and in October the grant was approved. Dad was thrilled with his new appointment. Later he said that recruiting Allan Tobin was maybe the best thing he ever did in the foundation.

At the time he joined the Hereditary Disease Foundation, Allan J. Tobin was an intense, energetic, emotional man, ambitious and hardworking, with a quick, earthy sense of humor. As an undergraduate at MIT, he had studied both science and literature and had written an undergraduate honors thesis on Niccolò Machiavelli. Later he had moved to Harvard, where he had earned a Ph.D. in biophysics and worked for a time as a postdoc at the Weizmann Institute in Israel and at MIT. Subsequently he had returned to Harvard as an assistant professor, before joining the UCLA Biology Department in 1975. An intellectual with wide interests outside science, he read voraciously, Mario Vargas Llosa as well as Richard Feynman, played the piano, backpacked in the Sierras with his two young sons, and took an active role in his synagogue. Unlike most molecular biologists, whose sartorial style was decidedly casual, Tobin dressed somewhat formally, and in workshops and meetings, where slacks and sweaters and Adidas were the rule, he was often the only person in a sport jacket and tie, albeit a wildly colorful tie. His friendly manner, however, was anything but formal. Despite the distance he had traveled from his childhood home in Manchester, New Hampshire, Tobin always retained a sense of his small-town origins and a deep sympathy for all underdogs and outsiders.

In accepting the position at the Hereditary Disease Foundation, Tobin acknowledged his attraction to interdisciplinary dialogue. "The business of doing science, of doing experimental science, is fundamentally dull," he told me once. "The ratio of ideas to experiments is very, very low. So the idea of being able to talk to a variety of people about a variety of ideas, of integrating different fields in science in a way that makes some kind of difference, is very appealing."

One of the people Allan Tobin most wanted to talk to was David Housman. They had met in Cambridge in the early 1970s, when they had both had the same baby-sitter for their kids. At that time Housman had been getting a degree in molecular biology at Brandeis, while also working in a lab at MIT. Later, he had moved to the Toronto Cancer Center, returning to Boston in 1975 to join the faculty at MIT. A big, youthful-looking man with a husky voice, quick wit, and a warm, gregarious manner, he had grown up on the Lower East Side of New York, where his great-aunt, a well-known anarchist organizer, had once lived for a while in a house with Emma Goldman. Housman was known as a bold, imaginative investigator who also had a gift for explaining his ideas to those outside his own field of specialization; he could be extremely persuasive.

Now, early in 1979, Housman was coming to California to give a seminar at Cal Tech in Pasadena and he asked Tobin to arrange one for him at UCLA as well. Even before Housman arrived in California for the seminars, Tobin had told him about his new appointment at the Hereditary Disease Foundation. He wanted to brainstorm with Housman about molecular biological approaches to Huntington's, which the foundation had not yet explored. Unlike Tobin, who had never worked on diseases, Housman had studied the genetics of cancer and the thalassemias, a group of inherited blood diseases, and might have some ideas on the subject.

Actually, Tobin had approached Housman at an opportune moment, when Housman and his extremely talented graduate student, James Gusella, were thinking about new ways to map disease genes. Housman had been an enthusiastic proponent of recombinant DNA from the beginning, but he had run into obstacles when he had arrived back in Cambridge from Toronto. He had found himself facing guidelines passed by the Cambridge City Council restricting recombinant DNA work such as cloning. In addition, though he had been working on thalassemia in Toronto, he was becoming convinced that enough researchers were already studying this disorder. He had begun thinking about a different set of questions. At that time, in order to isolate and clone a gene, it was necessary to know what that gene did biochemically. If you knew what protein product the gene produced, you could use the new techniques of somatic cell genetics to determine on which chromosome, and approximately where, the gene was located.

But what if you did not know the defective protein a disease gene produced, which was certainly the case with most genetic diseases, including Huntington's? Were there methods of localizing a gene to a particular chromosome without first knowing what that gene coded for? Could you find a gene without knowing what protein it produced? Jim Gusella, in fact, had crafted an ingenious technique using short repeated segments of DNA called *Alu* sequences—sequences that were highly specific to each species and functioned as a kind of genetic signature—to identify human DNA in the hybrid human-rodent cells that were the basis of the new somatic cell genetics. He and Housman were pondering the question how these or other classes of DNA sequences could also help localize genes whose protein product was unknown. As Housman put it, "Could you clone genes based on where they mapped rather than what they coded for?"

By early 1978, a number of researchers were asking that question. The new discussions grew out of the work begun in the early 1970s with restriction enzymes, the defenses mobilized by bacteria to "recognize" and splice out foreign substances at particular places in the DNA. By the mid-1970s, some investigators noticed that when they cut up human DNA from different individuals with a particular restriction enzyme, they produced sets of fragments that differed in length from person to person. The explanation seemed to be a variation in the DNA sequence where the restriction enzyme cut. Any change in the usual sequence of nucleotides that eliminated a cutting site or added a new one resulted in fragments of different lengths. For example, the restriction enzyme EcoRI recognizes the DNA sequence GAATTC and cuts it between the T and the C. An individual whose DNA possesses this sequence will produce two fragments wherever that sequence appears. But an individual with a different DNA sequence at the same spot, say GAATAC, will produce one longer fragment, since EcoRI will not cut that sequence. Particular sequences travel in families, much like any trait inherited in a Mendelian fashion.

The differences were visualized through the techniques of gel electrophoresis, Southern blotting, and autoradiography: that is, the DNA of different individuals was cut up with a restriction enzyme and the fragments, placed in separate channels, were run through a gel to separate them by size. Separated into single-stranded DNA, they were then transferred to a filter (Southern blotting). A solution containing a radioactively tagged probe was then poured over the filter, so that the probe would hybridize with its complementary DNA fragments. When the filter was exposed to X-ray film, these fragments would appear as dark bands on the film (autoradiogram). If the probe hybridized with fragments of different sizes for different individuals, then the bands on the film would also occupy different positions, with the longer (slower) fragments appearing as bands closer to the top, the shorter (faster) fragments represented by bands nearer the bottom. Because variable sequences in the DNA could be seen through the action of restriction enzymes, these sequences were called restriction fragment length polymorphisms, or RFLPs.

Actually, RFLPs had been used as tools in genetic analysis since 1974, in yeast and also in worms. RFLPs had only recently been identified in humans. By about 1978, however, a number of investigators independently began to observe variant places in DNA located near important genes, or sometimes right inside them.[1] Two researchers at the University of California at San Francisco, Y. W. Kan and A. M. Dozy, came up with the most influential finding. Early in 1978, they published a paper describing an RFLP located next door to the beta-globin gene. This is the gene that goes awry in sickle-cell anemia, a disease that in the United States predominantly affects African Americans and causes a painful and sometimes lethal distortion, or sickling, of the hemoglobin. Unlike Huntington's disease, which is caused by a dominant gene, sickle-cell anemia is caused by a recessive gene, which means that both parents have to pass the gene on to a child in order for that child to have the disease.

Kan and Dozy found that when they mixed human DNA together with the restriction enzyme *Hpa*I and then added a probe containing the beta-globin gene, the probe revealed several patterns of fragments, particularly in the DNA of some African Americans. The two researchers inferred that the differences resulted from an RFLP located right next door to the beta-globin gene. Individuals with the normal beta-globin gene usually possessed a cutting site for the restriction enzyme *Hpa*I that lay extremely close to the gene. In these people, digestion with the *Hpa*I enzyme produced a short fragment 7,600 nucleotides long. Individuals carrying the sickle-cell version of the beta-globin gene evidently lacked the neighboring cutting site. They therefore produced a much longer fragment, 13,000 base pairs in length. The RFLP itself caused no damage and had nothing functional to do with sickle-cell anemia except for the accident of a nearly similar address.[2]

The Kan and Dozy findings were crucial in dramatizing the potential usefulness of RFLPs as markers for disease genes in humans. Indeed, sickle-cell anemia became the first disease that could be diagnosed prenatally through the use of RFLP markers. But the sickle-cell gene had already been found before the RFLP next door was identified. The faulty protein it produced was also known. In fact, all the RFLPs identified so far were located near, or inside, known genes. But at a conference at Alta, Utah, in the spring of 1978—an event now famous in the annals of molecular biology—several other researchers, especially David Botstein from MIT, Raymond White from the University of Massachusetts at Worcester, Mark Skolnick from the University of Utah, and Ronald Davis from Stanford University, proposed using RFLPs for a much grander project. This group theorized that approximately 150 RFLPs spread at regular intervals throughout all the chromosomes might constitute a map of the human genome, a sort of grid placed over the entire three billion base pairs of human DNA. Like mile markers or signposts scattered across a continent, RFLPs located every twenty million base pairs or so should be enough to facilitate establishing the approximate chromosomal location of any specific gene through linkage with at least one RFLP. True, it might be necessary to test thousands of markers in order to pull out 150 that were evenly spaced throughout the genome. Only two RFLPs in humans had been identified so far. But once the map of markers was in place, virtually any gene could be localized through the techniques of genetic linkage.[3]

Genetic linkage, we should recall, was used to try to determine which genes were located close together on the same chromosome and how far apart they were. It was a technique for mapping genes, that is, determining their relative positions along the chromosome, by measuring how often they got separated through recombination events as they were transmitted from generation to generation. The maps resulting from these efforts were called linkage maps. Human geneticists particularly tried to link measurable biochemical markers such as blood type or serum proteins (as well as some forty other variable traits presumably caused by a single gene) with inherited traits such as disease genes, whose presence could not be ascertained clinically.

A major limitation of classical linkage techniques was the small supply of markers. Mike Conneally had exhausted all the available markers without finding any linkage to Huntington's. If Botstein and his colleagues were right about RFLPs, then here was a tremendous new supply of markers. RFLP markers spread throughout all the chromosomes would greatly aid the search for individual genes, such as disease genes, After a map was in place, locating any particular gene's approximate address would be a matter of finding a linkage with a marker, whose address would already be known. It would be like searching for a traveler lost somewhere in North America: finding her would be infinitely easier once you knew she was within fifty miles of St. Louis.

The idea caught on quickly. In November 1979, Botstein, Skolnick, White, and Davis submitted their classic paper to the *American Journal of Human Genetics,* where it appeared in July 1980 under the title "Construction of a Genetic Linkage Map in Man Using Restriction Fragment Length Polymorphisms."[4] According to Jim Gusella, the paper crystallized the fact that RFLP mapping was already happening, which those outside the field may not have realized. Indeed, at the time that Housman first spoke to Allan Tobin about Huntington's, in

January 1979, the paper had not yet appeared, though the ideas were being circulated at conferences and meetings. Certainly Housman's lab was already discussing the new phenomenon of RFLPs and the ways they might be useful for mapping genes. The discussions focused on two critical questions: how could you identify these RFLPs, and how could you find out if they were near a disease gene?

Late in January 1979, over coffee in the outdoor café at UCLA known affectionately as the "bomb shelter," David Housman and Allan Tobin quickly worked out a plan for a workshop to discuss these issues. At the very least, Housman felt that people interested in Huntington's should hear about the new RFLP technologies, and the possibilities they offered for a new approach to linkage. He himself had no plans to pursue such a study. His interests lay in more theoretical and methodological concerns, such as how you could find RFLPs in the first place; how you could identify RFLPs that did not contain any repeat sequences or occur more than once in the genome (a high priority at that time) and how you could use RFLPs to locate genes. But then another discussion in Boston changed his mind.

One day in the summer of 1979, Housman got a call from Joseph Martin, professor of neurology at Harvard Medical School and the chief of the Neurology Service at Massachusetts General Hospital, an affiliate of Harvard. Martin had decided to submit a grant proposal to the NIH for a Huntington's disease Center Without Walls. Martin wanted to include within the grant proposal a series of interdisciplinary research projects. He was reading Horace Freeland Judson's book on the development of molecular biology, *The Eighth Day of Creation,* and was thinking about how the new molecular techniques might bear on the research into Huntington's. He called David Housman and asked him to submit a proposal to include in the grant.

"To be absolutely honest with you," Housman told me later, "I was sort of reluctant to get drawn in." He already felt overworked, and his lab was too crowded. "But I really liked Joe Martin the first time I met him." Ever since his conversations with Tobin out in California the previous January, Housman had been mulling over the problem of Huntington's and how recombinant DNA techniques and RFLP markers might be used to find the Huntington's gene. He was concerned, however, about getting the right kind of families to study, although Martin assured him that they could find such families through the Boston CCHD chapter, as well as through the newly created Huntington's Disease Research Roster headed by Mike Conneally in Indianapolis. Housman knew that families were critical: if they were too small or did not consist of several living generations, the data collected would not achieve the statistical significance necessary to establish linkage.

And then RFLP mapping was still highly speculative. No one yet knew whether there were enough unique RFLPs to serve as useful genetic markers. No one knew if they were distributed fairly evenly along all the chromosomes or huddled together in particular regions, perhaps only on certain chromosomes, where they would be much less useful. No one knew if they were highly polymorphic—that is, if they came in enough alternative versions that differences between individuals could be tracked. But Martin liked the idea of developing RFLPs as potential markers for Huntington's disease and was willing to take the risk. He wanted to include a project in the center's grant.[5]

The deadline was a few weeks away, in the middle of September, and Housman had to work fast to draw up his proposal. Moreover, since he was at MIT and the grant would have to be carried out at Massachusetts General, Housman would have to find someone to supervise the day-to-day operations of the project, even though he would be principal investigator. He

told Martin, "I don't know who it will be, but I'll get someone."
He had that someone already in mind.

Allan, David, and Nancy had organized a workshop in
Bethesda in October 1979. They invited David Botstein, Ray
White, and a number of other geneticists and molecular biologists whose work was pertinent to mapping genes. The central
question on the agenda was just how much work was required
to identify an RFLP marker that was closely linked to the
Huntington's gene. "It was total pandemonium, total chaos,"
Nancy recalled years later. "Everyone was yelling and screaming. David Botstein would go to the board and scribble furi-
ously, then others would jump up and do the same."

The argument centered on priorities. Botstein and White
insisted that it was essential first to establish a grid of signposts before you started looking for linkage with particular
genes. Once they had completed this map, researchers could
start hunting for linkage with specific genes such as Huntington's. Botstein estimated that with the existing techniques,
a linkage with Huntington's could be found in about ten years;
rapidly advancing technologies might shorten this time significantly.[6]

Housman, on the other hand, argued that ten years was too
long to wait before even *starting* to look for the gene. Instead,
he proposed to test each newly identified RFLP for linkage
with Huntington's as he went along, using family pedigrees to
see if any particular form of the marker consistently appeared
in people with the disease. While working to develop RFLP
markers that would contribute to a map of the entire genome,
he would also be looking for the HD gene. True, the Housman
strategy would probably mean testing between 150 and 200
randomly selected markers, possibly even 300.[7] Testing each
probe for correlation with the disease was an enormously complex, time-consuming process. With luck, however, the strat-

egy could mean a shortcut to the gene, eliminating years from the difficult search.

David Botstein was not convinced. "I was absolutely opposed to this idea of leaping gazellelike through the genome," he said years later. "I thought it was nuts to do this without a map." Botstein considered the Housman approach too random and haphazard, like fishing for polymorphisms in a vast genetic sea. He feared that Housman was dreaming, or worse, taking advantage of desperation by making claims he could not possibly fulfill. The others at the workshop shared Botstein's skepticism about the likelihood of quickly homing in on the HD gene, though they were uniformly enthusiastic about the general approach.[8] Some also worried about the ethical implications of the Housman strategy, fearing that it would seem to raise hopes unrealistically. Those interested primarily in mapping the entire human genome did not want to get waylaid on one disease.

Nancy and Allan were willing to gamble. Botstein and White would go ahead with their efforts to identify RFLP markers throughout the genome in any case, whether or not they received funding from the foundation. Nancy felt that supporting the Housman strategy would increase the probability that the gene would be found sooner rather than later. She later recalled thinking that, even if it did take many years, they might as well start now, "because if nothing else worked, we knew this one eventually would." In addition, she had recently returned from Venezuela with ideas for a project that could combine with Housman's. As they talked that weekend, she grew increasingly excited at the prospects of a collaboration. "There have been few times in my life when I felt convinced that something was really right," she wrote later, "times when my heart has raced and leapt into my throat, times when I couldn't sit still and wanted to race as fast as I could, laugh wildly or explode. I had this feeling at the end of the workshop."[9]

Housman's enthusiasm also deepened during the workshop,

which turned out to have unexpected emotional repercussions. "I didn't go to Bethesda expecting to have something hit me in the face," he admitted later. For the first time he met someone with Huntington's disease, a woman who had been a computer programmer. She had been good at math, Housman recalled, "and now she could not count backward from a hundred by sevens—she really couldn't get past about eighty-six. She couldn't drive and was really dependent on people. So seeing her really had a profound impact on me." Housman liked Dad, and he especially liked Nancy, whose intelligence and charisma struck him immediately. He liked her rapport with the other scientists and the strong network she and Dad had already created within the scientific community. Most of all, he admired their courage in confronting this most traumatic issue in their lives. What had been an intellectual challenge for Housman now became an emotional commitment as well.

At the end of the Bethesda workshop, Nancy and Allan urged Housman to submit a grant proposal to the Hereditary Disease Foundation to start the project as soon as possible, since Martin would not know about NIH funding until the following spring. They also invited Housman to present his ideas at the forthcoming foundation workshop in January. Since they anticipated resistance from some members of the foundation's Scientific Advisory Board, they invited Mike Conneally as well, a crucial decision, as it turned out.

Conneally, of course, understood linkage only too well, given his own frustrating efforts to find a protein marker for Huntington's. (By the end of 1978, he and his student, Margaret Pericak-Vance, had begun to establish what they called an "exclusion map" of places in the genome not likely to contain the HD gene.) Although he had not been present at the October 1979 meeting in Bethesda, Conneally understood the potential of DNA markers. And he believed wholeheartedly in the utility of linkage. He would be, as Nancy put it later, a cru-

179

cial "crossover person" at the January 1980 meeting and, indeed, at many meetings to come.

Housman arrived in California in January sick with the flu and so hoarse he could hardly speak. But ill and feverish as he was, he managed to persuade most of the foundation's Scientific Advisory Board members of the usefulness of RFLPs. Mike Conneally too championed the new DNA markers, in language the nongeneticists could understand. Even the supercritical Ed Kravitz came away convinced of the value of the approach. Kravitz thought the RFLP strategy was "by far the most useful and far-reaching technology in relation to disease that we heard about. There seems little doubt that this will work." [10]

Nevertheless, even those board members like Kravitz who were excited about the RFLP technology doubted that a DNA marker specifically for Huntington's would soon materialize. They supported the theoretical innovation of RFLP mapping but were not convinced quick results would be forthcoming. They were willing, however, to vote seed money to Housman to start up the project, in this case $8,333 to run from February through June 1980, when they hoped Joe Martin's Center Without Walls would receive funding from the NIH. Housman was ready to roll. Back in November 1979, he had recruited his graduate student, Jim Gusella, who was just completing his Ph.D. Gusella, a Canadian from Ottawa, had met Housman at the University of Toronto, where he had done his undergraduate work, before going to MIT. Gusella recalled having read about Huntington's disease in high school and being fascinated by its late onset—"the idea that you could live for such a long time without anything being noticeable was neat. I thought it would be an interesting disease to work on." So when Housman suggested the linkage project, Gusella was immediately intrigued. The project would allow him to build on his earlier research, including the *Alu* work. Besides, he liked the open style of Housman's lab, where he could work on several projects at once. So as soon as they heard they had received the foundation seed money, Gusella began to set up his lab across the Charles River from MIT, at Massachusetts General Hospital. At the end of 1980, just a few months after the twenty-eight-year-old Gusella had completed his Ph.D., Housman made him principal investigator, though David continued to take an active interest in the work. The Boston Center Without Walls had received funding from the NIH, so support was assured.

By this time, though, Gusella was beginning to have second thoughts. He had turned down a postdoc at the prestigious lab of Leroy Hood at Cal Tech in Pasadena and wondered whether he had made the right decision. "I hadn't realized when I first started it," he told me later, "quite how much of a risk I was taking." If he found nothing after three years or so—a likely prospect—he would be without publications and, conceivably, without job possibilities, since these depend heavily on published scientific work. He was putting his entire career on the line. David Botstein thought finding a marker might take ten years; David Housman believed it could take less; Ron Konopka predicted "three or so years" to find the approximate location of the gene. But other scientists, including many geneticists, were far more skeptical. They believed that the late onset of Huntington's, and the lack of any clues as to which chromosome might hold the gene, made it an unrealistic choice for this approach. They thought it was "a shot in the dark, that it would take you half a century to do this." [11]

Ten

TRISTES TROPIQUES

The knowledge that he shared the city's secret, the city's guilt—it put him beside himself, intoxicated him . . .

—THOMAS MANN
Death in Venice

The project Nancy had in mind when she returned from Venezuela in July of 1979 focused on finding a homozygote, a recommendation of the Congressional Commission two years earlier. Only in the communities around Lake Maracaibo, with their high concentration of people with Huntington's, could she hope to find someone with a double dose of the gene. Over the course of the October workshop in Betheseda, however, she realized that the Venezuelan families might have a larger significance. For David Housman's linkage project, they might offer the crucial key.

A Venezuelan physician and biochemist, Americo Negrette, a long-time director of the Instituto de Investigación Clínica at the University of Zulia, first diagnosed Huntington's in Venezuela in 1952. After graduating from medical school, he came to practice in San Francisco, a suburb of the city of Maracaibo. "I saw a man coming down the street," he told me, "a robust, sturdy-looking man in his late thirties. He was staggering and weaving, and he kept falling down and picking himself up. I thought he was drunk." Negrette questioned some bystanders. "He's not drunk," they told him. "It's an illness we have here." They called it *el mal de San Vito,* or simply *el mal,* the sickness. The people who had it were *San Viteros.*

The next week, against the advice of his friends, Negrette went to visit the man in his house in San Luis, San Francisco's poorest barrio, which had a reputation for violence. "Everyone spoke badly of the people there," Negrette said, "including doctors, friends of mine, who told me that these people were very hostile, very aggressive, they had all kinds of problems." The man whom he had seen in the street was especially violent. He had repeatedly tried to kill himself by throwing himself in front of cars and trucks. When he failed, he tried to kill others. To Negrette, though, he was warm and affectionate. Negrette came from an impoverished background himself and felt empathy for these pariahs and outcasts. "I began with medical curiosity and ended with sympathy," he says.

Negrette visited other homes in San Luis, where he saw people with similar symptoms. He traveled to Barranquitas, a town several hours south on the shore of the lake, and even farther south to Laguneta, one of the *pueblos de agua,* villages built over the water. The people in these communities were all interrelated and recognized their common ancestry. Negrette soon diagnosed the illness as Huntington's chorea. An old woman known as the historian of San Luis told him the disease had started with a Spanish sailor who was hired on to a ship in Hamburg and stayed to raise a family in Venezuela. Negrette began recording their family histories and did what he could to help the people. He acted as their advocate with public health officials, although, influenced by eugenic ideas, he also for a time called for "eugenic sterilization," a practice he later repudiated. Mostly, he urged the people to practice birth control and, when IUDs and oral contraceptives became available, offered them to women who wanted them. He listened to their problems and became a friend.

Negrette described the catastrophe of Huntington's disease at the Sixth Venezuelan Congress of Medical Science in 1955. "For the first time, a disease which is neither infectious nor contagious is capable of mounting a serious public health threat," he warned. Eight years later, in 1963, he published a book on the illness, *Corea de Huntington: Estudio de una sola familia a través de várias generaciones (Huntington's Chorea: Study of a Single Family Through Several Generations).* A poet and painter as well as a physician, Negrette captures the voices of the people, who speak poignantly of their loneliness and isolation. A fifty-two-year-old man told him, "This disease is like nothing else. I am crazy with a desire to get rid of this trouble. I would rather have any other disease but this. There is nothing worse than this illness, this trembling all over my body, so that I cannot even talk to anyone. No, this is the worst." A fifty-six-year-old woman feels so tired she cannot even eat. There are nights when she cannot sleep for worrying about her children, "giving them over to the care of God and the blessed Virgin." She thinks a great deal about death, "because when one is alone, without having anyone to care for you, what else can you think about?"[1]

The people in these communities were expert diagnosticians. If they say of someone, *él está perdido,* he is lost, "we can already add one more person with chorea to the list." Sometimes they even diagnosed themselves; they recognized how the disease had changed them. "I used to be affectionate," said one woman. "Now I fight with everyone, for no reason." They could see themselves growing angrier and sometimes acting abusive. They suffered from marginalization, but especially from the rejection of those outside, who stigmatized the entire community. But they understood that *el mal* was an inherited illness "in the blood," as they put it, not a punishment from

God or a moral curse. They guessed that they had all inherited it from a single ancestor, even if they did not know the precise connections.

Negrette's 1955 paper on Huntington's, and his book *Corea de Huntington,* provoked controversy within Venezuela's medical community. Some refused to believe the diagnosis. They insisted Huntington's chorea did not exist in Venezuela. Outside the country, his work went unnoticed, perhaps because it was published in Spanish, in a Latin American country whose achievements in medicine were not often acknowledged in the United States or Europe.[2] The international Huntington's disease community learned about Negrette's work at the Centennial Symposium in Ohio in 1972, when Ramón Ávila-Girón, a psychiatrist and former student of Negrette, showed his film of the Maracaibo families. Though it stunned the audience at Columbus, several eminent researchers were still not persuaded that this was the same Huntington's chorea that existed elsewhere in the world; they thought it might be a genetic isolate—a version of the disease that existed only in this isolated region. Sometime after the Columbus meeting, André Barbeau traveled to Maracaibo during a sabbatical to look at the communities there, as did Loe N. Went, a neurologist from Leiden in the Netherlands. Both were convinced that what they observed was the same illness. And that was as far as it got.

That was as far as it got, that is, until Nancy joined the NINDS in the summer of 1978, determined to pursue a study in Venezuela. Ever since the Brown and Goldstein findings on hypercholesterolemia, Nancy had been eager to locate someone with two copies of the Huntington's gene. Someone whose father and mother were both stricken had a 25 percent chance of inheriting two copies of the gene. If a double dose had unlocked the genetic mystery of hypercholesterolemia, perhaps it would do the same for Huntington's.

Once installed in her Bethesda office, Nancy persuaded her

boss, Jack Brinley, and others in the institute, notably Tom Chase, to support an exploratory field trip to Venezuela. The following summer, in July 1979, Nancy and Tom Chase flew to Maracaibo. Through Negrette, they did indeed meet a large family in which both parents had the disease. Some of their fourteen children had a good chance of inheriting two Huntington's genes. But despite this outcome, Chase found conditions in Venezuela "hellishly uncomfortable" and had no desire to return. Nancy, on the other hand, found the whole experience exhilarating. She was impressed with the willingness of the Venezuelans to cooperate with a project that might ultimately eradicate the illness. She was struck, too, by the way in which people with Huntington's seemed to be better integrated into their communities than those in the United States, who were often overmedicated and hidden away in hospitals or at home. Back in Washington, Jack Brinley was also enthusiastic, especially since he spoke Spanish and was familiar with Venezuelan science and politics. He wanted to continue the quest for a homozygote.

Three months later, sitting in Bethesda at the October workshop listening to David Housman explain genetic linkage with RFLPs, Nancy grasped the possibility of a much larger, more ambitious project in which she could be a participant. And David Housman, listening to Nancy describe the Venezuelan families, also immediately recognized their significance for his proposal. Up until now, he had thought in terms of the families available through CCHD and the Roster, the largest of which was a group from Iowa that Mike Conneally had recruited. The Iowa clan, with some twenty-seven members, was extremely valuable for a genetic study, but they were only one family, and more were needed for unambiguous results. If only they were willing to cooperate, the Venezuelan families would be ideal. In the first place they were large, with many offspring—some with the disease and some without it—and with several generations all living near one another under similar conditions, not scattered like most families in the United States. The size of the families increased the likelihood of statistically significant results and made possible a more precise mapping of markers than could be achieved with smaller families. With large families you were more apt to have older people at risk who had no symptoms and were not likely to develop them in the future; you could compare these people with their siblings who did have the disease. Their geographical concentration meant that variations in symptoms were less likely to stem from environmental differences, since everyone shared the same climate and similar food and housing. In addition, all the Venezuelans with Huntington's had evidently descended from a single ancestor, which again helped limit the number of variables, since everyone would have inherited the same mutation—what geneticists call the founder effect.

Both David and Nancy, as well as Allan Tobin, left Bethesda with a new sense of excitement. David became a kind of Pied Piper at Huntington's meetings, patiently explaining RFLPs to anyone who would listen. Nancy too began showing slides and videos at every scientific meeting she attended, explaining how isolated towns such as Laguneta and Barranquitas almost certainly held the answer to the mystery of Huntington's, including its wide range of clinical variation, its devastating social consequences, its myths and folklore and people's strategies for survival. An international collaborative effort could delve into every aspect of the disease.

Not everyone, however, shared Nancy's enthusiasm. Shortly before the Bethesda workshop, she had presented a report of her first trip to Venezuela at a meeting of the World Federation of Neurology's Research Group on Huntington's Chorea in Oxford, England. While some of the most distinguished HD researchers, notably Andre Barbeau, Tom Perry, Tom Chase and Ntinos Myrianthopoulos, had been very supportive, other influential researchers had not seen the value of building a pedigree, especially an oral pedigree. They doubted that you could document paternity. Even if they were interested in the scientific aspects of the project, they doubted that Nancy could really do it. "It was sexism and ageism more than scientific disbelief," Nancy felt. "They thought I couldn't do it as a 'young girl.'" Meeting such sharp criticism, Nancy felt devastated on her return to Washington. "But one thing about Nancy is her stubbornness," recalled Ira Shoulson, who attended the Oxford meeting and later joined the Venezuela team. "You could see there was nothing that was going to deter her from this project." The criticism, however, rankled. What if she were going to collect quantities of blood to no avail, recruiting colleagues for a wild-goose chase that would serve no useful purpose?

In July 1980, Nancy returned to Maracaibo with Jack Brinley to negotiate a contract for a collaborative research project between the NINDS and the University of Zulia. The project still focused mainly on finding individuals with a double dose of the gene. But the Housman-Gusella linkage study added another layer of analysis in case the homozygote could not be identified or did not offer the hoped-for revelation. In March 1981, Nancy traveled to Venezuela for the first research expedition, this time staying for three weeks and taking with her a team of seven U.S. investigators who were joined, in Maracaibo, by five Venezuelan researchers. Many of these individuals would remain with the Venezeula project for more than a decade.

Later that year, Nancy found herself confronting yet more obstacles back in Bethesda. In the fall of 1981, the enthusiastic Jack Brinley moved into a different program within the institute and Carl Leventhal became Nancy's new boss. Surveying the programs within his jurisdiction (the Demyelinating, Atrophic and Dementing Disorders), Leventhal noticed that the Venezuela project, while extraordinarily interesting, seemed to be supported out of the "paper clip fund" in his office. In all other ways, too, it looked highly irregular, a sort of private bootleg operation, the sideline hobby of a couple of people. Leventhal decided that if the project were to continue it must be peer-reviewed, the standard mechanism for evaluating programs supported by the institute. No one really knew where the project was going, and Leventhal worried about possible conflicts of interest, since the NINDS, in its extramural dimension, was supposed to be supporting research, not actually conducting it. Though anxious at the prospect of peer review, especially after the rebuff at Oxford, Nancy recognized the legitimacy of Leventhal's demand. "There was every reason for him to believe this was a boondoggle," she said later, "and that I just wanted to get out of town."

Leventhal proved to be eminently fair and supportive in his handling of the evaluation. He recruited eminent scientists to review the project, including such distinguished geneticists as Luigi Cavalli-Sforza of Stanford University, who chaired the review panel, and Robert Sparks of UCLA. He even rehearsed Nancy for the presentation, which took place in June 1982.

The reviewers delivered a glowing report, giving the project a "high priority" in relation to other genetic research. Significantly, they expressed greatest enthusiasm for the linkage study, which now considerably overshadowed the search for the homozygote. This shift reflected the rapid advances that had occurred between 1979 and 1982 in the technology of mapping genes. No longer controversial, RFLP mapping was now widely practiced. The reviewers stressed that the linkage study could contribute not only to an understanding of Huntington's but to the field of genetics as a whole. They accorded particular value to the size and geographical proximity of the Venezuelan families to each other and also to the founder effect: if indeed those with Huntington's were descended from a single ancestor, any variation in symptoms or expression of the illness would still stem from the same original gene, located at the same spot on the same chromosome.[3]

Nancy was ecstatic, as was Carl Leventhal, who felt the review gave the whole thing legitimacy. He became an enthusiastic supporter, helping Nancy negotiate the hurdles toward long-term, regular funding. Later, when she applied for a five-year NIH grant, the Venezuela project received one of the highest possible evaluations. The second time she applied, the evaluation was even higher, one of the best in the entire history of the NIH.[4]

Half fishing village, half urban slum, San Luis hugs the shore of Lake Maracaibo on the sandy southern outskirts of the city, unremarkable except for Huntington's disease, which haunts almost every home. According to Negrette, the barrio used to be called *La Guajira* after the desert peninsula inhabited by the Guajiro Indians, across the border in Colombia. But one day the local priest decided the place needed a Christian name and it became San Luis, though outsiders still associate it with *el mal* and everyone is touched by the stigma of the disease.[5]

From downtown Maracaibo, Nancy's team traveled each day to San Luis, where they set up shop in the rooms of the *módulo,* a lakeside compound of low cinder-block buildings that serves as community center, school, grocery store, and clinic. From the outset Nancy wanted to secure the cooperation of the people in the barrio, since the team needed to draw blood and take small samples of skin to provide DNA for the linkage study. (Skin biopsies were soon discontinued since blood proved sufficient for extracting DNA.) Dr. Negrette went with them on their early visits, introducing them to people and bestowing his blessings. Ernesto Bonilla, an M.D.-Ph.D. physician and biochemist working on Huntington's at the Instituto de Investigación Clínica, and Ramón Ávila-Girón also worked with them, as did several other Venezuelans who became essential partners in the project.[6] But even Negrette and Bonilla had their doubts. "At first there was a lot of trepidation, even from our Venezuelan colleagues, that the families would not want to participate, especially in giving blood samples," Nancy recalled later. "We really wanted to enlist them as very active participants in the research as a source of pride," she said later, "because they were doing something that nobody else in the world could do. And also I felt personally that if they knew I was also at risk, they would feel that there was some bond between us and that I actually did know what they were talking about. I had seen it before, and I had a very strong reason to want to find some kind of treatment. So it would give us a little more credibility."

The team organized a party meeting in the barrio, where Nancy explained, in her pidgin Spanish, the purpose of the research. The families were amazed to hear that their disease also existed elsewhere; they had thought they were the only ones in the world to have it. "I said, 'It's also in my own family. My mother died of this disease and my grandfather and my uncles. I'm part of this same research. I've given blood and I've given skin. But our family is too small to study, and the families in the United States are not as good as yours for this research. You can open the door in a way that no other family can. And we really need your participation.' They were astonished and incredulous. They said, 'I don't believe you.'" So Fidela Gómez, the group's nurse, held up Nancy's arm and walked her around the room, pointing out the biopsy scar on her arm, and then they understood. "If I had not had that biopsy scar, they might never have believed me," Nancy said. "It really made a difference. After that, even if they thought the whole thing was crazy, at least they never doubted our sincerity."

I accompanied the team to Venezuela twice, in 1983 and 1984. Nancy had invited me to explore the archives in Maracaibo for clues to the origins of the Venezuelan communities, in Europe or elsewhere in Latin America. At first, though, I found myself caught up in the day-to-day work of the team, helping out wherever I could and getting to know the people.

March 10, 1983, 9:00am: The meeting room in the *módulo* takes on a slightly carnivalesque atmosphere as people from the barrio drift in, children darting underfoot, staring over shoulders, while the adults repeatedly shoo them outside, where they peer through the doorway or huddle at the windows. Gradually the room fills, with tired-looking women in worn polyester shifts and sandals or canvas *alpargatas,* their faces drawn and worried, and tense-looking men, and always the eager, barefoot, brown-skinned children, sometimes with the fair hair and blue or grey eyes that recall their European ancestry.

Taped around the walls of the room is the pedigree chart, a computer-generated system of lines, circles, and squares, like a Mondrian mural, that traces the relationships of all the local families with Huntington's. Polaroid photographs next to many of the names ensure accurate identification. Keyed to the pedigree is the P-list, a green and white computer printout of everyone in the growing pedigree, indexed by first names, since the surnames are relatively few, and indicating that person's relationship to the disease (affected, unaffected, or at risk). The P-lists are guarded jealously by all team members, who take them everywhere they go.

As the overhead fans turn lazily in the heat, people mill around outside on the concrete patio, small groups crowd around the tables inside, their heads together as Nancy or one of the others rehearses questions of genealogy: *"Como se*

llama su abuela?" (What is your grandmother's name?")
*"Dígame, por favor, los nombres de sus tíos, de sus hijos, de sus
nietos . . ."* ("Please tell me the names of your aunts and uncles, your children, your grandchildren, starting with the eldest . . .") and the families run down the names, shouting
above the din to be heard. At one table stands a thin man
whose shoulders twitch periodically and who holds his
hands very tightly clasped in front of him; near him a
woman with young children by her side rocks back and
forth on her heels, shifting her weight nervously from one
foot to the other and trying very hard to stand still. People
who cannot read or sign their name can recall the most complicated relationships, reciting their family histories with
ease and clarity. The women are particularly skilled at ge-
nealogies, perhaps because maintaining family connections
is defined as women's work.

Today is a "draw day," when those who have come earlier
for a neurological exam will return to give blood and a small
skin sample. Draw days, which come once or twice a week,
are especially intense, since the tissues must be obtained,
packaged, and taken to laboratories in Maracaibo, Caracas,
or Boston within forty-eight hours. The team schedules
these draw days to coincide with the staggered departures of
various participants who act as couriers, hand-carrying the
Styrofoam boxes of blood and skin to Miami for transship-
ment to Boston and elsewhere; sometimes they personally
deliver the tissues to Gusella's lab at Massachusetts General.

The "draw" takes place on the other side of the *módulo,* in
a closet-sized, air-conditioned examining room. Fidela
Gómez, an emergency room nurse who lives in Miami but
was born in the Canary Islands and grew up in Argentina, is
key to this operation. She is so quick-witted and skillful
with the needle that she draws blood before anyone knows
what is happening. As a native Spanish speaker, she acts as

diplomat and translator as well, and she especially has a way with kids, who adore her and follow her wherever she goes. Fidela clips a tiny square of skin from someone's arm and draws the six tubes of blood while bantering in rapid-fire Spanish, slowly shaking each dark red tube before handing it over to an assistant, who applies identifying labels and packs them gently into a Styrofoam box.

Outside on the sidewalk the neurological exams attract an audience of kids, who gather on the sidelines and comment on the action like a giggling Greek chorus. Soon they memorize the "neuros" and perform them on one another. "*Siga mi dedo* [follow my finger]," says Anne Young, an M.D.-Ph.D. neurologist and pharmacologist from the University of Michigan, where she shares a lab with her husband, Jack Penney, who is also a neurologist and part of the team. [In 1991, Young and Penney moved to Harvard Medical School, where Young is now Professor of Neurology and Chief of the Neurology Service at Massachusetts General.] Standing in her navy blue slacks and Hawaiian shirt, her long hair drawn to one side in a pony tail, she holds up a forefinger and moves it slowly back and forth, then up and down, in front of the faces of her subjects, asking them to follow her finger with their eyes, looking for the disturbances in fine eye movements that are often one of the earliest signs of the disease. As she pokes knees, prods elbows, scratches heels and toes to test reflexes, gently shakes an arm and bends it back and forth at the elbow to test muscle tone, Young converses in her pidgin Spanish, sometimes laughing at her own flat Yankee accent. Then she asks her subjects to walk for her, up and down on the sidewalk. "*Haga como yo* [do as I do]," she says as she walks heel to toe, heel to toe, and watches carefully for signs of chorea. Sometimes she writes "soft signs" in her report. Since the onset of Huntington's is so insidious, diagnosis is difficult in the early stages, when slight changes—altered movements of the eyes, increased depression or irritability, clumsiness or forgetfulness—might or might not be signs of the disease. Young especially wants to see the people with "soft signs" next year, since describing the natural history of the disease—tracing it from the first barely detectable signs to full-blown development—is another focus of the study. When a treatment for Huntington's becomes available, this information will be crucial for identifying when medical intervention should begin.

March 15, 1983. Notes from a visit to Barranquitas, a town two hours south of San Luis:

In our two big Chevy Malibus, we turn off the main highway onto a dusty, unpaved street and arrive in front of the *clínica,* a one-story aquamarine cinder-block building with a dirt yard enclosed by chain-link fence. Our arrival in Barranquitas arouses the neighborhood, and we are immediately surrounded by curious people, as if we were a visiting theater troupe. The clinic is locked. Across the street, facing the lake, a palm-thatched lean-to serves as a café, with a few chairs scattered out front. "Pablo" [not his real name], a man in his thirties with severe chorea, is having a beer, writhing and twisting and grimacing all the while. Here even people in the advanced stages of Huntington's are out in the streets, mixing with their neighbors. "*Vamos a hablar con la gente* [let's go talk to the people]," says Anne Young as she walks over to greet Pablo.

We open the clinic, which consists of a large, empty room opening onto two small examining rooms, with a bathroom in the back. We haul in boxes, valises, cartons, Styrofoam coolers full of Coca-Cola and *Chinotto,* a sweet Venezuelan soft drink. Today is another draw day. Soon people are milling about, waiting their turn, waiting, too, for the vitamins and *bolivares* that go along with the exam.

Inside the examining rooms or visiting people's houses,

Ira Shoulson, Anne Young, Jack Penney, and María Ramos, a young medical geneticist with an M.D.-Ph.D. from Bilbao, Spain, alternate between giving "neuros" to the individuals in the study and treating people for infections and injuries. In the big, crowded central room, Helen Travers, a genetic counselor from Miami, records pedigrees with accuracy and elegance, even with several children climbing all over her. Nancy stands at the entrance to the examining rooms for hours at a time, inspecting the lists of names, handing out labels to identify vials of blood, smiling, consulting, motioning people inside or out, urging some to wait just a little longer, advising others that they do not need to wait today. The work demands precision and accuracy, for one wrongly labeled vial of blood, one incorrectly diagnosed individual, can set back the molecular study for months. Nancy is physician, nurse, ethnologist, psychologist, diplomat, photographer, neurologist, geneticist, and general all rolled into one, a fact that does not escape some of the male members of the team, distinguished doctors themselves, who sometimes complain about having to take orders, especially from a young woman. "When you check in at the hotel, leave your *huevos* in the safe-deposit box," jokes Ira Shoulson. Yet the fact that many team members are female also disarms resistance among some anxious men, who fear giving blood will lower their sexual potency.

Outdoors I speak first with "Rogelia," an anxious-looking woman in her mid-thirties with short brown hair and a wide, worried face. She speaks rapidly to me about her mother, a woman of about fifty, gap-toothed, with short black hair and wearing a black cotton dress. The mother embraces me impulsively, with excessive clinging. Though she has relatively little chorea, her motions are exaggerated, floppy, and slow. She smiles too much, at inappropriate moments. Rogelia frowns. Her mother is impossible at home, she says. She fights with everyone, hits the children, and spends all day sweeping. Rogelia wants *calmantes*, tranquilizers, for her mother—perhaps also for herself. She is frantic. I promise to request the *calmantes* from the doctors. My job today is to go through a "staging" questionnaire with her, to determine how well her mother can function and which stage of the disease she might be in. The questionnaire, constructed by Ira Shoulson, is designed to test how well an individual with Huntington's can perform daily tasks, such as working outside or inside the house, handling money, making decisions about food, washing, and dressing, and how much assistance they might require.

We squat on a small ledge behind the clinic and immediately attract a small audience. The lack of privacy is disconcerting, but Rogelia is too upset to notice. She says her mother cannot contribute any work in the household. Her own husband has gone off with another woman. He too has *el mal* in his family, although he apparently is not affected. She gives me a good account of all his brothers and sisters and parents for the pedigree.

"José" saunters up unsteadily. He is a slight, handsome man of about forty-eight with broad, high cheekbones and thick, dark curly hair graying at the temples, a graceful man, smiling and swaying like a friendly drunk. He has the jerky gaze of many people with HD, a difficulty in shifting focus. He talks in sudden bursts. Later in the morning he leads me off to the house of Pablo, whom we meet walking toward us down the street. Pablo is fair-haired, freckled, and *flaco*, thin. We try to persuade him to come to the clinic. Although his speech is almost unintelligible, he understands our request. He turns abruptly toward his home. We follow him into a house with a large front room, bare except for a table in one corner. Pablo, twisting and writhing, disappears into the back room and returns, somehow managing to carry a chair. He disappears again and hauls out another chair, then another, making clear that he wishes us to sit down. His graciousness amid such dire poverty, and notwithstanding his extreme disability, suddenly move me to tears. Then Pablo's uncle appears, apparently one of the lucky ones who has escaped the disease. He is a man of about sixty, with several gleaming gold teeth and a gentle, resigned, matter-of-fact manner. This uncle has assumed total care of Pablo, whose mother and father are both dead. He obviously feels great sympathy for his nephew. I encourage them both to come to the clinic later in the day. Then José and I walk back to the clinic. José has nine children. One son died of juvenile Huntington's at the age of nine. Another son [whom we meet later in Laguneta], a beautiful blond sixteen-year-old, is gradually sinking into the weakness and rigidity characteristic of the illness in children and adolescents. José tells me firmly, "All my children are normal."

I speak in the afternoon to several teenagers who are worried and frightened about *el mal*. They say people make fun of the *San Viteros, hacen burla,* they ridicule them and tease them in the streets. I ask two cousins: If you could find out that a fetus would have the gene for *el mal*, would you seek an abortion? The girl, eighteen, says yes; the boy, no. A boy about twenty, looking very anxious, wants to know if there's hope for him. He thinks that since his father has *el mal*, he must get it too. I assure him he has a 50 percent chance of escaping the disease. Later a man whose family does not have *el mal* says that his mother told him never to marry a girl at risk for *el mal*, because she could get it and their children could get it. He took her advice, though his brother did not. People who are healthy do not want to marry those who inherit *el mal*, he says frankly.

The people here believe that everyone who has a parent with the disease always inherits it from that parent, but only some people actually develop the symptoms. Perhaps it is a way of acknowledging the anxiety and loneliness of being at risk and the worry of constantly wondering when and if you'll get the disease. Being at risk means feeling different from both those who are not at risk and from those with Huntington's. It's an emotional state all its own. The Venezuelans seem to understand this—better, perhaps, than North Americans, who do not tolerate ambiguity well.

It is dark when we pack up the blood samples, take Polaroid photos of the kids who are still hanging around the clinic, pass out candy, and then pile into the Chevys for the ride back to Maracaibo, where later that night we will pack the samples into Styrofoam boxes for the next morning's dash to the airport. We blast the Talking Heads on the cassette player in the car and do not talk.

Negrette's *viejita* had told him that a Spanish sailor named Antonio Justo Doria had brought *el mal* to Venezuela from Europe sometime in the middle of the nineteenth century. She said he had come on a ship from Hamburg engaged in the trade of *divi-divi,* a native tree whose fruit was used in the German dye industry. He had stayed in San Francisco and lived with a Venezuelan woman who had numerous children before the disease slowly consumed the sailor and, afterward, many of his children. No one knew if he really existed or if he really had Huntington's disease. I was to find out.

The documents were not difficult to locate. Like Spain, Venezuela began a Civil Registry in 1873, requiring that all births, marriages, and deaths be registered in duplicate. Each year one of the big bound volumes in which such events were carefully recorded was sent to the central registry in the capital of the province, in this case Maracaibo, while the other was stored in the local prefecture. It helped to know where an individual had died, since the records were organized geographically. We did not know where Antonio Justo Doria had died, but we decided to begin checking the death records for San Francisco, the Maracaibo suburb to which the barrio of San Luis formally belonged.

Soon after I arrived in Maracaibo in 1983, I went with Fidela to the downtown registry, the usual Kafkaesque Latin American archive. It was housed in a gloomy, warehouselike building on a dark narrow street off the Avenida Milagro, one of the central corridors of the city. Crowded around battered wooden tables in the front room as you entered, people thumbed anxiously through the pages of large volumes, searching for birth, death, and marriage entries to prove legitimacy or provide documentation for a *cédula,* the identification card required of all Venezuelans. For those who could not read, men in shirtsleeves, looking bored and distracted, read selected pages aloud for a few *bolivares.* The low, droning voices of the readers, the low ceilings and whirring of the overhead fans, somehow created an atmosphere of despair, as if petitioners and papers would never be united.

Behind a counter in the middle of the room, at desks cluttered with papers, neatly dressed clerks typed out official-looking forms, chatting casually over the din of their ancient, clackety typewriters. Standing in front of them at the counter, workers took requests from the petitioners, periodically ambling into the rear of the building with a pile of slips. We could see them retrieving the desired volumes from old metal shelves or sometimes disappearing for long minutes while they searched another part of the building.

Fidela and I joined the crowd of petitioners jostling for position at the counter. By dint of her persistence, we seized the attention of one of the employees, who brought us endless volumes of death records, proving helpful almost against his will. Negrette had written that Doria had arrived in Venezuela sometime between 1860 and 1870, so we decided to start with the earliest available death records in 1878 and work forward.

The registry closed each day at 1:00 P.M., so we had to work fast. We kept one eye on the clock at the entrance to the building, as if it were our enemy.

As we thumbed through pages upon pages of death records, the world of an obscure Venezuelan town in the late nineteenth century gradually opened to us, with its baptisms, drownings, its fistfights and dysentery, its fishermen and farmers and seamstresses and midwives and the women who performed the *"officios proprios de su sexo,"* tasks appropriate to their sex. From such dry records, a living world emerged without, however, any signs of Huntington's. Then, on the second day, toward closing time, I opened the book for 1887 and read the formulaic text, written in a flowing sepia script:

> I, Bartolomé Morán, the highest civil authority of the town of San Francisco, affirm that today, the second of January of the year eighteen hundred and eighty seven, Citizen Amable Soto, sailor and resident of this town, has come to me to report the death of Antonio Justo Doria, at three o'clock this morning, and from the information which I could elicit, it appears that the deceased was seventy years old, that he was also a resident of this town, the natural son of María del Rosario Doria, who lived in the town of Chiquinquirá. El Jefe Bartolomé Morán.[7]

We had found the Spanish sailor! I remember thinking as I showed the page to Fidela that I would never again feel such a thrill of discovery. We made photocopies, then grabbed a *por puesto* (a fixed-route taxi) back to the hotel. A few hours later, we drank toasts with Nancy and the others as we sat on the moonlit patio of a local Maracaibo fish restaurant and the cool evening breezes wafted up through the palm trees from the lake just below us. It was a small victory, to be sure, but in the search for the origins of Huntington's, even this clue felt deliciously sweet.

The next day Fidela and I returned to the registry to see if we could find other relatives of Antonio Justo Doria and link him with the ancestors of our informants in San Luis, none of whom was named Doria. If Antonio Doria were in fact the original progenitor, then the mother must have been named ——. In a community where many people did not legally marry, even though consensual unions were often quite stable, it was common for children to carry the name of their mother.

A few days later, we found a record for one Zoila ——, a woman who had died at the age of seventy-five in 1901. She had been a midwife, a *comadrona,* in San Luis, and she surfaced often, in many of the records, as one who reported deaths to the authorities. Clearly she was a person of some prestige and standing in the town, one whom other people sought out. She was also the widow of Antonio Justo Doria.

The pieces fit. Zoila, it seemed, had been the mother of the earliest generations of Venezuelans with Huntington's. They all carried her name, since she and Antonio Justo Doria had evidently not been legally married (though she was still described as his widow). We began now to find the records for the sons and daughters of Zoila, for she had had many children. We began to compile a pedigree from the archival records that could confirm the oral histories.

We also found records outside the registry. We learned that the prefecture of San Francisco, located on the Calle Principal bordering the barrio of San Luis, stored many of the same volumes as the downtown registry, as well as some that the registry was missing. The prefecture was more accessible, so we spent a few blazing afternoons in that bright blue stucco building, sitting in a tiny, airless office where the fragile volumes were stacked casually in a couple of metal cabinets. As we worked, people came in to request their *cédulas* or to visit relatives locked up in the jail in the rear of the building. We also discovered that Father Wílchez, the local priest, kept excellent records in his rectory across from the nearby Plaza Principal. Here we found a well-preserved set of volumes recording births and baptisms from about 1866. After the stifling heat of the prefecture and the registry, we sank gratefully into the big, vinyl-covered easy chairs of the air-conditioned rectory, and thumbed through pages of baptismal announcements while, in the next room, videotapes showing Father Wílchez delivering impassioned outdoor sermons to huge, cheering throngs played on an enormous television screen.

Encouraged by Father Wílchez's well-kept records, we decided to visit the old cathedral in downtown Maracaibo. We explained our mission to the priest, Father Guillermo González Fuenmayor, asking if we might see the baptismal records of the Parochial Archives, which he kept in his office in a locked mahagony cabinet. To our surprise, he refused. He was busy, he announced brusquely, preparing for *Semana Santa,* Holy Week. As we tried to explain the problem of Huntington's disease in Venezuela, he grew impatient and his voice rose. He did not have time to entertain us. "Besides," he shouted, "this is not my problem, this is a social problem!" We were simply acting out of "caprice." Apparently his church did not address social issues. Talking rapidly about the urgency of our project, Fidela managed to open a chink in his armor. With great reluctance, he unlocked the cabinet and took out one volume. "Just this one," he muttered, holding it open while we glanced down a few pages in search of some familiar names. After a minute or two, he slammed the book closed and shoved it back into the cabinet, practically pushing us out the door. From our quick survey of names, it seemed that no one from San Luis had gone to the cathedral to be baptized, but further investigation would have to wait.

Meanwhile, some disturbing discrepancies emerged, gaps between the written and oral records. None of Zoila's children, whose birth and death records we easily found in the archives, appeared in the pedigree constructed from the memories of living informants. Nor did Zoila herself appear. We had not yet found the link between Antonio Justo Doria and Zoila, on the one hand, and the people in the oral Huntington's degree pedigree, such as María Concepción, who had lived in Laguneta in the early 1800s. We assumed that it was just a matter of time before we could reconcile the information.

Now, with names from the civil and parochial records, we went back to some of the people in the barrio to try to sort out the differences. One afternoon, when we were in the middle of this effort, the two filmmakers who had accompanied our expedition—Steve Uzzell and Fred Burnham—decided to film Fidela and me reenacting our discovery of Antonio Justo Doria and, for dramatic effect, to stage the scene in the prefecture next door to the barrio, instead of the more impersonal registry where we had actually found his death record. Steve and Fred hauled their equipment out to the "location" and set up the lights and cameras. Meanwhile, Fidela and I paid a visit to Manuel, a thin talkative man in his seventies, a grandson of one of the earliest people who had died of Huntington's in San Luis, though he himself had escaped the disease. Antonio Justo Doria had never had *el mal,* he stated firmly, nor had any of Zoila's descendants. Hers was another branch of the family. She had been a prosperous, influential woman who owned considerable property in San Francisco. Doria too had been a wealthy man. They never had Huntington's disease in their family at all.

Manuel told us what we had already begun to suspect, and other sources soon confirmed his testimony. The people, it seems, had invented an important ancestor for themselves, taking a wealthy, powerful man like Antonio Justo Doria and making him the source of their misery. Perhaps it was a way of placing blame for a catastrophe that had no explanation, perhaps a way of transforming a disastrous origin into one more illustrious or even a way of making claims on his descendants. Or perhaps it was the fantasy of one old woman, Negrette's *viejita* with the memory like a computer, who had conjured up a romantic Spanish sailor and inserted him into a Venezuelan tragedy. Hoping for a Sherlock Holmes resolution, we found ourselves instead in a Borges story, where the suspect, a real man, is dreamed by the protagonists and given a history that corresponds not to the facts of his life but to their own.

When Fidela and I returned to the prefecture to call off the "shoot," we found Fred and Steve ready to roll. "Listen!" I shouted over the gathering crowd. "We have the wrong man! Antonio Justo Doria never had Huntington's!" Steve and Fred pretended not to hear. "Just stand over there and start walking," Steve commanded Fidela and me, motioning us to the other side of the Avenida Principal. He indicated that we were to cross the street slowly and enter the prefecture while he and Fred filmed. I don't know why we did not resist. Perhaps we wished to cherish for a few more minutes the romance of the Spanish sailor. Or perhaps we did resist, and I no longer remember. In any event, we reenacted our false "discovery" with the unexpected help of the prefect. This slow, somnolent man had been indifferent to all our earlier research efforts. But when he saw the movie cameras, he suddenly grew excited and eager to cooperate. He posed and preened under the lights, holding the big volume of death records on his knees and smiling proudly into the camera. I am sure he did not have the faintest idea what it was all about, but after that we were treated with great respect, and we could see the records whenever we liked.

March 22, 1983. On board our orange Lagoven launch heading toward the lagoon of Laguneta, we strain toward that flat, naked little skyline. In 1499, the Florentine Amerigo Vespucci entered a similar harbor at the mouth of the lake, "where we found a town built over the water, like Venice." From this vision had come the name of Venezuela, though we know from that early chronicler, Father Pedro de Aguado, that the province already had a name and the town was nothing at all like Venice. With that metaphoric name, suggests the historian Arturo Uslar-Pietri, began the conquest of Tierra Firme and the first imposition of a "reality seen from outside" that marked what he called "the invention of Venezuela."[8] Yet, like those sixteenth-century explorers mapping America to the geographies of Europe, we too bend experience to myth, imagining ourselves in a Conradian heart of darkness framed by water, jungle, and silence.

We move into our two rented houses on stilts over the lake, in this *pueblo de agua* of about twenty houses clustered a hundred yards from the shore, dense with palm trees and foliage. Laguneta today has about two hundred residents, most of them children. The town has shrunk over the past decades, down from a population of eight hundred back in the 1950s, when Negrette first visited this lagoon. Today most of the houses are melancholy hovels with rusting roofs and rotting porches, though some are painted bright colors and boast plants and flowers and pigs as well. The children say it is lonely here, there is no school, no place to walk, no way to earn money. There are no books in Laguneta.

Our work begins. Ira Shoulson and Robert Snodgrass, a pediatric neurologist from Children's Hospital in Los Angeles and the most intellectual member of the team, set up a clinic in the "church"—one of the *casas*—to treat ordinary illnesses and infections. Anne Young and Jack Penney begin to give "neuros" on a nearby porch, watched by an audience of anxious adults and always the squirming, smiling kids who can also be surprisingly somber, fixing us with their penetrating stares. Inside another *casa* Fidela Gómez draws blood. Nancy negotiates among all these sites, determining who is needed for the "draw," sending us to visit certain casas to try to persuade people to participate in the project. Often she goes herself, and sometimes, when people are reluctant to go out, Fidela and the neurologists make house visits. Here is Nancy in her blue jeans and pink T-shirt, her long blond hair pulled back under a green baseball cap with "Freud" embroidered on the front. No matter how busy she is, she always has time to hug a child, comfort a worried parent, pass out candy and Polaroid snapshots to the *niños*. "A lot of what Venezuela means to me is having kids," she told me once. "I always thought if we could find a marker, then I could have children. And there, it's like having a thousand kids for a month each year."

We visit the separate *casas* of "Ramón" and "Carlotta," both in their fifties, both sick with *el mal*. They are the couple with fourteen children whom Nancy met on her first visit to Venezuela; each child has a 75 percent chance of inheriting their parents' illness, including a 25 percent chance of a "double dose." So far only two show symptoms. The team members believe that at least one of the fourteen is likely to have two hits of the HD gene, unless of course a double dose is lethal. They are careful to check for abortions and miscarriages. Ramón and Carlotta are extremely handsome, despite advanced chorea, Carlotta with her tall, slender body, her haughty manner, and fits of *rabia,* and Ramón, with his fine, high cheekbones, aquiline nose, and chiseled lips. Their children too are remarkably good-looking, including three pretty daughters in their thirties, sad and slow like plump stones, caring for their parents and for their own children in an endless round of work.

We visit Jesús, the nephew of Ramón and Carlotta, the son of José who lives in Barranquitas. Jesús has a Botticelli face and an advanced case of juvenile Huntington's. He moves slowly and stiffly and falls frequently, though he can clean fish with astonishing grace. His delicate thirteen-year-old sister looks much younger, a thin, freckled girl with limp blond hair and brown eyes and a beautiful face full of sadness. Although she poles her *piragua* with languid ease, she too shows the suspicious stiffness characteristic of juvenile Huntington's. Within a few years the team hears from her family, and sees for themselves, that, like her brother, she too is *perdida*.

With their beauty, grace, and ruin, the family of Carlotta and Ramón embodies the paradox of Laguneta, half terrestrial paradise, half tropical hell. Within a few years, the people will abandon these rotting shells of houses with doors open to lake and wind and stars. But here, perhaps, in this gorgeous, shattered setting, is the inner truth of the European conquest of America: a few dying families in a desolate stilt village, children who will carry on the curse of their grandparents and fathers and mothers for generations to come.[9]

By midday, the air is stopped, a blazing sun reflects off the water, and a fetid stench rises from the lake. You try not to breathe. Even the catfish gasp at the surface of the water, their big mouths gaping and blowing restless dirty bubbles, their barbels like whiskers probing the air. They lurk under houses, waiting for our garbage or human waste, which they devour instantly in an explosion of floundering silver bodies. I feel as if I will die in this place and cannot wait to leave. But by late afternoon, when a breeze rises, the palms sway, and the sun hangs like a jewel on the horizon, Laguneta changes into an enchanted village floating over the water, the open doors of shacks turned toward the sun like eyes watching God.

One year, the team almost did not return from Laguneta. They were caught in a violent storm on Lake Maracaibo while traveling by boat at night, tossed for sickening hours by waves and wind, and menaced by unseen oil rigs sprouting up out of the darkness of the lake. "Nancy was a saint," said Anne Young later. "She was up making sure everyone was alive, trying to reassure people. I think she was the strongest person there, she was really tough." A worker on the rig where they finally managed to dock expressed his amazement at their survival. "I've seen many boats go down in the lake, and many people drown," he said. "You were extremely lucky."

In the middle of the storm, when he was certain they were all going to die, Nelson Marsól, one of the Venezuelan members of the team, made a vow to San Benito that, if they survived this night, he would reward the saint generously. The way you reward San Benito, Jack Penney said, is to dance for two hours. And so, when they all returned to San Luis, they organized a big dance and invited the entire barrio to come and celebrate.

Nancy was thinking, she told me later, that if they had survived that dark night on the lake, perhaps they really were going to find a cure for *el mal* after all. But for a long time she did not want to talk about what had happened. And when the team returned to Laguneta after that, they traveled only by daylight.

Eleven

G-8

> ... and he began to decipher the instant that he was living, deciphering it as he lived it, prophesying himself in the act of deciphering the last page of the parchments, as if he were looking into a speaking mirror.
>
> —GABRIEL GARCÍA MÁRQUEZ
> *One Hundred Years of Solitude*

The traveler who commutes between the high-tech molecular biology labs at the Massachusetts General Hospital and the steamy wooden porches of Laguneta crosses distances not easily measured in miles. Yet, by the spring of 1983, powerful bonds of common interest linked these two sites, each marked in different ways by Huntington's disease. For certain scientists at Massachusetts General, the people of Laguneta, Barranquitas, and San Luis were becoming a focus of intense interest. Many difficult technical obstacles to mapping the Huntington's disease gene had been solved, problems relating to cell lines and storage. Researchers were now convinced that the Venezuelan communities offered the kind of families needed for such a study. In addition, the number of RFLP markers was rapidly growing, confirming the predictions of Botstein, White, Housman, and others that RFLPs would be numerous and distributed evenly enough throughout the genome to serve as useful markers for mapping genes. Back in 1980, only two such markers had been known. By now, there were nearly two hundred RFLP markers, and RFLP mapping was well under way. Some geneticists estimated that a linkage map of the entire human genome would be completed within three or four years.[1]

Still, one of the major challenges for Gusella lay in generating more RFLP markers. Even more daunting was the prospect of testing each newly developed marker for a possible correlation with Huntington's. Gusella expected that they might have to test 150 to 200 markers—an immense amount of work—before they found one close to the Huntington's gene.[2] As one of Gusella's technicians, Rudolph Tanzi, put it, "We were really in the random boat."

For several months, Gusella's group had been testing each newly created marker against two different Huntington's disease pedigrees, hoping to find a consistent difference between people with Huntington's and those without it. They were using DNA from the Iowa family, which was theoretically large enough to yield statistically significant results.[3] They were also using DNA from the rapidly expanding Venezuela pedigree, which now numbered some 3,000 people, of whom about 1,200 were living.[4] By the spring, they had constructed thirteen new genetic markers and had tested eleven of them for linkage, without coming up with significant results.[5] Gusella wasn't discouraged. He knew he was still in the initial phase of the work.

Sometime in April, they decided to test the twelfth probe, called G-8 after the technician named Ginger Weeks, who had designed this probe from DNA plucked arbitrarily out of a human DNA library—a collection of short segments of DNA. G-8 was a little swatch of DNA about 17,600 base pairs in length. It was an anonymous sequence, which meant that no one had yet identified the particular chromosome from which it came. And it was ideal as a probe since it was one of a kind—a sequence of nucleotides that occurred only once on one chromosome. (In fact, G-8 was only the third such "single copy" probe of the twelve they tested.) As they did with each probe, they first tested G-8 to determine if it picked up any variable regions in the DNA. When they mixed the G-8 probe together with DNA fragments from the Iowa family—fragments that had been chopped up by the restriction enzyme *Hind*III, they saw that G-8 revealed fragments of several different sizes. That meant that G-8 was indeed picking up two different RFLPs— that is, two places in the DNA where individuals varied. These variations, which were extremely close together, occurred at spots where the *Hind*III enzyme happened to cut. Hence they gave rise to four different fragment lengths.

Some individuals produced fragments that were 15,000 nu- cleotides in length; these people possessed the first sequence recognized and cut by the *Hind*III enzyme. Others produced longer fragments, of 17,500 nucleotides; these people lacked the first *Hind*III cutting site. There was a second variable spot as well. At this spot, those individuals whose DNA was cut by *Hind*III produced two different fragments, of 3,700 and 1,200 nucleotides. Other people, who lacked the second cutting site, produced one longer fragment, of 4,900 nucleotides. Altogether, G-8 picked up two sites of variation, with four pos- sible combinations determined by the presence or absence at each site of a sequence cut by *Hind*III.

It sounds complicated, but it was actually straightforward: four possible patterns of fragments, technically called haplo- types, that Gusella's group called A, B, C, and D. Each individ- ual in a family inherits two haplotypes, one from the father, one from the mother. This is true in families without Huntington's as well as those with the disease. The critical question for Gusella was whether any of these haplotypes might be correlated with the illness *in families affected by the dis- ease.* (In unaffected families, the haplotype would be insignifi- cant.) In other words, do individuals who have the disease consistently have a particular haplotype? Does a particular pattern of fragments always travel together with the disease?

When Gusella looked at the distribution of patterns with G-8 in the Iowa family, it did look as if there might be a relationship. Individuals who were known to have the disease seemed consistently to have the A haplotype, though there were many individuals without the disease who also had the A haplotype. (Since these four haplotypes occur in people with and without Huntington's in the family, and since everyone has two haplotypes, it is quite possible for healthy people in a family with Huntington's to have an A pattern as well. It is also possible for someone *with* Huntington's to have two A haplotypes, one from the parent with the illness and one from the other parent.)

The LOD score for the Iowa family came out of the computer at 1.8. A LOD score is a statistical calculation geneticists use to determine the likelihood that two genes—or any two segments of DNA—are actually linked, that is, physically located on the same chromosome, and not merely inherited together by chance; they consider a LOD score of 3 as establishing genuine linkage. (Technically, a LOD score is the logarithm of the ratio of the odds for or against linkage.) The higher the LOD score, the closer together on the chromosome the two points are likely to be. A score of 3 means the odds are a thousand to one that linkage is not a chance result.

So a score of 1.8 was good, but not startling: it meant that the odds were 65 to 1 against chance that G-8 was linked with Huntington's in this family. Gusella was not impressed. "There's not a geneticist in the world, especially in a case like Huntington's disease," Jim told me later, "who wouldn't say, well, that score will go away with more data. So we weren't particularly excited about it." He wanted a LOD score of at least 3. Still, after Mike Conneally in Indianapolis got the data from Jim and did a statistical analysis, he called Boston and said, "Jim, it looks promising. Why don't you stick with that one, G-8, and do the Venezuelan family." At that point, though, Gusella did not have enough DNA extracted from any of the Venezuelan families, and isolating the DNA from the nuclei of white blood cells takes time. He and Rudi Tanzi decided to prepare a large subset of the Venezuelans that they knew would be informative because of all the people with Huntington's in it. That process continued until the beginning of July.

Meanwhile, they already had some DNA ready from a much smaller subset of the Venezuelan family that they had been using for something else. In early June they decided to run gels on this group with G-8. "It was a very simple little pedigree," Jim recalled. "All it involved was a mother and father and four children. And it was the only case, the only set of people where we had a grandparent available and already made into DNA. By itself it wouldn't give you very much of a LOD score. But it's one that's very easy to look at and see what's going on." In this little pedigree there were two children with the disease and two without it. Both children with Huntington's had the pattern or haplotype called C, while the unaffected children had a different haplotype. (That the individuals with Huntington's in the Iowa family had an A haplotype while the Venezuelans with Huntington's had a C haplotype was insignificant: the critical question was whether, in each family, only one haplotype traveled consistently with the disease.)

"At this point," recalled Mike Conneally, "the LOD score went up to 2.2. Now, that's odds of about a hundred twenty to one against chance." It still wasn't highly significant; but at least the scores were going up. "I had hardly heard about it," said Mike, "hardly gotten the run out of the computer, when Nancy called. And I said to Nancy, things are looking good, they're looking promising, I think we're getting somewhere. I think we've got a marker. And Nancy said, oh terrific! And when I hung up I thought, Mike, you damn fool, you should never have said that, you really put your foot in it, you'll have to eat crow later. I thought, why didn't I have the fortitude to hold back and not tell her that? because I'd been so frustrated in the past, I really didn't believe it myself."

But Jim too was impressed by the results. "Of course it was not definitive," he admitted later; the pedigree they had used was too small. And one of the unaffected children was quite young and could still develop the disease in the future. "But I looked at that," said Gusella later, "and my mind went from saying that the 1.8 was merely being tested to thinking, maybe the 1.8 is really right. And we better get this tested fast."

Feeling a new sense of urgency, Jim and Rudi rushed to prepare the DNA from the other Venezuelan subset, which was quite large and therefore more informative. Gusella felt increasingly pressured, since he was scheduled to attend a week-long meeting in Aspen, Colorado, at the end of July and really wanted to get the data out to Mike before he departed. "On the Friday afternoon before I had to leave we got the autoradiograms, got them all dried, and Rudi and I sat down and read them all," Jim recalled later. "And then we took the data and put it on the pedigree to send to Mike. And it was just obvious, from the pedigree, that this was going to make the LOD score go up rather than down, because it matched perfectly. Everybody who was affected had a C [haplotype], and virtually nobody else did." Looking at the pattern on the pedigree spread out in front of him, Gusella knew he had found the linkage even before the data went through the computer. He could see from the pedigree that G-8 picked up two RFLPs that were right next door to the Huntington's gene.

As soon as he realized the linkage result, Jim tried to call Nancy in Washington, but he was unable to reach her. He decided to wait until he got the LOD score back from Mike Conneally before trying her again. Meanwhile, in Indianapolis, Mike Conneally took a fast look at the data Jim had sent him and saw that, superficially, it looked good. He too was about to leave for the West, for a vacation in the Grand Canyon, so he instructed his graduate students to feed the new data into the computer. "Then I'm in Grand Canyon National Park on Tuesday night," Mike recalled, "sitting by my campfire having a beer with my wife and daughter. And I see this cop coming back and shining a light on our car. At least I thought he was a cop. He was really a park ranger. When he saw we had Indiana plates he came over and said, are you Dr. Connally? They always call me Connally! I said, yes I am. And he said, I have an emergency, an important message for you to call Peggy [Pericak-Vance] or Beth—these were my graduate students. It was now eleven o'clock at night. At that time, it would have been one in the morning in Indiana. I thought, well, of course I can't call them tonight. Little did I know they were waiting up for me to call. So I didn't call until the next morning. But I knew. I was convinced. I said to my wife, we've got it! At last it has happened! And the next morning when I called, of course, there it was. The LOD score was six point something, and there was absolutely now no doubt, the odds were a million to one, and you know, that was it."

"How'd you feel when you heard the news?" I asked Mike Conneally later, though the answer was pretty obvious. "Oh, elated!" said Mike. "Absolutely elated. I had a few more beers that night, I can tell you. I was almost crying, because I thought, at long, long last, the search is over. I felt so good. And you know who I felt good for? Nancy. I thought, that's great for Nancy, because she worked so hard on it. Then I talked to her, two nights later. It was the greatest feeling I've ever had, I know, in my life."

Back in Washington, Nancy had been waiting in suspense ever since her earlier conversation with Mike in June, when he had hinted that they might be onto something. She had kept closely in touch after that and had called in late July. By that time, however, Mike had already left for the Grand Canyon. The next time she called, Mike was still away, so one of his graduate students read her the computer results over the phone. "I let out a shriek that could be heard up and down the halls," Nancy told me later. "And as you know, I'm not normally the most restrained and quiet person. Everyone came rushing in to see what was wrong!" She raced upstairs to tell the people who had worked so hard on the Venezuela project, and later, at home, spent hours on the phone, lying on the floor of her Bethesda apartment, trying desperately to contact Jim, "and no one could reach him, he was out in Aspen!" But that night, Nancy called from a Washington restaurant and surprised him with how much the LOD score had risen. Before speaking to Jim, though, she reached David Housman, who happened to be in his office at MIT. She told him the score she had heard from Indianapolis. "Does this mean what I think it means?" she asked, still incredulous at the news of a marker. "Yes, it does," David said. "It definitely does!" Later David recalled feeling the way he always felt when he got good news—like going out and having a beer. "I felt very gratified," he told me later. "Especially since many people had been so skeptical."

Mike Conneally did have one haunting fear. "The thing that really bothered me," he confided, "—I even had a nightmare about it—was the possibility that when they found a DNA marker, and I knew DNA would do it, it would be linked to a marker close to one of the ones we had looked at but hadn't looked at closely enough." By this time, Conneally and his group had analyzed thirty-five protein markers for linkage with Huntington's and had managed to eliminate some 20 percent of the genome for linkage. "Didn't that help Jim, by showing him where not to look?" I asked. "No, it didn't help," said Mike. "Jim didn't know where the twelve he looked at were located. Down the road it would have helped, if he had been unlucky and had had to look at a lot of markers, but as it tran-spired, it didn't help a bit. I mean, Jim just took twelve at ran-dom. All our work, to be quite frank about it, did not help in pinpointing the marker. This one would have been found even if there was never a linkage looked at before."

I was lying in bed reading *One Hundred Years of Solitude* when Nancy called with the news, early in August. She had already spoken to Dad, and then I called him too, just to share his pride and excitement on the phone. I had two immediate reac-tions, first the thrill of anticipation, and second, the desire to write the story. Still, the news didn't really sink in until a few weeks later, at a workshop in Rochester, New York. Several months earlier, Allan and Nancy had planned this Hereditary Disease Foundation workshop on "The Clinical Impact of Recombinant DNA Research on Neurogenetic Diseases." They anticipated that the discussion would be purely theoretical. But here was Jim Gusella, standing in a darkened room at the Marriott Hotel, in his gray slacks and shirtsleeves, pointing to a series of blurry bands on a screen. "What we've done—and we've only done this in the last three weeks, so a lot of this is still jelling in my mind as well as in the computer," said Jim, "we've tested this probe [G-8] against somewhere around seventy-five individuals from a very large Venezuelan pedigree that Nancy and her colleagues are assembling on the shores of Lake Maracaibo in Venezuela. I can't show you a slide of that pedigree because it would never fit on a slide. . . . We fed that into the computer and what we got was a LOD score that in-creased for this marker. Using the haplotype that I'm going to explain to you from the next slide, that LOD score went up above six. It made us a little worried about our interpretation of things because we wanted to be absolutely sure." He was speaking slowly, as if even he couldn't believe his fantastic re-sults. "Where we are now," he said carefully, "is that we have a marker which is at an unknown distance from the gene." Suddenly everyone was talking at once, except Nancy, who was grinning from ear to ear. As one workshop participant exclaimed over dinner that night, "It's really almost unbelievable! It's totally changed the situation for research in Huntington's disease."[6]

The paper "A Polymorphic DNA Marker Genetically Linked to Huntington's Disease," appeared in the November 17, 1983 issue of the prestigious British science journal *Nature,* accompanied by two enthusiastic editorials. *The New York Times, The Wall Street Journal,* the *Los Angeles Times, The Boston Globe,* and *The Washington Post* ran the story on the front page. Magazines such as *Newsweek* and *Time* carried it, as well as the popular science press. Jim Gusella appeared on the *Today* show, and Nancy too was interviewed on a number of radio and television programs. Everyone lauded the astonishingly rapid localization of the Huntington's gene to the short arm of chromosome 4 as the first significant breakthrough in the entire history of Huntington's disease. Gusella's group had clearly shown the usefulness of the new RFLP technology, and, in doing so, they had been the first to use this technique to localize a gene for an inherited disorder whose chromosomal address was completely unknown. As *Science* magazine put it, "This is the first time anyone has used restriction enzyme markers to locate a gene that could have been anywhere on the genome. Always before they at least knew on which chromosome to begin looking."[7]

The discovery revived traditional Mendelian genetics by demonstrating the power of a whole new set of genetic markers available to geneticists. As *Nature* magazine observed, "Mendelian genetics is once again the major tool for mapping the human genome."[8] According to Ralph J. Greenspan, a biologist at Princeton, the discovery was revolutionary, not in a conceptual sense but because it opened a new door to studying human hereditary defects. "It gives a major experimental foothold to simply being able to do genetic analysis, and that's incredibly important." David Housman's vision and bold gamble back in 1979 had paid off, as had Jim Gusella's skill and his daring in pegging his career on a high-risk experiment that many people thought was "nuts." "They had no idea what they were in for," reflected David Botstein years later. "But they were right. Like the guy who goes in to play the slot machine and hits the jackpot."

This jackpot, however, was not the gene, and Gusella estimated that the Huntington's gene lay at least four million base pairs away from the G-8 marker. How would you get from the marker to the gene? How would you know when you had arrived at the gene? How would you recognize your quarry? Chromosome 4 was one of the largest, thought to contain some 200 million base pairs, and not many of the genes had been specified so far. Would Jim Gusella's Midas touch continue to hold?

The discovery of a marker did mean that within a short time it would be possible to test *some* of the people at risk to see if they carried the deadly gene. But not everyone *could* be tested by this means. Here was an important limitation, as Gusella and others repeatedly emphasized. The marker test required a certain kind of family structure to be genetically informative.[9] According to Mike Conneally's Huntington's Disease Research Roster, as of April 1984, only about 20 percent of the 150,000 people at risk in the United States had the family makeup that would yield meaningful results with the techniques then available (that is, a 95 percent probability that they did or did not have the Huntington's gene). The linkage test also required blood samples from several family members, and sometimes from many, which often required complicated emotional negotiations. Moreover, the results were always a matter of probabilities, not an either-or proposition. Because the marker was some distance away from the gene on chromosome 4, there was always the possibility that a recombination event might have separated them; in that case, an individual might test positive for the marker but still not carry the Huntington's gene. Conversely, a person might test negative for the marker but in fact carry the lethal gene and hence be fated to develop the disease. But then, as the widow and mother of several individuals who had died of Huntington's asked, "Do you really want to know that in 10 to 15 years, you too will be stricken by the disease, or would you rather live in uncertainty?"[10] Even Allan Tobin, who had worked so hard to achieve this outcome, found himself fearing the possible implications. As Allan recognized, this event dramatized the distance between the power of scientists to predict diseases and their limited ability to cure or to treat them. It opened an abyss in all our lives, a vast space between prediction and prevention.

Despite such concerns, many scientists and Huntington's activists were optimistic that the dilemmas of testing would be worked out. Even Nancy, in a trenchant editorial in the *Archives of Neurology* spelling out the psychological and social risks of testing, noted that, because one's odds improved with age, "two-thirds of those at risk will be free of the HD gene and can lead their lives unchained." (While each child of a parent with Huntington's is born with a 50 percent chance of inheriting the gene, those odds decline as a person grows older and remains healthy. Individuals who have no symptoms in their forties usually have significantly less than 50 percent odds of inheriting Huntington's. Given that some people taking the test will be older and their odds will be lower, more people are likely to test negative than positive.) Even if the present was "a painful and taxing hiatus," she urged that the problems "should not overwhelm attention to the tremendous benefits this new knowledge can bring." With all the inevitable difficulties, "it is also probable that many who wish to take the test to face the future knowledgeably will use the information constructively to consolidate life plans. Hopefully they will be galvanized to lead a fuller life while they are able." [11]

Whatever the risks of presymptomatic testing, there was no question that a reliable test indicating which individuals carried the gene could offer scientists valuable data about the early pathology of the illness, allowing them to study subtle changes long before symptoms became apparent. Such early diagnosis in itself could point toward the development of effective interventions. Most of all, as the *Nature* article emphasized, "The discovery of a marker linked to the Huntington's disease gene makes it feasible to attempt the cloning and characterization of the abnormal gene on the basis of its map location." [12] Whatever the difficulties surrounding the marker discovery in terms of prediction, it was clear, as one observer put it, that "This is a unique historical moment. . . . What's going to happen in the next ten years won't ever happen again." [13]

Twelve

TESTING FATE

Fate takes pleasure in repetitions, variants, symmetries.

—JORGE LUIS BORGES
"The Plot"

The ambiguous condition of 50% risk is extremely difficult to maintain in one's mind, if not impossible. In practice, a 50–50 risk translates to a 100% certainty that one will or will not develop the disease . . .

—NANCY WEXLER
"Genetic 'Russian Roulette' "

I dreamed I went to visit C., who had moved to a large house in Hillsborough, somewhere near Palo Alto. The house was not yet finished, and the floorboards in the living room were only partially installed. Under the floorboards was a sort of pond or pool. I plunged in, not realizing there were fish in it. Suddenly I found myself in an embrace with masses of seaweed and a large, flapping fish. I couldn't get out for a long time and was terrified. Later, I tried to explain to some of John's colleagues at the university my fear of fish. John had given me a beautiful edition of a medieval text with pictures of houses or horses in it. One of the colleagues said maybe the fish is the equivalent of the horse. "But I'm not afraid of horses," I said. I dove again into the pool, which widened into Lake Maracaibo. Instead of fish, I saw the faces of those who had died of Huntington's. Their bodies had settled onto the lake bottom like the hulls of sunken galleons, their hair streaming out behind them. I swam among them searching for my mother, but when I found her and held her in my arms, what I saw was my own ruined face.

The psychologist Schlomo Breznitz said that the moment when a predictive test becomes a real possibility marks a decisive emotional shift for the person at risk for Huntington's disease—and perhaps for any fatal, untreatable illness. At that moment the anticipation changes. And from that moment until the actual taking of the test is also a distinct time, quite unlike the period when one can fantasize about a test that does not yet exist.[1]

Fragments from a diary:

April 13, 1984. The immensity of it scares me shitless. The idea of really knowing—and what if it is positive? Or if Nancy is? Once we do know, there's no going back. John thinks we are crazy to go ahead with this.

April 28, 1984. A workshop on genetic testing in New York. Nancy invited me to come as recorder. The doctors and scientists are cautious, careful. They offer sober reminders about the many issues that remain to be resolved. The question of heterogeneity looms large. Is the HD gene on chromosome 4 in all families, everywhere in the world, or is it on other chromosomes, in some other place, in other families? Does the gene malfunction in the same way in all cases, or are there different kinds of malfunctions, different errors in the genetic script that lead nonetheless to similar symptoms? Are there several different HD genes? How accurate is a predictive test based on a marker near the gene, rather than the disease gene itself? How big does a family have to be in order to get a reliable result?

The scientists are wary of offering a test before the protocols are in place, anxious about the possibility of suicide in those who get a positive result, worried about the "pseudo-volunteer" who may feel pressured to take the test. Many people's families are too small for testing. They will not be "informative," as the geneticists say, because there are not enough relatives to determine which pattern (or haplotype) of the marker travels with the HD gene in that particular family. But what of people from big enough families whom those administering the test consider too emotionally vulnerable? Should some people be told they cannot take it? The HD activists, such as Madeline Bates and Sam Baily—two of the mainstays of both CCHD and HDSA—warned against the dangers of medical paternalism. "I would be enraged to be told I couldn't take it," Bates said. Even though they acknowledged all the difficulties, they want the test to be available as soon as possible for those people at risk who wish to take it. "Who is this test for," Baily asked, "the families themselves or the medical profession? Is the thought of suicide always an irrational response that should disqualify a person from taking the test?"

May 14, 1984. Today's the day Mom died—6 years ago. It was Mother's Day that year. Yesterday at Papi's—where I took John, Nancy, Dad, and Herb [Pardes] for Mexican food en route home from Palm Springs—we talked about the test and about Mother. . . . Talking about it concretely—moving from the realm of abstract possibility to planning the logistics of it—terrifies me. I keep telling myself I have only a 25%–30% chance of a positive test—I think that's the only reason I'm taking it. If it were 50% I wouldn't. But the thought of learning that I carry that gene—that my brain is already deterioriating—is just too horrendous. I'm not sure I could go on. Nevertheless we all made plans to bank our blood until the time comes to do it. And John and I are already trying to conceive.

June 10, 1984. Alternately exhilarated, depressed, elated, overwhelmingly anxious, and frantic. I find it hard to think about the test at all. My mind tries to escape to other things. I only want to take this test to find out I *don't* have the illness. Cheerful predictions that people could use a positive diagnosis to make rational life choices mystify me. Yet I am a pessimist, and maybe some people really could assimilate that kind of information. I doubt if I'd have the confidence to continue. To think that my brain was slowly dying, never to know if thoughts or feelings were artifacts of a diseased brain—how to live with that and keep on working? At least there are still many more issues the scientists have to resolve; taking the test is a long way off.

February 5, 1985. Went into LA yesterday, had lunch with Nancy. We talked about THE TEST. Nancy said, "I have to get it into my head that there could be a bad result."

June 24, 1985. Now the plan is for us all to get together to *talk* about the test—get everything clear before we do it. I feel in a way the time for talking is past. Also, I'm not sure Dad is really prepared for this. He's doing it because he feels 95% confident we don't have the gene, but that 5% is beginning to worry him. What if he's wrong? He says he wants to know about error rates, timetables for finding the gene, for developing a treatment. I don't want to be blanketed with his optimism the day we get the test results. I don't want to feel as I did in 1968 that I have to respond in a way that will ease his feelings.

I'm not at all sure we should be pressing hard for testing. Counselors and therapists can help people learn to live with ambiguity—there's no way to accept a sentence of death like this one. . . . I feel very worried about the whole business. And yet I'd like a child—and John and I are going ahead full steam trying. The stress is almost unbearable.

June 30, 1985. A dreadful weekend. We were all to get together at Maryline's to talk about the test. Nancy and I were hours late, since Nancy was working on a grant proposal that was due the next day. Dad was furious, said he'd come over when he was ready. We started to talk without him. An hour later he walked in, sat down, and glared at us. "I want to stay out of this discussion," he said. "I'm not participating." He felt we were treating the test cavalierly, putting off this vital discussion on account of a mere grant proposal. He had no trust, no confidence in the process, he wanted no part of it. He'd support us if we decided to get the results, but he didn't want the rest of his life ruined by a false positive. He didn't have that many years left to live, and he wanted to enjoy them.

Nancy began explaining how the test would be done, and the possible sources of error: it isn't a 100% prediction. more like 95%, because of the slight possibility of a recombination event separating the marker from the gene; in that case you could test positive for the marker and still not carry the gene, or vice versa.[2] The test is more a matter of changing probabilities than of absolute prediction.

Now Dad became even angrier, insisting he did not trust the results. He was tired of our treating him so casually, keeping him waiting all day. His needs didn't matter. I said I thought there were two separate issues here and we needed to keep them separate—his rage at us for keeping him waiting, and his feeling the test was still too unreliable. Also, that his anxiety over error perhaps masked his deeper fear of the possibility that one or the other of us has the gene. Maybe he wasn't being entirely honest with himself. ("Oh, thank you for your psychological insight," he said coldly.) He insisted that I wanted to hear his opinion only if it agreed with mine, that he wasn't allowed to have his own opinion. Are you the only one allowed to make psychological judgments? Herb asked.

Dad's rage filled the room, blasting us whether he spoke or not, so that it was impossible to think or feel. John and Herb tried to be supportive without adding to Dad's fury, but he was beyond listening to anyone. I didn't know what I felt. Finally Dad marched out the door, without saying good-bye.

For a while after that nightmare weekend, we didn't speak much about the test. It was as if Dad's outburst had stunned us into silence and we needed to regroup and gather our thoughts. Old angers kept erupting to mix with the new ones until it seemed impossible to sort out which was which. Certainly Dad had spoken our own doubts and fears, though he tended to stress the dangers of an error in the test results while I worried more about the dangers of the truth. Since the test was not yet available in any case, we put the subject on hold. Nancy and I talked more often now about our fractured relationship with Dad, trying to sort out what had happened. Was he being preemptive or protective, we asked ourselves?

Over time, Nancy came to feel that Dad's anger was understandable, that it stemmed from his feeling that we were being cavalier about a decision that would have immense consequences for all of us; that we were about to get this life-changing information that might not even be true. Nancy said later that, since the marker discovery, she had considered in an intellectual way the possibility that one or both of us might have the HD gene, but it had not really penetrated emotionally. Suddenly seeing Dad dealing with the possibility "opened my inner eyes," as she put it. "It finally got through on an emotional level. It became patently clear that whatever we did would have enormous consequences for the rest." Even if he had exploded in ways that were not helpful to us in thinking through our choices, she felt he had forced us to address what we had not really confronted in any sustained way.

I was not convinced. For a long time I was furious that Dad had managed to usurp an occasion that should have been about Nancy and me, not about him. Instead of helping us make our own decisions, he had made things incomparably more difficult. And then, Nancy always seemed eventually to come around to Dad's basic point of view, even when she and I were the target of his attacks; I wished that she would take my side more strongly. I was angry at her, too, for setting the stage for this crisis by deciding to work on her grant proposal and making everyone wait for her.

And yet, what if we had gone ahead? I had to admit that I had been drifting into the testing situation with strong feelings of anxiety, persuaded more by the optimism of my sister and father than by my own feelings of confidence about a good result or a conviction that I could live with a bad one. Dad's sudden about-face, which had been uncharacteristically violent, had at least forced me to acknowledge the strong resistance I felt to going through with the test. In his own way, he was actually validating the doubts I had been trying to deny.

March 24, 1986. Nancy back from Venezuela. Good trip. She had a cold, was hoarse, exhausted. The crew from *60 Minutes* was down there. They want to interview Nan, Dad, and me talking together about the test. Diane Sawyer would do it. . . . At first I thought OK but the more I think about it the less I like the idea. It would be awful to break down and cry and hard not to be very emotional, since we are far from having sorted out all the issues.

April 14, 1986. Dinner in LA with Joel Bernstein, producer from *60 Minutes.* Joel is nice, an easygoing, red-haired guy in Reeboks, very warm and friendly. He thinks it's a terrific story—family that has helped to arrive at this great scientific advance—this test—now pulling back from results, deciding not to take the test or at least facing it with great ambivalence. He sees the program as a story about 1. the successful Venezuela project and the search for the HD gene. 2. a story of two sisters courageously facing a very difficult dilemma—

unmarried on account of HD. 3. a dilemma regarding genetic knowledge soon to face many people.

Dad feels strongly now against our taking the test, he hopes we won't take it. Joel sees paradox, irony in the fact that having moved forward so rapidly, now we're pulling back from results, that we're now having to face the implications of our own efforts, in our own lives.

April 16, 1986. Feeling very low. Odd how the prospect of filming our family on TV has precipitated a turning point. Each time Nancy comes out to California there's some new information, something else to consider. Here I am, trying to get pregnant, but it's only now that I begin to understand the nondisclosing prenatal test—what David Housman devised as a way of testing a fetus without the parents having to find out their own genetic status. It's like this: a fetus inherits one chromosome 4 from its father and one from its mother. In our case, that means one from John and one from me. The one from me could have come either from Dad or from Mom. If I'm pregnant, the test can tell us which of my chromosomes the fetus has inherited. If it's from Dad, then no problem. If it's from Mom, then there is a problem, since it could be either Mom's normal chromosome 4 from *her mother* or the one with the HD gene from her father. The fetus would be at 50% risk, since we wouldn't know which of Mom's chromosomes it carries. I'd have to decide at that point whether to go ahead and test the fetus for the marker; but if the fetus carries the marker for HD, that means I too must have the marker, and therefore the HD gene. I could abort the fetus at 50% risk, or go ahead and have the baby, not knowing its genetic status. It's an awful dilemma. Somehow it was not brought home to me that if you test the fetus in this way, you might be in a position of deciding on abortion without knowing the status of the fetus, or you might have to go through with the test yourself.

Dad keeps emphasizing—to Joel—that he never thought about Nancy and me taking the test. He only thought of finding the marker as one giant step toward therapy and a cure. I don't remember that he was so opposed to the test before that awful weekend at Maryline's. What puzzles me is that he was so optimistic about our not having HD, saying his "clinical intuition" told him we didn't have it. Could it be that my "decision," if it was that, to go along with the test was really based on Dad's denial, his insistence that we did not carry the gene? He's not saying that anymore. When I told this to Joel he seemed surprised. He said, "You mean you'd persuaded yourself that you weren't going to get Huntington's?" "Yes," I said.

The other day I got a copy of my medical records from my new gynecologist. "Patient has a high probablity of developing Huntington's disease," he wrote on the record he submitted to the insurance company. I was furious and called him to protest. "I'm sorry," he said. If I had asked him earlier to delete the disease from the record he would have done so, but now it was too late. "But it's not true," I said, "I don't have a *high probability* of getting Huntington's disease, I'm forty-four years old and my odds are going down." "I'm very sorry," he said, "but there's nothing I can do." Doesn't he know that risk for Huntington's is one of the conditions, along with sickle-cell anemia, muscular dystrophy, insulin-dependent diabetes, AIDS, for which insurance companies unconditionally deny medical coverage? Between infertility and Huntington's, I feel a little like a diver who can't come up for air. I dreamed of a cracked watchface, my watch, that had broken once again—no doubt a reference to not getting pregnant.

April 18, 1986. Yesterday I felt like I'd been punched hard in the stomach, no air left. Joel said at dinner, surprised I guess at our calm, "So the test is not really a crisis for you?"

I said, "Yes, it *is* a crisis." This new realization now—and why didn't I think this before?—that it's really Russian roulette this way, taking the test. I don't want to play, and that means, no kids. Well, if by some fluke I do get pregnant, then I'll have to think about it all over again.

I keep asking myself, but what's changed? There's really no new information. Is it only that Dad's no longer so willing to gamble on his intuition that we both don't have the illness? Was that the *sole* basis on which we were going ahead?

Dad was extolling the virtues of denial the other night—that denial can be a very useful defense for an at-risk person, allow them to keep on going. But a positive test result removes that denial, or makes denial almost impossible to sustain.

April 20, 1986. Spoke to Maryline this morning re *60 Minutes* and the test. I asked her, what's changed? She said, well, it's natural and normal that your father says you don't have HD. Because he wants to believe that. But he could be wrong. That's only his opinion. She says she wouldn't want to take the test and seems strongly aware of the dangers. But then, having children was never a high priority for her. "Was it ever?" I asked her. "No," she said. She says she can't imagine how Nancy and I would have time for a child, we have so much in our lives already. Have good lives without children, like she does. I asked, "But what would it be like to reach seventy and think, well I could have had children after all?" She said, "You know, it's possible to reach seventy and not have children and still have a good life."

She is realistic about the fact that there is a possibility we could develop the illness. Oddly enough, it was reassuring to hear her say that, in contrast to Dad's persistent denial. I guess now he realizes it's denial, his saying over and over, I don't think you have it, either of you. As if by repeating the litany often enough he could make it come true.

April 23, 1986. Spent Monday in LA filming for *60 Minutes.* A nine-man crew—no women, except for the assistant producer and Diane Sawyer, who is smart, attractive, and a very lively character. . . . We spent a lot of time sitting around waiting. Then we filmed on the Santa Monica beach, Diane asking questions. Later, in Dad's apartment, she posed more questions—"What would make you take this test?" "How would you feel if you discovered you had the gene?" "What is your fantasy about what you would do on the day after a cure was found?" (Nancy: "I'd go door to door in Venezuela—where six hundred kids are going to get the disease—and pass out pills to them. I would be ecstatic!") To Dad: "Did you notice any changes in your wife?" Dad: "No, I didn't. She'd changed, but I attributed it to any number of things—aging, the marriage. God knows what. But not Huntington's." Diane said at one point to Nancy and me: "You two sound like people who are not going to take the test." Nancy demurred, said she really didn't know. Diane wanted to know what would make her take it—Nancy said, if they found a cure. What would precipitate a decision? Nancy wasn't sure, but having a child was a critical issue. . . .

Dad says he's quite happy with things as they are, he could live the rest of his life very content, feeling confident we don't have the illness. He told Diane, "What I have now is joyousness. If I knew they [Nancy and I] were free of the disease, I'd feel ecstasy. It's not that great a gain. But there's an immense difference between joy and discovering one of them carried the gene. It's not worth the gamble."

Diane kept asking about the value of certainty, the importance of knowledge for its own sake. Nancy said, "Yes, I've always believed in knowledge for its own sake. And it is ironic that after working for precisely that, I'm now finding it much more complex than I ever thought it would be."

Diane: "Did you think you'd take the test when the linkage was discovered?" Nancy: "Absolutely. Yes. I never doubted it. And now I'm not sure."

After the *60 Minutes* program we continued to talk about the HD test, but in a desultory, interrupted fashion, in fragments of conversation over the phone or at dinner. Nancy kept us informed about new scientific developments. Researchers had now determined that there was only one Huntington's disease gene, located on chromosome 4 in all families. And as they found new markers closer to the Huntington's disease gene, the accuracy of the test was increasing. More people were able to get results. But I wasn't tempted, not seriously.

The decision not to take the test—at least for the moment—meant learning once again to live at risk, with no thoughts now of a final release, no fantasies of freedom from the possibility of HD. Our odds would go down as we got older, but then the age of onset tends to run in families, and Mom was not diagnosed until she was fifty-three. The most frightening part of being at risk is not the possibility of death but the manner of dying, not so much the loss of physical control, devastating as that is, but the loss of mental and emotional control. The intellectual decline that could precede the physical illness by years or even a decade especially haunted my mind, as I imagined slowly losing the ability to organize a paragraph or an article, much less write a book.

A dancer with Huntington's disease, in her early forties, described how, long before there were any other symptoms, she began having difficulty learning dance sequences; whereas once she had had no problem memorizing complicated routines, she gradually found it more and more difficult to master a series of different steps. Later on she found it increasingly difficult to organize a meal, coordinating the different dishes so that they would all come out together. Living at risk undermines confidence, for there is no way of separating the ordinary difficulties and setbacks of life from the early symptoms of the illness. It is not like any other physical illness, where consciousness can at least continue in the knowledge that one is still oneself, despite severe pain and physical limitation. Huntington's means a loss of identity. The husband of a patient once said as much. "Our marriage is over," he said frankly, though his wife was still in the early stages. "She's not the same person she was before."

Testing programs began around the country and in Canada, Great Britain, and Europe. But relatively few people actually completed the test, despite the enthusiasm for a predictive test in the days before the marker was discovered and the euphoria of the discovery in 1983. By the end of 1990, about 248 people had completed the testing process in Great Britain; by early 1992, about 300 in the United States, for a total of about 1,400 worldwide.[3] Nonetheless, the media, and sometimes the doctors and counselors who administered the test, engaged in subtle psychological pressure, portraying those who took the test as somehow stronger, braver, more optimistic, more "normal" than those of us who chose not to know. But isn't it also possible that those who opt not to know are more able to live with uncertainty and ambiguity? As Nancy says, the test does not really resolve the uncertainty, because you still don't know when the symptoms will appear, only that they will come at some time in the future. But it could be years, decades away, and by then you will have lost all that time.

I spoke to people who had taken the test. Why did you decide to go ahead, I asked? Some had never questioned that when a test became available, they would take it. It was something that many in the Huntington's disease community had been anticipating for years. It just seemed like the right thing to do, said one young woman, it just fell into place. One theme came up again and again: people said they had taken the test because they felt they probably had the gene, so getting confirmation wouldn't be that bad.[4] Some were convinced they were already experiencing symptoms. Why did you feel you were going to get HD? Because I looked like my mother, who had Huntington's, said one young woman. Because I was the youngest in the family and none of my brothers or sisters had it, said a man. "I knew right away I would take it," said one forty-year-old man. "That's my nature: if I know what it is I'll be able to handle it. I don't like surprises. I wanted to be able to plan. I'm not the kind of person who'll panic, say my life is over." Another fifty-year-old man concurred. "My feeling was that I did have it, so it would not be that awful to find out for sure."

The issue of control loomed large. Knowledge one way or the other appeared to give a measure of control, or at least of choice, over how one lived one's life: at the very least, knowledge of one's future in relation to Huntington's seemed to increase the terrain on which one could knowledgeably make decisions. Some people wanted to take the test in order to make decisions about having children or, more often, to inform the children they already had about their own risk, particularly if those children were themselves approaching childbearing age. Many people emphasized the extent to which testing involved everyone in the family, not just those who actually got tested.[5]

Nearly everyone mentioned the need to escape the oppressive uncertainty. I was surprised to discover that people shared my own experience of increasing anxiety over time, even though statistically the odds of becoming sick decreased with age. A man close to fifty felt the uncertainty becoming an obsession. "You think about this constantly," he said. "I wanted to set my mind at rest one way or another. The older you get, the more you worry about it." But the older you get, the lower your odds, I reminded him. "Yes," he said, "but I'm approaching the age when it occurs in my family." A young writer, Sally Spaulding, observed, "As I planned my future, I never looked past the age of 40, which was about the time both my father and grandmother first began exhibiting symptoms."[6]

Although motivated by a desire to end the painful ambiguity of their lives, several who came out with a positive result—they learned that they did carry the gene and would inevitably develop the disease, even though they were entirely free of symptoms when they took it—acknowledged that the test did not really halt the worry. "There is no question that the worst part about being told you have the gene is the watching and the waiting. It would be wonderful if someone could tell you when the symptoms will first appear and what they will look like."[7] "Now it's just a matter of when," said another woman with a positive result. Those who had tested positive acknowledged that it had been more traumatic than they had expected, even though, before the test, they had believed at some level that they were carrying the gene. "I didn't expect to take it as hard as I did," said one woman frankly. "You can't anticipate how hard it will hit you. There are a lot of issues to think about that you don't foresee." For the first two years afterward she felt a little numbed by it, just trying to deal with the result. Even after that she felt the need for personal therapy to take off some of the pressure, to help her answer the question "What do I do now?"

The lucky ones who got a negative result—no HD gene— felt relief and joy, though it was not necessarily immediate or unalloyed. A woman who tested negative felt her life had changed radically. She had avoided getting married, avoided commitments, both personal and professional. After taking the test she bought a house and committed herself to a job she really liked. "I was able to make peace with my [affected] mother," she said, "accept my mother in ways I hadn't been able to do before." And she became more of a Huntington's disease activist, in part because of two brothers who were not as fortunate as she. Many, if not most, of those who found themselves free of the gene had siblings who learned they would develop the disease.

Adjusting to a negative result also required time and patience. One man who tested negative felt as if he were missing a limb, a part of his identity. "I had lost my creative terror," he said. He had always been driven to seek out death-defying situations—on motorcycles, mountains, airplanes. Soon after getting the good news and knowing he was safe, he had found himself under arrest for writing bad checks.[8] A woman whose husband had tested negative said that after having lived with this for twenty years, "you just don't go home and forget about it. The thoughts and fears were there for a long time. It took me a long time not to think about it every day."

Choosing not to take the test is a decision one can easily revoke, unlike the situation after testing. As Geri Harville said, "You and your family will be affected by this information forever. Once you have the information, you cannot give it back." I have made my peace, more or less, with uncertainty, though sometimes I wonder if I have let it invade other areas of my life as well. Unlike many people who opted for testing, I have never felt convinced I was going to get Huntington's. Neither am I persuaded absolutely that I won't. Perhaps I even enjoy the ambiguity, resisting sharp categories and binary definitions, the border guards insisting that we place ourselves in one camp or the other.

And Mom, part of the attraction of writing this book is the connection I feel, not to your illness but to your strength, to the memory of that lively young woman long ago who pondered *Drosophila* at Columbia University, and studied bugs up at Woods Hole. I have developed a completely unexpected passion for nature. While I always scoffed when you tried to explain to Nancy and me the names of trees and flowers, I find myself now with an insatiable curiosity to know the names of everything I see. I collect field guides to trees, flowers, cactuses, stuffing my backpack with a small library each time we go hiking. The names take on a magical resonance, brittlebush, buckwheat, palo verde, ocotillo, ceonothus, agapanthus, penstemon, and monkeyflower, all the beautiful oaks and agave. Knowing the names brings me closer to you, Mom, I remember, I speak this language too, there are no more secrets and you and I are no longer strangers.

My mother embraces me at the bottom of Lake Maracaibo, her hair streaming out behind her. "Speak to me!" I shout at her, shaking her thin shoulders and flashing my jade ring in her face. "What other gifts have you left behind for Nancy and me?" But in that vast underwater terrain, no sound escapes, there is only her embrace of tenderness and longing, the eyelids closed for eternity. Gently I let go of her arms and she releases me from her hold. As she falls away toward the floor of the lake, she turns into a beautiful golden fish with silky scales and emerald eyes. With a flick of her tail, she vanishes into the depths, while I swim up toward the surface of the water and emerge into the sunlight of the Venezuelan tropics.

GENETIC DESTINATIONS

The Huntington's Disease Collaborative Research Group and members of the advisory committee at Dennis Shea's retreat at Islamorada in the Florida Keys. From left to right standing: Nancy, John Wasmuth, Marcy MacDonald, P. Michael Conneally, David Housman (behind Conneally), Francis Collins (behind Housman), James Gusella (in glasses), Julia Richards, Allan Tobin (with profiterole tee-shirt designed by Claes Oldenburg), Michael Altherr (in baok), Hans Lehrach (in dark glasses), Robert Moyzis, Gillian Bates (looking to her right), Robert Horvitz, Glen Evans, and Herb Pardes. Seated in front: Lynn Doucette-Stamm, Anna Maria Frischauf, Jan-Fang Cheng, and Norman Doggett.

Thirteen

"THE SINGLE MOST IMPORTANT PIECE OF INFORMATION"

Evolution is a tinkerer.

—Francis Crick

On Friday, January 6, 1984, eleven young molecular biologists crowded into a small conference room at the offices of the Hereditary Disease Foundation in Santa Monica to discuss ways of accelerating the search for the gene. Nancy, Allan Tobin, David Housman and Jim Gusella, who had organized this meeting, hoped to persuade those present to apply the new technologies they were developing to Huntington's disease: technologies such as chromosome hopping and jumping, pulsed-field gel electrophoresis (a method of analyzing large chunks of DNA), and new techniques of somatic cell genetics. Over the next several days of intense discussions, the group decided to form a research collaboration of seven (later six) laboratories and to share probes, information, and reagents to speed travel from the G-8 marker to the gene. The foundation agreed to supply $30,000 annually (subsequently increased) to each participating lab to cover the cost of a technician or postdoc and materials. Three or four times a year, they would meet to map out progress in an informal setting. The cooperative arrangement, and the spontaneous way in which it came about, impressed some members of the foundation's Scientific Advisory Board as extremely novel, or even unnatural, in part because of the size of the group and the great range of approaches that were going to be needed. Collaborations usually begin as an agreement between two people in different labs who decide to share resources to progress toward a certain goal. This one differed in that the group decided all at once to collaborate under the aegis of an outside foundation. "The degree of planning and organization is familiar to high-energy physicists," commented one scientific board member, but it is "an unfamiliar experience for most biologists." Another board member even thought it to be a historic moment. "What you're doing now is a scientific experiment, in point of fact," said Harvey Herschman of UCLA. "I don't know where this has ever been done before."[1]

At first, relations were somewhat tense, as people slowly got to know each other. "It certainly goes against the grain of the average scientist," Jim Gusella told me. "The average scientist is in science partly because they have control. And you relinquish control. You're willing to do so on a one-to-one basis. However, it's not so clear when you get into a group situation." Part of the difficulty arose because the necessary technologies were still being developed. "The direct approach wasn't there," recalled Gusella. "It was more difficult to work out the collaborative arrangements because the natural thing was to have people working on their own while they explored the technology." In Gusella's view, the collaboration did not really get under way until 1986, when people became more comfortable with the technologies then available and there was a natural coming together of the labs, "where people really had a reason to talk to each other about data and to move on from data that came from other places, rather than just from themselves."

By early 1986, the group had narrowed the location of the Huntington's gene to the top 3 percent of chromosome 4, called 4p16, a region of some twenty million base pairs, or .5 percent of the total genome, extending from the G-8 marker to the tip of the chromosome. They were focusing now on finding a flanking marker—that is, a marker on the other side of the gene from G-8 that would define the target region. Conrad Gilliam, at that time a postdoc in Jim Gusella's lab, had discovered another marker, called C4H, which looked for a while as though it might be the longed for flanking marker. But then they decided it wasn't; the individual whose DNA had provided the evidence, who had been diagnosed with Huntington's, probably didn't have the disease after all.[2]

Still, C4H was important, since it was closer to the HD gene than G-8 was. Working with C4H and other markers, the group had targeted the top .5 percent of chromosome 4 by the following year. The Venezuela team had also established conclusively that having two Huntington's genes did not change the clinical manifestation of the disease. The homozygote was not more severely affected than the heterozygote, making Huntington's a true dominant disease and opening an entirely new line of inquiry. Things seemed to be moving along nicely, so much so that several participants at the workshop in January 1987 predicted enthusiastically that the gene would be cloned within the next year or two at the most.

But then new evidence from two Venezuelan siblings with Huntington's threw a monkey wrench into the works. The evidence from one of them placed the HD gene far out at the tip of the chromosome, where everyone already suspected it was. But the DNA from the other sibling pointed toward a different, slightly more internal location, a little farther down toward the center of the chromosome, called the centromere. That area showed signs of linkage disequilibrium with Huntington's, a phenomenon that usually indicates that two regions are extremely close together on the chromosome. Meanwhile, things were also getting messy out at the end. The tip of the chromosome was proving to be a strange, intractable region with lots of repeated sequences. Some people raised the possibility that Huntington's might represent a chunk of some other chromosome that had been displaced onto the tip of chromosome 4. By the time of the January 1988 workshop, the mood of the group had grown somber, and expectations of an imminent discovery had diminished.

By now a number of other individuals offered contradictory evidence similar to that of the two Venezuelan siblings. Chromosome 4 from some of them still showed the Huntington's gene in a relatively small area far out toward the tip—in the last hundred thousand base pairs of the chromosome. Although they appeared to suffer from Huntington's disease and therefore to have the HD gene, chromosome 4 from these people showed none of the usual marker patterns associated with the disease gene. The absence of neighboring markers suggested that a recombination event must have occurred extremely far out toward the tip. In other words, the part of chromosome 4 that was usually inherited along with the Huntington's gene must have switched places with a normal chromosome 4, leaving only a tiny segment out at the tip containing the gene itself. But chromosome 4 from other individuals still implicated the more internal area, which was much larger, more than two million base pairs. These individuals, who also had the disease, had the marker patterns usually associated with Huntington's up to and just a little above the G-8 marker. Above that, though, they had a normal pattern. This finding, and the growing evidence of linkage disequilibrium, increasingly suggested that the gene did not lie far out at the tip but lower down on the short arm, in a vast, uncharted landscape. But if linkage disequilibrium often meant you were on the right track, the absence of linkage disequilibrium did not rule out a region. The situation was so confusing that Francis Collins, a collaborative group member from the University of Michigan, likened it to a Keystone Kops movie, where everyone first rushes to one place, then madly dashes to another, then races back to the first, and so on and on.

When Gillian Bates, in Hans Lehrach's lab at the Imperial Cancer Research Fund in London, finally cloned the tip of chromosome 4 in the spring of 1989, everyone hoped that this piece would contain the elusive gene. As it turned out, the tip of chromosome 4 from a person with Huntington's (a homozygote, who had the HD gene on both chromosomes) looked exactly like a chromosome 4 from someone without it—indeed, it resembled the tips of several other chromosomes, unless the difference was too subtle to detect.

By now, though they were making impressive strides in mapping the five million base pairs of the short arm of chromosome 4, the collaborative group was feeling increasingly frustrated. They were racing, not only against time but against several other research groups who had opted not to join the collaboration, though relations with them remained friendly and generally cooperative.[3] Moreover, while the Huntington's gene still eluded its hunters, other groups using the RFLP mapping techniques that had produced the Huntington's marker in 1983 were finding other important disease genes. A group headed by Louis Kunkel of Children's Hospital in Boston discovered the gene for Duchennes muscular dystrophy in 1986; the group of Lap-Chee Tsui of the Hospital for Sick Children in Toronto, and Francis Collins, who was also part of the HD collaboration, found the gene for cystic fibrosis in 1989. Clearly the HD gene posed formidable obstacles.

On the fund-raising front, however, 1989 brought substantial rewards. The efforts of the Hereditary Disease Foundation, of HDSA, and especially of Dennis Shea, a former Wall Street broker, yielded a million dollars for research from a benefit dinner held in November at the World Financial Center in New York. Shea's Foundation for the Care and Cure of Huntington's Disease had funded numerous research and educational projects since the early 1980s; Shea, an extremely effective fund-raiser, now directed that $725,000 of the money he raised from that dinner be used for the Huntington's Collaborative Group, to augment its support from the Hereditary Disease Foundation. These funds were especially crucial now, since money from the NINDS—the major government support for research on Huntington's—had actually declined during the 1980s.[4] Indeed, as the collaborative group closed in on the gene, both foundations increased their support.[5]

By the summer of 1990, David Housman was becoming convinced that the gene lay in the more internal region, which he also believed was preferable. A gene far out in the "twilight zone" was much less likely to code for a conventionally expressed gene product that would be potentially remediable. The more internal region, although much larger, was potentially more fixable. Another collaborative group member, John Wasmuth of the University of California at Irvine, described the tip as a vast jigsaw puzzle where a lot of the pieces looked alike and it was hard to see how they fit together. The internal region was more easily cloned, unlike the moonscape out at the tip, an area where the work, according to Gusella, was "not fun."

A certain amount of exhaustion was setting in, which in Jim Gusella's wry view facilitated the teamwork. "The more tired you are, the easier it is to get the collaboration to work," he said. As Hans Lehrach put it, "Everybody realized it was enormously difficult. At some point you get sick of banging your head against a brick wall. You don't mind a little help." Despite the obstacles, the group was feeling proud of its accomplishments, including the development of important new technologies.[6] "Even though there were always a few tense moments about authorship on manuscripts, et cetera, et cetera, I think the collaborative group made incredible progress dealing with an awful lot of pieces of DNA and a much larger physical region of the genome than we suspected," said John Wasmuth. "We really compiled a pretty complete long-range restriction map of about five or six million base pairs of DNA on the short arm of chromosome four, all the way from G-8 to the absolute end of the chromosome, an exciting milestone." Wasmuth could not imagine the task having been done without the collaborative arrangement. "This large a region of the genome has not been this well mapped by any single person or group of persons to this point," he said. "There's just no way one lab or two labs collaborating could have done that."

In developing a cooperative way of doing science, some felt the group had also established a paradigm for work on the human genome generally. Even scientists who felt they might not wish to work in such an arrangement, such as Louis Kunkel, viewed it as a model, since the resources and technologies available today are so numerous that one lab often cannot master them all. The frequent meetings were invaluable, said Wasmuth, who had initially been skeptical. "You have to face these people two or three times a year, and if you're not doing what you're supposed to be doing, it's hard. At the same time, it's really great to sit down and talk to them because the enthusiasm and excitement go from one person to another."

The group had resolved the tricky question of authorship by agreeing to a collective signature, the Huntington's Disease Collaborative Research Group, with members of each lab listed separately in an order to be determined by each principal investigator. They had developed what Francis Collins called "a culture of collaboration," a sense of shared struggle and camaraderie, that helped keep up morale. As Marcy MacDonald, a senior member of the Massachusetts General group, put it, "You go to one of these meetings and you want to show what you've done for the common effort. You want to say, 'Oh, look here what we have in our suitcases for you!' "

Those who stayed in the group tended to be unusually self-confident and cooperative people, willing to expose themselves to group scrutiny and to give up individual fame for collective achievement. "By collaborating," reflected Mike Conneally, "regardless of whether you clone the gene or not, you become part of a much larger group, and so your efforts will seem diluted. Whereas if you don't join and somebody else finds it, then you get no recognition at all. And so, do you want all or nothing? Do you say, well, I'll share and be part of it. Or do you say, I absolutely want the whole pot or nothing." Especially for postdocs at the start of their careers, who have to establish themselves with a piece of original research, participating in the collaborative group could pose problems; some postdocs were not willing to do it. Yet for those who were, the rewards were also substantial—the opportunity to work on a truly important project and to interact with some of the leading scientists in the field.

Mike Conneally recalled with some awe a moment at one of the collaborative group meetings, which he described as the epitome of collaboration. Mike Altherr, a postdoc in John Wasmuth's lab at the University of California at Irvine, was discussing a new probe he had isolated that looked very promising. "In fact," recalled Conneally, "there was a very slight hint that it might be the gene itself. . . . But after he talked about it, he put his hands into his pocket and pulled out five or six vials with the probe in there and passed it around to all the participants." Actually, Allan Tobin sometimes called people before the meetings and suggested the sharing of probes; such sharing was not always altogether spontaneous. And occasionally members of the group reacted sharply to such "management" by Allan or Nancy, disliking the sense of interference from outside their own lab and the fact of having to be accountable to so many other people. The politics could be exhausting. "There are times when everybody's been aggravated over some aspects of the collaboration," said Wasmuth frankly. "Having people look over your shoulders all the time. Some people have felt a bit manipulated, to conform more to the group. But if you look right now at what's been accomplished, especially in the last year and a half [1988–89], it couldn't have been done [any other way]."

With a collaboration involving some fifty-eight individuals at ten different institutions, it was essential that the postdocs, who did the hands-on work, communicate directly with one another. Including the postdocs, technicians, and grad students in the collaborative meetings, especially at the annual April meeting at Islamorada in the Florida Keys, served to facilitate their relationships and ease tensions. A small advisory committee also helped reduce stress, since the committee was not part of the collaborative group but attended all its meetings and kept communications open with Allan, Nancy, and the scientific advisory board on the one hand, and among people in different labs, on the other. This committee—whose membership over the years included Mike Conneally, Richard Mulligan of the Whitehead Institute, John Minna, Glen Evans of the Salk Institute, and Robert Horvitz of MIT—proved skillful in working through grievances and conflicts as they arose. Horvitz, who had worked collaboratively on *C. elegans*, especially drew on that experience in his association with this group. He stressed the importance of troubleshooting competitive issues quickly as they came up. It was essential to remind people, he said, that "this is not about fame and glory."

Now some investigators were beginning to worry that the gene might be only transiently expressed at some early moment in development, leaving its devastating effects to be felt twenty or thirty years later. There was discussion of a position effect, in which a normal gene is altered because it gets switched to some abnormal position on the chromosome. Or possibly some normal rearrangement that is supposed to take place during development does not occur, so that a gene that is supposed to turn off remains turned on and therefore becomes toxic and dangerous to all around it. Or maybe there is a suppressor gene that is supposed to turn off another gene, but the suppressor gene gets knocked out and whatever it was supposed to suppress remains operative. Maybe there are double recombinants or "ghost recombinants" pointing in the wrong directions.

And there was still the persistent question of how to recognize the Huntington's gene once it was actually cloned. After all, there are many variations in human DNA—the whole concept of RFLPS is based on that fact—yet most differences have little to do with disease. On the other hand, some differences, such as an extra chunk of DNA stuck inside an otherwise normal gene, a sequence missing from that gene, or even a single nucleotide change, can cause devastating illness in some instances. And how would you find out if the Huntington's mutation affects only the brain, or particular regions of the brain, or if it really aims its poison at some other part of the body whose malfunction only secondarily destroys brain tissue (like Wilson's disease, in which an excessive accumulation of copper in the liver ultimately affects the brain's function)? In 1989, the foundation decided to organize another collaborative research group to work on the neurobiology of Huntington's. (Although the foundation had always funded grants in this area, most of its resources were going toward the gene hunt.) Such a group would be useful to have in place once the gene was discovered, and intensified emphasis on the brain might open up new avenues for treatment in the event that the gene remained uncaptured.[7]

There was talk of more than one original mutation, possibly as many as five, which meant that the linkage disequilibrium data would be far less useful. David Housman expressed another worry. "There's going to come a day when we do find it," he said, "when the mists clear and it's going to become more or less likely, depending on what the gene actually does, that it can be fixed. And I know that everybody's hope is that it will be something fixable. But I don't think there's any way to know where it sits in that spectrum, from very easy to fix to impossible to fix, until you actually see it. It's a concern I've had for the whole ten years, to tell you the truth." Francis Collins compared the situation to that of buying a house sight unseen, knowing that something is wrong with it but not knowing exactly what. "You don't know if it's something major, a structural thing that you're not going to be able to repair, or if it's just one rotted-out beam and you will be able to go in there and shore it up and live in the house for a hundred years. Until you have actually seen the house and gone down into the cellar and looked at the structure, you don't know what the answer is going to be."[8]

Those not participating in the search for the gene, especially the neurobiologists, were even more cautious, warning that "The isolation of the gene itself gives us a possible, but not certain, route to understanding the disease." Even understanding the pathogenesis may not immediately point the way toward a cure. Glen Evans, risking "hereditary ridicule," speculated that while he thought "sequencing the HD gene will tell us relatively little about how the gene works and what it does and may tell us absolutely nothing about the pathogenesis of Huntington's disease," that gene was still "the single most important piece of information which could be obtained."[9]

At the January 1992 foundation workshop, David Housman, who had been one of the discoverers of the gene for myotonic dystrophy, suggested that the mechanism of error in

Huntington's might be similar. In the myotonic dystrophy gene, a short sequence of three nucleotides that is usually repeated just a few times undergoes abnormal expansion. This expanded nucleotide repeat, lodged among the many thousands of nucleotides that make up the normal gene, manages to screw up its entire functioning, thereby producing the disease. Might there also be abnormal repeat sequences in HD, Housman asked? He was developing techniques to scan for large expanded repeats.[10]

By this time, the collaborative group had cloned all the DNA within the more internal region, some 2.2 million base pairs of DNA, an awesome achievement in itself.[11] They had homed in on a stretch of some 500,000 base pairs, which everyone now accepted as the most likely. And they had started to identify genes in the region that might possibly be the one for Huntington's—candidate genes, they called them. They were using a variety of techniques, some of them newly developed in the course of the collaboration and others that had been around for a while, like zoo blots for example. Zoo blots depend on the fact that any gene with an important function tends to be conserved through the evolutionary process; some critical human genes can also be found in simpler organisms, like mice or fruit flies or yeast. And if a human gene is roughly homologous to that of a mouse, for example, then a single strand of human DNA will hybridize to its complementary segment from the mouse. The resulting zoo blots are a means of pulling out unknown genes from human DNA by seeing if they will hybridize to known genes from other organisms. They also give important clues to genes that are functionally significant. The area within the short arm of chromosome 4 that the collaborative group was studying was especially rich in genes, containing perhaps as many as a hundred, so looking at all these genes to determine which one might be the gene for Huntington's was not a trivial operation. The one collaborative member willing to speculate about when they might actually land on the Huntington's gene was Francis Collins, who made his guess late in 1992. He put the date of discovery around the end of 1994. No one else was making any predictions.[12]

Ironically, the very success of the marker discovery, which led to the focus on finding the gene, caused some investigators to reflect with nostalgia on the earlier days of the struggle. "I was struck," said John Minna in 1986, "how, on the surface, this workshop would have gotten an A plus from scientists, whereas probably many established scientists would have walked out of all of the first workshops as being too childlike. But it was that kind of childlike enthusiasm that led to the current success. It's interesting to think about what has happened in a decade. I think that nobody would have predicted with a high degree of certainty that the results of these workshops were going to lead to the type of successes that they indeed have." Yet Minna felt that the current workshop marked a moment that was both happy and sad. "It was happy because while the HD problem has not yet been conquered, it was clear that all of the tools were on the way to identifying the gene. It was also happy because over the twelve years that I've known the foundation, the foundation and the discussions have become incredibly sophisticated and also focused." But in other ways, Minna continued, the workshop seemed more like a conventional scientific meeting, with all the hallmarks of the formal scientific establishment. "Yet, if you look back, it was just the opposite of this that Milton was trying to establish."

"Where has the greatest impact been?" I asked. "I think it was mainly in terms of getting people at a formative phase of their career involved in this research," said Minna. In addition, "The thing that's so potentially exciting is that if one could crack the Huntington's problem, it would open up parallels in other neurogenetic diseases, or in other developmental diseases as well. If you work on a relatively obscure disease, the results from that can then be generalized to other diseases. I think that's a major underlying philosophic point. The other amazing thing is how the workshops have gotten diverse groups of people who otherwise, even if they were working on the HD problem, would have worked on it in a competitive and probably not a productive fashion, to work on it in a cooperative fashion. In fact, it's hard to think of any other area in biologic sciences where people are working toward a very specific common solution where they have been so willing to pool resources, from so many different labs."

"What's the reason for that?" I asked. "I think it has a lot to do with the familial atmosphere that is generated by the workshop," said Minna. "One really felt part of the family. I think that any of the people working on that would feel, if somebody in the family succeeded, then they would have succeeded too." But in his view, "The person that made all of the HD thing work and brought it to fruition was Nancy. Nancy's big contribution was not only participating in the workshops but this whole process of setting up the pedigrees. There were various HD groups and foundations, but it was Nancy who focused down in terms of the [Venezuela] pedigree. And actually, by the bootstraps, collected the pedigree and served as a glue and catalyst between other people working on pedigrees and people working in the laboratory . . . plus she got people to start applying the new recombinant DNA techniques to the pedigrees. It was her acting as this glue and go-between, doing whatever was necessary, that was the real key, in a very practical sense, and made the discovery of the linkage possible. . . . Nobody had the guts or the fortitude to focus in on this one particular disease and do it the way Nancy did."

"How will you feel when the gene is discovered?" I asked John Wasmuth one day in his Irvine lab. "Oh, I'll be ecstatic," he said. "I have two very strong feelings about this. The first is that it's just like reading a great mystery novel, you're up to the last chapter and it's been so involving and exciting you want it to continue, and yet you can't wait to find out who did it. We've been involved in it, everybody, for so long, the anticipation is just really remarkable. And at the same time, [when the gene is discovered,] I'll be a little bit sad because it's the end of the most exciting project that's ever gone on in my lab. Not the end—obviously there's so much more to do—but getting this far has been so exciting and frustrating and taken so much effort that in a way it's going to be, not disappointment at having achieved it, but disappointment that that part of the effort is over. Almost like postpartum depression. Like Buzz Aldrin, the second guy to walk on the moon, says, well, what the hell do I do now, I've walked on the moon, what's next?"

Fourteen

REPEAT SEQUENCES

> . . . for it was foreseen that the city of mirrors (or mirages) would be wiped out by the wind and exiled from the memory of men at the precise moment when Aureliano Babilonia would finish deciphering the parchments . . .
>
> —GABRIEL GARCÍA MÁRQUEZ
> *One Hundred Years of Solitude*

February 24, 1993. Nancy called. They found the Huntington's gene!! Jim Gusella calls it IT15, for Interesting Transcript. I didn't know genes had names. He calls the protein huntingtin. As usual Nancy just slipped this news into the conversation, low-key and all—it didn't seem real.[1] John Wasmuth said later he was "literally stunned," it took him several days to realize what had happened. And Marcy MacDonald told me, "When we called people their first reaction was relief—thank God it's over!—and the second one was pure joy!" In total agreement was David Housman. As usual, he went out and had a beer.

So there it is—at last! Dad called up thrilled and delighted. He was worried he might not live to see the discovery—and here it is!

March 24, 1993. Today the newspapers all carried the story of finding the gene. They called it "the longest and most frustrating search in the annals of molecular biology." The gene lies about 3.5 million base pairs from the tip of chromosome 4, in the more internal region and not out at the end, where the team first thought it must be. It's a big gene too, over three hundred thousand base pairs, and its normal version produces a protein unlike any other protein yet identified. The normal gene contains the nucleotide triplet CAG—that is, a sequence of the nucleotides cytosine (C), adenine (A), and guanine (G)—which is repeated anywhere between eleven and about thirty-three times within the gene; the average number of repeats is around twenty. But people with Huntington's have more than this number, from thirty-seven to as many as one hundred or occasionally, even more. Those with between thirty and forty repeats are in a range that geneticists consider noninformative, since it may be nearly impossible to predict if they will develop the disease. Evidently the distinction between the "normal" and the "abnormal" is not entirely clear.[2]

What is clear, though, is that the extra repeats—which they call an expanded trinucleotide repeat—do something to wreck the normal functioning of the gene, leading to the awful effects called Huntington's disease. Extremely high numbers of repeats may be correlated with an earlier age of onset, though the link is still very tentative. Apparently the number of these CAG repeats can change when transmitted from parent to child. If researchers can unravel the mechanism of change, they will understand why these repeats are unstable, and hopefully how to reduce the number. The CAG nucleotide triplet spells out the amino acid glutamine; just why the same amino acid should be repeated inside a protein in this way, and how the body utilizes the protein are central mysteries of the disease.

Interestingly, there are other diseases that are also characterized by expanded trinucleotide repeats, such as myotonic dystrophy, spinobulbar muscular dystrophy (Kennedy's disease), and fragile X syndrome, a form of mental retardation. Unlike Huntington's, these disease genes are characterized by a much greater number of extra repeats. But some of the other genetic diseases linked specifically with expanded CAG repeats, such as Kennedy's disease, are also degenerative neuromuscular disorders. Under-standing the Huntington's gene may illuminate them as well, and vice versa. In fact, Huntington's may be an example of a kind of mutation quite common in human genetic disease.

Now the two tracks of Huntingon's research—neurobiology and molecular genetics—can come together to determine just how this gene disrupts brain functions. Already the scientists have found that the Huntington's gene is expressed in all the tissues of the body, though the brain is the organ most devastated by the disease. Apparently the normal version of this gene is very old; it is found in mice and *Drosophila* and even in yeast. Now researchers can look at what it actually does, put it into a mouse or other organism and see what kind of protein it produces, and what effect that protein has. They can explore how those extra CAG repeats interfere with the normal functioning of the gene. They may even be able to calculate when the first mutation appeared.[3]

The most immediate result, however, is to simplify the process of presymptomatic testing. Now people at risk, if they wish, may take a test for the presence or absence of the gene, rather than for a complicated set of markers. It will no longer be necessary to get blood from numerous family members. Those whose parents have died, orphans, adopted individuals, and people with small families will be able to get tested. The process will be far less expensive. It will amount to a simple blood test.[4] Will we maintain the caution about testing that has prevailed so far? Will we ensure that the ability to test not be translated into the imperative to test? Will the decision not to take the test be respected as a legitimate choice and not represented as a failure of courage or a desire to "remain ignorant," as *Time* magazine wrote?[5]

For those already ill with Huntington's, identifying the gene does not immediately transform the medical landscape or translate into effective therapy. What has changed is the psychological landscape, the wider horizons of hope before us. Now researchers begin yet more journeys, of discovery, invention, but no longer capture, the favorite metaphor of many "gene hunters." As Francis Collins put it, "This is a big fish that finally got caught after many close scrapes. This time it didn't get away."

fish dreams (ii)

Several years ago our father acquired a beautiful lamp in the shape of a fish. Perched delicately on its stand, with translucent white scales lit from within, it seemed an icon or a spirit, a protector of souls. Later the fish was sold, moved on. My sister and I often speak of that fish not as a threat but as a promise. On certain nights it swims into memory, lighting our sea of dreams with a radiant glow.

NOTES

The following abbreviations have been used in the notes:

AW   Alice Wexler
LSW   Leonore Sabin Wexler
MW   Milton Wexler
NW   Nancy Wexler
CCHD   Committee to Combat Huntington's Disease
HDF   Hereditary Disease Foundation
HDSA   Huntington's Disease Society of America

"THAT DISORDER": AN INTRODUCTION

1. George W. Huntington, "On Chorea," *Medical Surgical Reporter* 26 (Philadelphia, 1872): 317–321.

2. Robert Mullan Cook-Deegan, "The Human Genome Project: The Formation of Federal Policies in the United States, 1986–1990," in Kathi E. Hanna, ed., *Biomedical Politics* (Washington, D.C.: National Academy Press, 1991), 102.

3. The literary critic Marjorie Garber has written recently, "The 'third' is a mode of articulation, a way of describing a space of possibility. Three puts in question the idea of one: of identity, self-sufficiency, self-knowledge. . . . The third deconstructs the binary of self and other that was itself a comfortable, because commutable, and thus controllable, fiction of complementarity." Garber posits an analogy between the marker for the Huntington's disease gene and the transvestite, or cross-dresser: one points to genetic trouble somewhere else, while the other indicates gender trouble; Marjorie Garber, *Vested Interests* (London: Routledge, 1991), 11–12.

4. See Jacques Lacan, "The Mirror Stage," in Jacques Lacan, *Écrits: A Selection* (New York: W. W. Norton, 1977), 1–7; D. W.

Winnicott, "Mirror-Role of Mother and Family in Child Development," in *Playing and Reality* (1971; New York: Routledge, 1991), 111–119.

5. Michel Foucault, *The History of Sexuality,* vol. 1 (New York: Pantheon, 1978), 27.

6. Arthur Kleinman, *The Illness Narratives: Suffering, Healing, and the Human Condition* (New York: Basic Books, 1988), 31.

7. Testimony by John Arcotta, April 19, 1977, in *Report of the Commission for the Control of Huntington's Disease and Its Consequences,* vol. 4, pt. 4 (Washington, D.C.: National Institutes of Health, 1977), 109; testimony by Martha Barnett, March 23, 1977, *ibid.,* 133.

8. *Report of the Commission,* vol. 1, 7–10.

9. Evelyn Fox Keller, "Genetics, Reductionism, and the Normative Uses of Biological Information," conference paper, "Genes 'R' Us" conference, University of California, Irvine, May 1991. See also Donna Haraway, "When Man Is on the Menu: Technical Products as Social Actors," conference paper, "Genes 'R' Us" conference, University of California, Irvine, May 1991.

10. See for example Thomas Laqueur, *Making Sex: Body and Gender from the Greeks to Freud* (Cambridge, Mass.: Harvard University Press, 1990).

CHAPTER 1: AFTER WOODS HOLE

1. Joan Kelly, "The Social Relations of the Sexes: Methodological Implications of Women's History," *Signs* 1 (1975–76): 816.

2. On the history of the Menninger Clinic, see Lawrence J. Friedman, *Menninger: The Family and the Clinic* (New York: Alfred A. Knopf, 1990), 224–232. For a discussion of the radical origins of psychoanalysis in Europe, see Russell Jacoby, *The Repression of Psychoanalysis* (Chicago: University of Chicago Press, 1983).

3. LSW to Alene Mintz, February 19, 1942.

4. LSW to Alene Mintz, August 1, 1942.

5. LSW to Alene Mintz, March 15, 1951.

6. LSW to Alene Mintz, March 15, 1951.

7. LSW to Alene Mintz, October 17, 1951.

CHAPTER 2: SILENT SUBJECTS

1. Morris B. Bender to Dr. David Rubenfine, September 30, 1950.
2. LSW to Alene Mintz, March 15, 1951.
3. LSW to Alene Mintz, November 8, 1948 and October 1, 1951.
4. LSW to NW, July 17, 1965.
5. NW to MW, September 21, 1967.
6. NW to MW, spring 1968.
7. LSW to AW, August 7, 1964.

CHAPTER 3: 1968

1. G. W. Huntington, "Recollections of Huntington's Chorea as I Saw It at East Hampton, Long Island," *Journal of Nervous and Mental Diseases* 37 (1910): 303–305, quoted in A. Barbeau, T. N. Chase, and G. W. Paulson, *Advances in Neurology*, vol. 1: *Huntington's Chorea, 1872–1972* (New York: Raven Press, 1973), 37–39.

2. See G. W. Bruyn, "Huntington's Chorea—Historical, Clinical and Laboratory Synopsis," in P. J. Vinken and G. W. Bruyn, eds., *Handbook of Clinical Neurology*, vol. 6 (Amsterdam: North-Holland Publishing Company, 1968), 298–378, cited at 299. The historical origins of Huntington's disease have been the subject of much speculation, mostly by neurologists and geneticists. The influential account by P. R. Vessie, written in the 1930s, claimed to trace the disease in the United States back to three men, allegedly half brothers, from the village of Bures, in Suffolk, England, who had come to America with the John Winthrop fleet in 1630. Vessie cited as evidence the fact that a number of the descendants of these men had Huntington's disease and that legal difficulties and accusations of witchcraft were allegedly raised against some of them; P. R. Vessie, "On the Transmission of Huntington's Chorea for 300 Years—The Bures Family Group," in *Journal of Nervous and Mental Disease* 76 (December 1932): 553–573.

Elaborating on Vessie, MacDonald Critchley, an eminent British neurologist, decided that it was not Vessie's three men but their mother, "that gay lady of Bures," who bears the blame!

"Personally I am inclined to regard that local light o'love 'Mary H.' as the villainess of the piece," writes Critchley, "and the probable source of the tainted germ-plasm"; Critchley, "Huntington's Chorea and East Anglia," *Journal of State Medicine* 42 (1934); 575–587. Subsequent research has discredited both Vessie's and Critchley's claims, showing them to rest on faulty identification and the too-ready interpretation of witchcraft charges as evidence of Huntington's; see Mary B. Hans and Thomas H. Gilmore, "Huntington's Chorea and Genealogical Credibility," *Journal of Nervous and Mental Disease* 146 (1969): 5–12; also Peter Harper and Michael Morris, "Introduction: A Historical Background," in Peter S. Harper, ed., *Major Problems in Neurology,* vol. 22: *Huntington's Disease* (Philadelphia: W. B. Saunders, 1991), 14–15.

3. See "Notes on the Temporal, Geographic, and Racial Distribution of Huntington's Chorea," *Neurographs* 1 (1908): 150.

4. William Osler, *On Chorea and Choreiform Affections* (Philadelphia: Blakiston, 1904); for a long time, doctors disagreed about whether hereditary chorea differed fundamentally from other kinds of temporary choreas.

5. On hereditarian social thought, see Daniel J. Kevles, *In the Name of Eugenics: Genetics and the Uses of Human Heredity* (Berkeley: University of California Press, 1986); see also Mark Haller, *Eugenics: Hereditarian Attitudes in American Social Thought* (New Brunswick, N.J.: Rutgers University Press, 1963).

6. Duchenne described muscular dystrophy in the 1850s; Gilles de la Tourette described the disease that took his name in 1885; "Editorial," *Neurographs* 1 (1908): 88. The three were Charles Oscar Waters, Charles R. Gorman, and of course George Huntington; all were in their twenties when they described the disease.

7. G. W. Bruyn, "Huntington's Chorea," 313.

8. Osler included George Huntington's account in his widely used 1893 textbook *The Principles and Practice of Medicine,* thereby lending Huntington his authority and associating that name with this disease. Osler's monograph *On Chorea and Choreiform*

Affections included a long section on hereditary chorea, which he, unlike Jean-Martin Charcot, described as a fundamentally distinct entity; Osler, *On Chorea;* see also William Osler, "Remarks on the Varieties of Chronic Chorea, and a Report upon Two Families of the Hereditary Form, with Autopsy," *Journal of Nervous and Mental Disease* 18 (February 1893): 97–111: Jean-Martin Charcot, *Leçons du mardi à la Salpetrière. Notes de cours,* 543 (Paris: Bureaux du Progrès Médical, 1887). One of the early Freudians in America, Smith Ely Jeliffe, was also fascinated by the illness; in 1908, he organized an entire issue of the journal *Neurographs* around articles on Huntington's chorea, "in view of the world-wide interest that has been shown in the subject"; Smith Ely Jeliffe, "A Contribution to the History of Huntington's Chorea: A Preliminary Report," *Neurographs* 1 (1908): 116–124. See also S. Weir Mitchell and C. W. Burr, "Unusual Cases of Chorea, Possibly Involving the Spinal Cord," *Journal of Nervous and Mental Diseases* 15 (1890): 427–431.

9. Charles B. Davenport, "Huntington's Chorea in Relation to Heredity and Eugenics," *American Journal of Insanity* 73 (October 1916): 215.

10. William Osler, "Case of Hereditary Chorea," *Johns Hopkins Hospital Bulletin* 5 (1894): 119–129; Clarence King, "Hereditary Chorea," *New York Medical Journal* 104 (1916): 307–308. See also Frank K. Hallock, "A Case of Huntington's Chorea . . ." *Journal of Nervous and Mental Diseases* 25(12) (1898): 851–864; *Major Problems in Neurology,* vol. 22, 18; Wharton Sinkler, "Two Additional Cases of Hereditary Chorea," *Journal of Nervous and Mental Disease* 14 (February 1889): 90; Huet, *De la Chorée chronique,* 235–236.

11. NW to LSW, January 29, 1971.

12. NW to LSW, July 17, 1972.

13. MW, "It Runs in the Family," unpublished ms., 9; Maya Pines, "In the Shadow of Huntington's," *Science* 84 (May 1984), 34; Jerry E. Bishop and Michael Waldholz, *Genome* (New York: Simon and Schuster, 1990), 43.

14. NW to LSW, February 2, 1973.

CHAPTER 4: DREAMING CHOREA

1. See Judith P. Zinsser, *History and Feminism: A Glass Half Full* (New York: Twayne, 1992), for an account of this project.
2. Margaret Anderson, *My Thirty Years' War* (London: Alfred A. Knopf, 1930), 54–55.
3. "The grotesque body is the open, protruding, extended, secreting body, the body of becoming, process and change. The grotesque body is opposed to the classical body, which is monumental, static, closed, and sleek, correspondent to the aspirations of bourgeois individualism; the grotesque body is connected to the rest of the world." Mary Russo, "Female Grotesques: Carnival and Theory," in Teresa de Lauretis, ed., *Feminist Studies/Critical Studies* (Bloomington: Indiana University Press, 1986), 219.

CHAPTER 5: NEDDA AND HOPE

1. See MW, "The Structural Problem in Schizophrenia: Therapeutic Implications," *The International Journal of Psycho-analysis* 32 (1951); 157–166; Karl Menninger to MW, August 24, 1989.
2. Ntinos C. Myrianthopoulos, "Huntington's Chorea," *Journal of Medical Genetics* 3 (1966): 312. Also, Harold Stevens to Romi Greenson, June 12, 1968; N. C. Myrianthopoulos et al., *A Centennial Bibliography of Huntington's Chorea, 1872–1972* (Louvain: Leuven University Press, 1974), 10, for publication figures over the decades.
3. Horace Freeland Judson, *The Eighth Day of Creation* (New York: Touchstone, 1979), 225.
4. Drugs such as haloperidol (Haldol), for example, which helps relieve choreic movements, act to block the dopamine receptors.
5. Henry Wexler to MW, July 24, 1968 and October 7, 1968.

CHAPTER 6: "TAINTED BY SMOG AND HOLLYWOOD"

1. MW to Marjorie Guthrie, May 6, 1970.
2. MW to Leon Freeman, December 14, 1970.
3. MW to NW and AW, 1971; MW to B. Fritts, March 16, 1971.

4. John H. Menkes, "Summary of a Workshop: Huntington's Disease," Brain Research Institute and Biomedical Library, UCLA, BIS Conference Report no. 17, October 29, 1971. On the higher proportion of paternal inheritance in juvenile cases of Huntington's, see A. D. Merritt, P. M. Conneally, N. F. Rahman, and A. L. Drew, "Juvenile Huntington's Chorea," in A. Barbeau and J. R. Brunette, eds., *Proceedings of the Second International Congress of Neurogenetics and Neuro-ophthalmology of the World Federation of Neurology,* vol. 1 (Amsterdam: Excerpta Medica Foundation, 1969), 6545–6650.

5. At the time he was recruited by Dreyer and Benzer, Konopka had just discovered a specific genetic locus governing circadian rhythms in *Drosophila,* a benchmark discovery that showed that even such complex behaviors as circadian rhythms could be affected by single gene mutations; R. J. Konopka and S. Benzer, "Clock Mutants of *Drosophila melanogaster,*" *Proceedings of the National Academy of Science* 81 (1971): 2142; see also Rick Weiss, "Time Flies: Circadian Cycles and the *per* Gene of *Drosophila,*" *Journal of NIH Research,* June 1990: 63.

6. MW, "Random jottings to whomever with love," "Sunday," 1967.

7. Artists such as Ron Davis, Kenneth Price, Larry Bell, Claes Oldenburg, Coosje van Broogen, Chuck Arnoldi, and especially the painter Ed Moses and the architect Frank O. Gehry, donated their works, and attended numerous foundation events; Gehry also opened his home to foundation dinners. Actors, artists and writers on the board of trustees of CCHD/HDF included, over the years, Frank Gehry, Carol Burnett, Ed Moses, Sally Kellerman, Julie Andrews, Blake Edwards.

8. NW to MW, March 27, 1973.

9. NW to MW, September 1973.

10. NW, "Genetic 'Russian Roulette': The Experience of Being at Risk for Huntington's Disease," in Seymour Kessler, ed., *Genetic Counseling: Psychological Dimensions* (New York: Academic Press, 1979); "Living Out the Dying: HD, Grief and Death," *ERIC Reports* (Washington, D.C.: National Institute of Education, 1975).

11. The chairperson of the 1972 symposium was Sigvald Refsum, a

neurologist at the University of Oslo Rikshopitalet in Oslo, Norway. For an overview of research presented at the symposium, see A. Barbeau, T. N. Chase, and G. W. Paulson, eds., *Advances in Neurology,* vol. 1: *Huntington's Chorea* (New York: Raven Press, 1973).

12. See, for example, Loe N. Went to NW, September 19, 1976, in *Report of the Commission for the Control of Huntington's Disease and Its Consequences,* vol. 2 (Washington, D.C.: National Institutes of Health, 1977), 102–104. Went and Bruyn wanted to include in the international workshops only "those investigators and medical people that have worked on Huntington's Chorea for at least the last several years."

13. David S. Barkley, "Autoimmunity and Huntington's Disease," Workshop Report, California chapter, CCHD, 1972.

14. Marjorie Guthrie to MW, August 20, 1971.

15. Ibid. Dad protested that the film and record had become "vast unmentionables. They are not discussable." He wanted to hear Marjorie's plans "cold turkey." "We are not in a business deal; we are in the struggle to save lives and in that I don't hold any subject too sacrosanct for invasion." From Dad's point of view, Marjorie had no real science program: "Your program is getting people fired up with no place to go"; MW to Marjorie Guthrie, April 7, 1971.

16. Minutes of the California chapter, CCHD, January 24, 1972. At the end of 1971, the California chapter had about $200,000 cash on hand.

17. Sidney Katz to MW, August 7, 1971, September 1, 1971, and 23 June 1972.

18. MW to Marjorie Guthrie, May 6, 1970.

19. Richard Branaghan to MW, April 16, 1974.

20. There was some overlap: between 1969 and 1977, CCHD spent about $48,000 on basic research. During the same period, the California chapter, and later the Hereditary Disease Foundation, spent about $657,000 for research; *Report of the Commission,* vol. 2, 43–46. From 1986 to 1990, HDSA funded some thirty-four research awards totaling close to $900,900. In 1990, HDSA

spent about $310,570 on research and $922,894 on all other programs: $200,569 on education; $569,540 on patient services; $142,280 on community resources; and $152,785 on chapter development. During the same year, HDF spent about $594,500 on research, apart from workshops and collaborative group meetings. See Minutes of the Scientific Advisory Board, HDF, January 21, 1991; Annual Report of the Huntington's Disease Society of America, 1990.

21. CCHD split into two organizations in the late 1970s, reuniting in 1986 to form a new organization, the Huntington's Disease Society of America, the name it retains in the mid-1990s.

22. Ntinos C. Myrianthopoulos, "Huntington's Chorea: The Genetic Problem Five Years Later," in Barbeau et al., *Advances in Neurology*, vol. 1, 149–160.

CHAPTER 7: THE TEST FOR "HD-NESS"

1. For an overview of Huntington's research in the 1970s, see A. Barbeau, T. N. Chase, and G. W. Paulson, eds., *Advances in Neurology*, vol. 1: *Huntington's Chorea, 1872–1972*; *Advances in Neurology*, vol. 23: T. N. Chase, N. S. Wexler, and A. Barbeau, eds., (New York: Raven Press, 1979).

2. See Minutes of the Scientific Advisory Board, HDF, January 14, 1977 and January 13, 1978. See also I. Shoulson et al., "Huntington's Disease: Treatment with Muscimol, a GABA-mimetic Drug," *Annals of Neurology* 4 (1978): 279–284.

3. J. H. Menkes and N. Stein, "Fibroblast Cultures in Huntington's Disease," *New England Journal of Medicine* 288 (1973): 856–857.

4. He took lymphocytes from people with and without Huntington's, mixing them with brain tissue from some who had died of Huntington's and testing for the presence of something called migration inhibition factor—MIF—a substance that suggests the presence of an antigen.

5. The arguments against HD as an autoimmune disease were: (1) HD is an autosomal dominant disease; (2) it is noninflammatory; (3) it is slowly progressive without exacerbations and remissions; and (4) it is not associated with other clearly defined

autoimmune phenomena. "Although it is possible that the immune response could be a very low-grade, slowly destructive one, at present we have no examples, either in humans or animals, of such a process": Larry W. Kwak, "Immunology and Neurodegenerative Disease," Workshop Summary, HDF, June 21–22, 1980.

6. In this process, proteins are separated out on the basis of charge and molecular weight, labeled with radioactive isotopes, and then exposed to film so that patterns from people with and without Huntington's can be compared. David E. Comings's efforts to identify the mutant protein in Huntington's disease, through a process called two-dimensional gel electrophoresis, had also failed to yield results so far, although for a while it looked as though he might have found something—a protein he called HD-Duarte after the location of City of Hope, where he worked.

7. André Barbeau, Summary Report, HDF, January 1978.

8. C. D. Marsden, "Animal Model of Huntington's Disease—A Review," in Chase et al., *Advances in Neurology,* vol. 23, 570.

9. See Oliver Quarrell, "The Neurobiology of Huntington's Disease," in Peter S. Harper, ed., *Major Problems in Neurology,* vol. 22: *Huntington's Disease* (Philadelphia: W. B. Saunders, 1991), 165–168.

10. Barbeau, Summary Report, HDF, January 1978.

11. Ntinos C. Myrianthopoulos, "Huntington's Chorea," *Journal of Medical Genetics* 3 (1966): 307.

12. The Hereditary Disease Foundation also funded several other researchers who were looking for linkage in Huntington's, specifically Anne Campbell Spence of UCLA in 1971 and William J. Kimberling of the University of Colorado in 1975. See Minutes of the Scientific Advisory Board, HDF, July 1, 1971, and July 30, 1975. Linkage studies of HD began in the early 1950s.

13. See M. A. Pericak-Vance, et al., "Genetic Linkage in Huntington's Disease," in Chase et al., *Advances in Neurology,* vol. 23, 59–72.

14. Christopher Wills, *Exons, Introns, and Talking Genes: The Science Behind the Human Genome Project* (New York: Basic Books, 1991), 201–202.

15. The other commissioners were Stanley M. Aronson, M.D., Dean of Medicine, Brown University; Ching Chun Li, Ph.D., Department of Biostatistics, University of Pittsburgh; Guy McKhann, M.D., Chair, Department of Neurology, Johns Hopkins University School of Medicine; Alice E. Pratt, Huntington's Chorea Foundation; Lee E. Schacht, Ph.D., Human Genetics and Health Resources for the Handicapped Unit, Minnesota Department of Health; Jennifer Jones Simon; Stanley Stellar, M.D., Director, Neural Sciences Research Institute, St. Barnabas Medical Center, New Jersey.

16. Minutes of the Scientific Advisory Board, California chapter, CCHD, January 25, 1973, 6.

17. *Report of the Commission,* vol. 2, p. 113; see also Jerry E. Bishop and Michael Waldholz, *Genome* (New York: Simon and Schuster, 1990), 188–191.

18. See *Report of the Commission for the Control of Huntington's Disease and Its Consequences,* vol. 1 (Washington, D.C.: National Institutes of Health, 1977), 24–25; vol. 2 (1977), 333–341.

19. *Report of the Commission for the Control of Huntington's Disease and Its Consequences,* vol. 2, 21.

20. A National Genetic Diseases Act in 1978 allocated $3.24 million for information, service, and referrals to families with inherited diseases.

21. David E. Comings, "Editorial: The Ups and Downs of Huntington's Disease Research," *American Journal of Human Genetics* 33 (1981): 155–165.

22. G. W. Bruyn, "Huntington's Chorea—History, Clinical, and Laboratory Synopsis," in P. J. Vinken and G. W. Bruyn, eds., *Handbook of Clinical Neurology,* vol. 6 (Amsterdam: North-Holland Publishing Company, 1968), 298–378, quoted at 353.

23. See F. Arthur McMorris, Workshop Report, HDF, October 1975 and January 1978; Malcolm S. Steinberg, Workshop Report, HDF, November 3, 1975. See also Chase et al., *Advances in Neurology,* vol. 23, vii–viii.

CHAPTER 9: "LEAPING GAZELLELIKE THROUGH THE GENOME"

1. See David Botstein et al., "Construction of a Genetic Linkage Map in Man Using Restriction Fragment Length Polymorphisms," *American Journal of Human Genetics* 32 (1980): 314–331, A. F. Jeffreys and F. Flavell, "A Physical Map of the DNA Regions Flanking the Rabbit Beta-Globin Gene," *Cell* 12 (1977): 429–439; T. Maniatis et al., "The Isolation of Structural Genes from Libraries of Eucaryotic DNA," *Cell* 15 (1978): 687–701; Ellen Solomon and Walter F. Bodmer, "Evolution of Sickle Variant Gene," *Lancet* 2 (1979): 923.

2. Y. W. Kan and A. Dozy, "Antenatal Diagnosis of Sickle-Cell Anemia by DNA Analysis of Amniotic-Fluid Cells," *Lancet* 2 (1978): 910–912.

3. See David Botstein et al., "Construction of a Genetic Linkage Map"; and David Botstein, "Genetic and Physical Maps: What Are They and What Can They Tell Us?" and "Human Genome Project: Boon or Bane?," Stanford Centennial Symposium, January 11–13, 1991, Palo Alto, California. For a popular account of the Alta conference where RFLP mapping was first proposed, see Jerry E. Bishop and Michael Waldholz, *Genome* (New York: Simon and Schuster, 1990), 49–68.

4. There is some irony in the title of this paper, which both acknowledges genetic diversity and obliterates it at the same time by referring to only one map and one gender.

5. According to Christopher Wills, a molecular geneticist at the University of California at San Diego, "Population geneticists . . . had expected RFLPs to be everywhere, but their prevalence came as a surprise to molecular biologists, who were nevertheless very quick to exploit them"; Christopher Wills, *Exons, Introns, and Talking Genes* (New York: Basic Books, 1991), 201. Alec Jeffries estimated that 1 to 2 percent of human DNA is polymorphic; Minutes of the Scientific Advisory Board, HDF, January 11, 1980, 8. See also Brenda Fung, "New Directions in Neurobiology," Workshop Report, HDF, January 8–9, 1983, 8.

6. Minutes of the Scientific Advisory Board, HDF, January 11, 1980, 8.
7. See David Parker, "Gene Expression in the Brain," Workshop Report, HDF, April 4–5, 1981, 10; also Rudolph Tanzi, interview, May 31, 1984.
8. "All in all this is perhaps the most exciting and ambitious project in human genetics today underway to study molecular linkages," wrote one participant at the October 1979 HDF workshop. "It has a tremendous potential to pay off in all areas of genetic diseases"; W. Ted Brown, Workshop Report, HDF, November 7, 1979.
9. NW, "50/50: Genetic Roulette," unpublished ms., 31.
10. Ed Kravitz, comments on an HDF Workshop, January 1980.
11. Ron Konopka to MW, December 26, 1979; Anne Young, personal communication, October 14, 1993; David Housman, personal communication, January 1990.

CHAPTER 10: *TRISTES TROPIQUES*

1. Americo Negrette, *San Francisco: Informe Rural* (Maracaibo, 1958); *Corea de Huntington* (Maracaibo: Universidad de Zulia, 1963).
2. It was not reviewed in U.S. medical journals or listed in the *Index Medicus,* the standard international listing of medical publications. Neither Myrianthopoulos nor Bruyn included it in their influential reviews of 1966 and 1968.
3. See "Report of the Ad Hoc Review Committee of the Huntington's Disease Venezuela Project," NINDS, June 22–23, 1982.
4. The priority score for the second grant proposal was 104; NW, personal communication, May 1990.
5. Americo Negrette, *Corea de Huntington,* 205.
6. These included especially Iris de Quiroz and Nelson Marsól.
7. Record of Deaths, State of Zulia, Municipality of San Francisco, January 2, 1887; Registro Municipal, Maracaibo, Venezuela.
8. Arturo Uslar-Pietri, "Letras y hombres de Venezuela," in *Obras Selectas* (Caracas: Ediciones Edime, 1953), 855–859.
9. The Venezuela pedigree in 1992 numbered about 11,000 indi-

viduals both living and deceased. Of these, approximately 370 had HD, and about 3,600 were at risk. Of the 9,000 living individuals, most are under forty. The pedigree (numbering 14,000 in 1995) has yielded much important information about the natural history of Huntington's disease. It has revealed the extremely gradual "zone of onset" of the disease, as well as the similarity between the homozygote, who has two genes for the disease, and the heterozygote, who has only one gene. The lack of clinical difference between the heterozygote and the homozygote makes Huntington's the only known human hereditary disorder that is completely dominant. See Nancy Wexler et al., "Homozygotes for Huntington's Disease," *Nature* 326 (1987): 194–197. On the Venezuela study see Anne B. Young et al., "Huntington's Disease in Venezuela: Neurologic Features and Functional Decline," in *Neurology* 36 (1986): 244–449. See also Nancy S. Wexler, "Clairvoyance and Caution: Repercussions from the Human Genome Project," in Daniel J. Kevles and Leroy Hood, *The Code of Codes: Scientific and Social Issues in the Human Genome Project* (Boston: Harvard University Press, 1992), 211–243.

CHAPTER 11: G-8

1. See Ellen Solomon and Peter Goodfellow, "Human Gene Mapping Rolls Along," *Nature* 306 (17 November (1993), 223–224; Brenda Fung, "New Directions in Neurobiology," Workshop Report, HDF, January 8–9, 1983, 8; Daniela S. Gerhard et al., "What Can Be Learned About Huntington's Disease Once the Gene Has Been Located?" Workshop Report, HDF, May 21–23, 1983, 5.
2. See Fung, "New Directions."
3. It happened, however, that this family's DNA contained unusual patterns that made them somewhat less informative; Mike Conneally, personal communication, July 30, 1993.
4. See Fung, "New Directions."
5. Ibid.
6. Robert Williamson, personal communication, August 17, 1983.

7. Gina Kolata, "Huntington's Disease Gene Located," *Science*, November 25, 1983: 915.

8. *Nature,* 306 (1983): 223.

9. Families had to be large enough, with enough living relatives and enough heterozygosity—that is, people who had different forms of the marker—to make it possible to determine linkage.

10. Matt Clark, "Decoding a Killer Disease," *Newsweek,* November 21, 1983: 107.

11. Nancy Wexler, "A DNA Polymorphism for Huntington's Marks the Future," *Archives of Neurology* 42 (January 1985): 22.

12. J. F. Gusella et al., "A Polymorphic Marker Genetically Linked to Huntington's Disease," *Nature* 306 (17–23 November 1983): 238.

13. Richard Doherty, comments at an HDF Workshop, August 17–18, 1983.

CHAPTER 12: TESTING FATE

1. Schlomo Breznitz, comments at an HDF workshop, April 28–29, 1984.

2. There was always the slight possibility of a recombination event separating the marker from the gene. In that case, an individual might inherit the haplotype usually associated with the HD gene in his or her family but still not inherit the gene; conversely, an individual might not inherit the haplotype associated with the HD gene yet still possess the gene for the disease.

3. See Kimberly A. Quaid, "Presymptomatic Testing for Huntington's Disease in the United States," *American Journal of Human Genetics* 53 (1993): 785–87; David Ball, Audrey Tyler, and Peter Harper, "Predictive testing of Adults and Children: Lessons from Huntington's Disease," in Angus Clarke, ed., *Genetic Counseling: Practice and Principles* (London: Routledge, 1994), 63–94, cited at 69.

4. Panel discussion, annual convention, HDSA, St. Louis, Missouri, July 31, 1994.

5. See Catherine V. Hayes, "Genetic Testing for Huntington's

Disease—A Family Issue," *The New England Journal of Medicine* 327 (1992): 1449–1451.
6. Sally Spaulding, "Living with Bad News," *The Marker,* Summer 1991: 5.
7. Ibid.
8. See Patrick Cooke, "Sentenced to Live," *Health* 7 (July/August 1993): 80 ff., cited at 84.

CHAPTER 13: "THE SINGLE MOST IMPORTANT PIECE OF INFORMATION"

Two published articles by Leslie Roberts were especially useful in preparing this chapter: "Huntington's Gene: So Near, Yet So Far," *Science* 247 (1990): 624–627, and "The Huntington's Gene Quest Goes On," *Science* 258 (1992): 740–741. Apart from these articles, interviews with the participants, and sources cited elsewhere, information for this chapter comes from the reports of HDF workshops and of meetings of the Collaborative Research Group of the Hereditary Disease Foundation (until mid-1990, this group was called the Collaborative Research Agreement, or CRA).

1. Senior members of the original collaborative group were James F. Gusella at Massachusetts General Hospital and Harvard Medical School in Boston; David E. Housman at the Massachusetts Institute of Technology in Cambridge; Hans Lehrach and Anna-Maria Frischauf at the Imperial Cancer Research Fund in London; Keith Fournier at the University of Southern California; John Wasmuth at the University of California at Irvine; and Charles R. Cantor and Cassandra Smith at Columbia University. Subsequently Cantor and Smith and also Fournier withdrew from the collaborative group and Francis S. Collins of the University of Michigan, and Peter S. Harper and Duncan Shaw of the University of Wales College of Medicine in Cardiff joined.
2. After the HD gene was discovered, researchers learned that C4H was in fact a flanking marker; NW, personal communication, August 14, 1994.
3. These were Richard M. Meyers and David R. Cox of the

University of California at San Francisco and Michael R. Hayden at the University of British Columbia.

4. NINDS spending declined from $4 million in 1983 to $3.5 million in 1989; Minutes of the Scientific Advisory Board, HDF, May 22, 1990.

5. In 1990 their total support jumped to $431,500; for 1991 and 1992, it was about $447,000 each year for the collaborative group. In addition, both foundations maintained other programs. Besides sponsoring four meetings of the collaborative group, the Hereditary Disease Foundation continued to hold five or six workshops annually, with participants numbering between 50 and 100 each year. In 1990, of 99 scientists who participated in these workshops, some 48 had never before attended such a meeting, and many of these were new to Huntington's research altogether. The HDF also continued to fund grants and postdoctoral fellowships; in 1990 it awarded $163,000 to seven projects, apart from the collaborative group. Dennis Shea's foundation also sponsored educational materials and training programs for health care workers, while HDSA continued to fund literature, social workers, and support groups, as well as research. See Minutes of the Scientific Advisory Board, HDF, January 15, 1990, May 22, 1990, January 21, 1991, February 3, 1992, and January 11, 1993.

6. Marcy E. MacDonald, HDSA meeting, Dallas, July 28, 1993. These included chromosome jumping and hopping, and exon amplification.

7. Interestingly, while all of the principal investigators in the gene hunters' collaborative group were men (though there were many women involved within each lab, as senior investigators, postdocs, and technicians), several of the principal investigators in the neurobiology collaborative group were women. Indeed, the workshops on neurobiology always had more women participants than the molecular biology workshops did.

8. Francis S. Collins, "In My Corner," *The Marker*, Summer 1987: 2.

9. Glen A. Evans, quoted in Donald R. Gehlert, "Molecular Approaches to the Treatment of Neurodegenerative Diseases,"

Workshop Report, HDF, October 24–25, 1987, 27; see also Constance Cepko, quoted in Mary A. Nastuk, "Cellular, Molecular, and Developmental Mechanisms Underlying Specific Patterns of Cell Death in Neurodegenerative Diseases," Workshop Report HDF, September 7–8, 1984, 2.

10. See Helen G. Harley et al., "Expansion of an Unstable DNA Region and Phenotypic Variation in Myotonic Dystrophy," *Nature* 355 (1992): 545–546.

11. Gillian Bates had in particular made a heroic effort in this part of the project; NW, personal communication, May 1994.

12. See Leslie Roberts, "Huntington's Quest," *Science* (1992): 741.

CHAPTER 14: REPEAT SEQUENCES

1. See Huntington's Disease Collaborative Research Group, "A Novel Gene Containing a Trinucleotide Repeat That is Expanded and Unstable on Huntington's Disease Chromosome," *Cell* (March 26, 1993): 1–20.

2. Anne Young, "Keynote Address," HDSA Research Luncheon, Dallas, July 31, 1993; see also *Guidelines for Genetic Testing for Huntington's Disease* (rev. 1994), HDSA; also NW, personal communication, October 1994.

3. Geneticists once thought that Huntington's began with a single original mutation, which multiplied through many generations. Subsequently they theorized the origin in several different mutational events, all probably centered in Europe. By the mid-1990s, the possibility of as many as a hundred separate mutations was becoming accepted; P. Michael Conneally, personal communication, July 30, 1994.

4. In a trenchant essay on the genome project, Evelyn Fox Keller argues that "despite the repeated emphasis on health care, on the diagnosis, treatment, and prevention of genetic disease, it is in fact primarily the possibility of diagnosis that is considered of practical relevance for the near future by even the most enthusiastic proponents of the human genome project"; Evelyn Fox Keller, "Nature, Nurture, and the Human Genome Project," in Daniel J. Kevles and Leroy Hood, eds., *The Code of Codes:*

Scientific and Social Issues in the Human Genome Project (Boston: Harvard University Press, 1992), 281–299, quoted at 295.

5. See Philip Elmer-Dewitt, "The Genetic Revolution," *Time,* January 17, 1994: 48. Equating an individual's wish not to know his or her genetic status with a desire for "ignorance" is itself a subtle form of pressure, a means of devaluing that desire. Health professionals also unwittingly use language that, while claiming to be neutral and descriptive, is both manipulative and prescriptive. In 1994, a clinical psychologist noted that "at long last predictive testing for HD will be widely available, accurate, and financially possible for most people. After years of uncertainty, at-risk individuals may make plans for the future. . . . An increased sense of control will now be possible both for gene-carriers and those who find that they are no longer at risk." Such commonly used language implies that testing is highly desirable, that people at risk who choose not to test cannot plan for the future, and that those who do take the test will enhance their sense of control over their lives—all of which is highly uncertain. Randi Jones, "Genetic Testing for Huntington's Disease— What's New?" *The Marker* (Spring 1994), 6–7.

A NOTE ON SOURCES

First, I wish to mention two books that do not deal with Huntington's disease but were extremely useful for suggesting insights about the symbolic dimensions of illness and about the process of creating an "illness narrative." Though aimed at clinicians, Arthur Kleinman's *The Illness Narratives: Suffering, Healing, and the Human Condition* (New York: Basic Books, 1988), and Evan Imber-Black, ed., *Secrets in Families and Family Therapy* (New York: Guilford Press, 1993), helped me to think about the multiple meanings of Huntington's in our family and the ways in which it shaped our lives even before we knew of its existence.

The literature on Huntington's is surprisingly rich. Though I have included many references in the notes, a few important sources, as well as ephemeral, official, and personal materials not mentioned in the notes merit acknowledgment here. A basic reference for the history of medical discourse on the disease is G. W. Bruyn, F. Baro, and N. C. Myrianthopoulos's *Centennial Bibliography on Huntington's Disease* (Louvain: Louven University Press, 1974), which contains a vast number of references up to 1972. The two volumes of *Advances in Neurology* cited in the notes, volumes 1 and 23, chart the progress (or lack thereof) of research in the 1960s and 1970s. More recent overviews include Michael Hayden, *Huntington's Chorea* (Berlin: Springer-Verlag, 1981); Susan Folstein, *Huntington's Disease: A Disorder of Families* (Baltimore: Johns Hopkins University Press, 1989); and especially Peter S. Harper, editor, *Major Problems in Neurology*, vol. 22: *Huntington's Disease* (Philadelphia: W. B. Saunders, 1991). This volume, collectively written and surprisingly readable, offers the most comprehensive and politically informed overview to date. Each chapter contains extensive bibliographies.

The Congressional Commission for the Control of Huntington's Disease and its Consequences issued an extensive report (October 1977) that remains a valuable resource, particularly for its volumes of public testimony and the position papers. Especially notable are Ira Shoulson's "Clinical Care of the Patient and Family with Huntington's Disease," and "Living with a Time Bomb" by Maya Pines, as well as Pines' summary of public testimony. The volume of technical papers offers useful insights into the early debates over presymptomatic testing and the genesis of the Venezuela Project and the Centers Without Walls.

The newsletters, annual reports, and other literature of the Committee to Combat Huntington's Disease (CCHD) and, since 1986, the Huntington's Disease Society of America (HDSA) offer useful information about the organization and concerns of the Huntington's disease community. In 1989, the HDSA published *Guidelines for Predictive Testing for Huntington's Disease,* which were revised in 1994 after the gene was identified.

One of the goals of the Hereditary Disease Foundation, since its inception as the California chapter of CCHD, has been to stimulate the exchange of information about Huntington's within the medical and scientific communities. To that end, the foundation has circulated reports of its workshops since March 1971. Particularly since 1980, when Allan J. Tobin became executive director, these reports have offered an overview of research-in-progress. I have also drawn on the Minutes of the Scientific Advisory Board of the foundation, as well as the Minutes of the Executive Committee of the board of trustees. The Huntington's Disease Collaborative Research Group, organized in 1984, also recorded its deliberations after each meeting.

The National Institute of Neurological Disorders and Stroke (NINDS) has also issued reports of institute-sponsored research.

Since 1980, the literature on Huntington's has mushroomed, both in the science and in the popular press. Leslie Roberts' two articles "Huntington's Gene: So Near and Yet so Far," *Science* 247 (1990): 624–627, and "The Huntington's Gene Quest Goes On," *Science* 258 (1992): 740–741, are excellent on the Collaborative Research Group. Maya Pines, "In the Shadow of Huntington's," *Science '84* (May 1984): 32–39, discusses the Venezuela communities where Huntington's is found, as does Donald Drake in "The Curse of San Luis," *The Philadelphia Inquirer Magazine,* August 26, 1984: 20 ff. Marlene Cimons, "It's All in the Family," *Los Angeles Times Magazine,* February 10, 1991: 7 ff., includes an autobiographical essay by Nancy Wexler. Catherine V. Hayes, a former president of CCHD, has written both personally and professionally on genetic testing; see "Genetic Testing for Huntington's Disease—A Family Issue," *The New England Journal of Medicine* 327 (1992): 1449–1451. Susan Ager, "Daring to Know," *The Philadephia Inquirer Magazine,* September 10, 1989: 18ff., sensitively explores the experiences of a young woman undergoing the predictive test. Andrew Revkin's "Hunting Down Huntington's," in *Discover* 14 (December 1993): 98ff, profiles Nancy Wexler, as does Mary Murray's "Nancy Wexler's Test," *The New York Times Magazine,* February 13, 1994: 28–31. Patrick Cooke's portrait of a man at risk who learns he will not get Huntington's is especially compelling; see "Sentenced to Live," *Health* 7 (July/August 1993): 80ff.

Huntington's disease is discussed in many articles and books on gene mapping, genetic testing, genetic disease, and the Human Genome Project. Despite its grandiose title, *Genome: The Story of the Most Astonishing Scientific Adventure of Our Time—The Attempt to Map All the Genes in the Human Body,* by Jerry E. Bishop and Michael Waldholz (New York: Simon and Schuster, 1990), contains several readable chapters on the search for the HD gene. Daniel J. Kevles and Leroy Hood, eds., *The Code of Codes: Scientific and Social Issues in the Human Genome Project* (Boston: Harvard University Press, 1992), includes an essay by Nancy Wexler, "Clairvoyance and Caution: Repercussions from the Human Genome Project," that focuses on the example of Huntington's; many other essays in this excellent book are also relevant.

The recent publicity surrounding Huntington's disease has inspired fictional treatments of people at risk, including segments on the television program *L.A. Law* and a play called *Can I Have This Dance?* by Doug Haverty. The 1985 novel *The Dancing Men* by Duncan Kyle (Glasgow, Scotland: Fontana Collins, 1985) centers on a presidential candidate whose hidden risk for Huntington's forms the central mystery of the plot. The noted British mystery writer Ruth Rendell (writing as Barbara Vine) created a narrator at risk for Huntington's in her novel *House of Stairs* (New York: Harmony Books, 1988).

Presymptomatic testing has also motivated a number of people at risk to write, both about the testing experience and about the larger meanings of Huntington's in their families. Sally Spaulding's haunting memoir, *Autumn Patience* (unpublished at this writing), evokes a father whose personality changes defy the understanding of his young daughter until she undertakes a journey of her own. See also Spaulding's "Living with Bad News," *The Marker* (Summer 1991), 5. Joanne Wilke's "The Dance" describes taking the test during a period of fourteen months in Montana. Sharon Dunn's powerful poems grieve for her mother and brother with Huntington's and convey her ambivalent responses to the testing process. Gabrielle Hamilton describes the ambiguity of a noninformative test in "Left Wondering," *The Marker* (Spring 1992), while Geri Harville writes about getting a positive result in "Life Goes On," *The Marker* (Spring 1994). While narratives of personal experience are influenced by medical discourse, journalistic stories, television, movies, and other forms of popular culture, they nonetheless offer a different kind of entry into the emotional world of the person at risk. Until recently nearly all such accounts were mediated through the neurologist, the psychiatrist, or the genetic counselor. The new HD narratives, written outside any medical/therapeutic institutions, represent an important alternative in the literature of Huntington's disease and the contemporary history of the body.

INTERVIEWS

Anderson, Mary Anne, Massachusetts General Hospital and Harvard Medical School: June 1990, Boston.

Barbeau, André, deceased; formerly at the University of Montreal: January 8, 1984, Santa Monica.

Barkley, David S., consultant, Los Angeles, formerly at UCLA: October 5, 1989, Los Angeles.

Barnard, Maryline. November 26, 1983, Santa Monica.

Benzer, Seymour, California Institute of Technology: January 22, 1990 (telephone).

Bick, Katherine L., Centro SMID USA; formerly at the National Institutes of Health: January 11, 1988, Santa Monica.

Botstein, David, Stanford University: January 12, 1991, Palo Alto, California (informal conversation).

Buckler, Alan J., Massachusetts General Hospital and Harvard Medical School, formerly at MIT: June 1, 1990, Boston.

Collins, Francis S., director, National Center for Human Genome Research, Washington D.C., formerly at the University of Michigan: November 27, 1990 (telephone).

Conneally, P. Michael, Indiana University School of Medicine: January 7, 1984, Santa Monica; June 2, 1990, Boston.

Dreyer, William, California Institute of Technology: January 23, 1990 (telephone).

Gilliam, T. Conrad, Columbia University: June 13, 1990, New York City.

Greenspan, Ralph J., New York University: March 1987, Princeton, New Jersey.

Gusella, James F., Massachusetts General Hospital and Harvard Medical School: May 31, 1984, Boston; January 1987, Santa Monica; June 1990, Boston.

Housman, David E., Massachusetts Institute of Technology: January 6–7, 1984, Santa Monica; June 1990, Boston.

Konopka, Ronald, consultant, Pasadena, California, formerly at the California Institute of Technology and Clarkson University: June 13, 1990, Saratoga, New York.

Kravitz, Edward A., Harvard Medical School: January 5, 1984, Boston.

Kunkel, Louis M., Childrens Hospital, Boston, and Harvard Medical School: June 4, 1990, Boston.

Lehrach, Hans, Imperial Cancer Research Fund, London: January 19, 1991, Santa Monica.

Leventhal, Carl M., National Institutes of Health: January 11, 1987, Santa Monica.

MacDonald, Marcy E., Massachusetts General Hospital and Harvard Medical School: June 1990, Boston.

Matthysse, Steven W., Harvard Medical School and McLean Hospital: January 9 1984, Santa Monica.

McKay, Ronald, NINDS, formerly at Cold Spring Harbor Biological Laboratory: January 8, 1984, Santa Monica.

Menkes, John H., UCLA (emeritus): February 11, 1986, Santa Monica.

Minna, John D., University of Texas Southwestern Medical Center, (formerly National Institutes of Health): January 11, 1986, Santa Monica.

Mulligan, Richard, The Whitehead Institute: January 6–7, 1984, Santa Monica.

Myrianthopoulos, Ntinos C., National Institutes of Health: January 6, 1984, Santa Monica.

Negrette, Americo, University of Zulia: March 29, 1984, Maracaibo, Venezuela.

Roberts, Eugene, City of Hope: November 16, 1989, Duarte, California.

Shoulson, Ira, University of Rochester School of Medicine: January 11, 1985, Santa Monica.

Tanzi, Rudolph E., Massachusetts General Hospital and Harvard Medical School: 31 May 1984, Boston.

Tobin, Allan J., UCLA and Hereditary Disease Foundation: July 11, 1984, February 3, 1989, October 2, 1989, Santa Monica.

Walters, Judith R., National Institutes of Health: January 7, 1984, Santa Monica.

Wasmuth, John J., University of California at Irvine: February 8, 1989, Irvine.

Wexler, Milton: November 26, 1983, February 9, 1987, Santa Monica

Wexler, Nancy S., Columbia University and Hereditary Disease Foundation: November 13–14, 26, 1986, 17 April 1987, Santa Monica.

White, Raymond L., University of Utah: January 23, 1986, Riverside, California.

Young, Anne B., Massachusetts General Hospital and Harvard Medical School, formerly at the University of Michigan: January 7, 1984, and April 4, 1985, Santa Monica.

ACKNOWLEDGMENTS

This book is about collaborative science, and is itself a kind of collaboration. All of the investigators who are part of this story graciously shared their memories and interpretations and patiently tutored a beginner in the ways of molecular genetics and neurobiology. I owe a special debt to Allan J. Tobin and Edward A. Kravitz for their explanations and their enthusiasm for this project over many years, and for their trenchant criticisms of the manuscript. In addition, David E. Housman, James F. Gusella, Marcy E. MacDonald, P. Michael Conneally, and John J. Wasmuth made time for my questions on numerous occasions, showed me around their labs, and in the case of Mike Conneally, generously arranged a visit to Indianapolis so I could see the Huntington's Disease Research Roster. Anne B. Young read the manuscript at a critical moment and has been an inspiration throughout the writing of this book,

For their generosity in offering recollections and interpretations, I wish to thank Mary Anne Anderson, David S. Barkley, Maryline Barnard, Gillian P. Bates, Seymour Benzer, Katherine L. Bick, David Botstein, Alan J. Buckler, Marie-Francoise Chesselet, Francis S. Collins, William Dreyer, T. Conrad Gilliam, Ralph J. Greenspan, Peter S. Harper, H. Robert Horvitz, Ronald Konopka, Louis M.

Kunkel, Hans Lehrach, Carl M. Levanthal, Steven W. Matthysse, John C. Mazziotta, Ronald McKay, John H. Menkes, John D. Minna, Richard C. Mulligan, Ntinos C. Myrianthopoulos, Americo Negrette, John B. Penney, Eugene Roberts, Ira Shoulson, Rudolph E. Tanzi, Judith R. Walters, Leslie P. Weiner, Raymond L. White, and the late André Barbeau.

A number of people, in very individual ways, offered astute readings of the manuscript at various stages and insightful editorial suggestions. Joan G. Baily and Samuel L. Baily, outstanding leaders in the Huntington's community, gave me the benefit of both their professional acumen and personal experience, as well as deeply appreciated emotional support. Christina Benson helped me untangle many of the knotted threads of this story, through her finely honed capacity to listen and understand. Elizabeth Lord's faith in the project and her comments at an early stage illuminated questions both scientific and psychological. I was fortunate to have the keen editorial insights of Jeffrey Escoffier, who at an early stage raised crucial questions and pointed me in the right directions.

The critical responses of several historian and writer colleagues who read drafts of the book were absolutely essential. Ellen DuBois kibitzed, encouraged, criticized, and cared, as well as inspired me by her own example as a historian and biographer. I am grateful also to Robert Rosenstone for encouraging me to take risks in writing and for his own path-breaking practice as a biographer. Our continuing conversations about personal narrative and "experimental history" have been an invaluable accompaniment to this project. Ella Taylor's wonderful wit and humor, as well as her keen critical eye and confidence in this book, helped me through many an anxious moment. Both Lois Banner and Sharon Salinger commented in detail on the manuscript, generously offering both incisive historians' insights and feminist sensitivity.

I also wish to thank Stephanie Kay for her unquenchable enthusiasm, concern, and friendship through all the vicissitudes of this work. Thanks also to Wini Breines, Alice Echols, and Ellen Krout-Hasegawa for their lively and enlightening conversations about writing as I was completing this book. John Ganim's encouragement and generosity, both emotional and intellectual, helped make this book a reality. Participation in several groups also stimulated my thinking about gender, science, and writing, especially the Research Seminar on Gender and Power at the University of California at Riverside, the Women's History Teaching Workshop at UCLA, and my biography group. I am grateful to other colleagues whose ideas and vision have contributed to my thinking, especially Janet Brodie, Robert Dawidoff, Ellen Dwyer, Barbara Epstein, Carole Fabricant, Nina Gelbart, Stephanie Kay, Daniel Kevles, Herbert Pardes, Daniel Rubey, David Schickele, Bryant Simon, Moshe Sluhovsky, Sarah Stage, Kay Trimberger, Devra Weber, and Deborah Willis.

The staffs of the Hereditary Disease Foundation and the Huntington's Disease Society of America helped with information and materials, especially Edy Shackell, Judith Lorimer, Phil Cohen, and Andrew McInnes. I am grateful also to the trustees of the Hereditary Disease Foundation, especially Berta and Frank Gehry, Eppie Lederer, Edward C. Moses, Donna and Richard O'Neill, Claes Oldenburg, and Coosje van Bruggen. I also wish to thank Julie Andrews, Jan and Gerald Aronson, Larry Bell, Buster and Debbie Blethen, Carol Burnett, Betty Borman, Jay Chiat and Donatella Brun, Jean Hale Coleman, Meg and William Dorn, Blake Edwards, Jodie Evans, Marjorie and Michael J. Fasman, Peter Feibleman, the Fritts family, Arthur Golding, Kiyo and Robert Higashi, Sally Kellerman, Harry Lieberman, Rebecca Marder, Elaine May, Evelyn and Morris Ostin, Kenneth Price, Jennifer Jones Simon, and Susan Spivak for their generosity in supporting the foundation. Thanks also to Alice Pratt and the Wills Foundation, and to Dennis Shea and the Foundation for the Care and Cure of Huntington's Disease, special friends and allies in the fight against HD.

Other members of the Huntington's disease community, especially Catherine V. Hayes, Sally Spaulding, and the Wieske family, helped by their own courageous example to give me the determination to complete this book. I also wish to thank Kimberly Quaid and Jacqueline Gray for sharing information relating to the Roster and testing.

The suggestions of my editor, Ruth Fecych, at a very early stage of this project, were crucial in transforming a shapeless draft into a book. I appreciate immensely her patience, perceptiveness, and enthusiasm during a much longer period than she bargained for. Thanks also to Robbin Schiff, Martha Schwartz, Laura Taylor, and Lynn Anderson of Times Books/Random House for their elegant input. Finally, I am deeply grateful to my wonderful agent, Frances Goldin, who believed in this book when it was only a fantasy, read and critiqued it in several versions with her usual discerning eye, and offered not only the advocacy of an agent but the warmth and caring of a friend.

In conclusion, I wish to express my deepest appreciation and love to my father and sister for their generosity and grace in supporting this project. The book became part of our ongoing conversation, another strong-minded member of the family. Besides engaging in this dialogue, Nancy shared memories and information, read several different versions of this manuscript, and took time from her own numerous commitments to devote her attention to mine. My father courageously respected my family narrative even when it did not agree with his. His willingness to see himself, in print, through a daughter's eye, is only one of his many gifts.

INDEX

ABOUT THE AUTHOR

ALICE WEXLER is the author of *Emma Goldman in America* (1984) and *Emma Goldman in Exile* (1989). She has taught most recently at Occidental College and UCLA, where she is currently affiliated with the Center for the Study of Women. She lives in Los Angeles.